PRAISE FOR

The Woman
Beyond the
Attic

"Andrews's fans will appreciate this insightful glimpse into her mysterious life."

—*Kirkus Reviews*

"Neiderman . . . uses letters and family interviews to set the record straight. . . . Using flowery, dramatic language that is the hallmark of Andrews's novels, Neiderman presents a woman who never let her disability get her down. . . . [T]he text of an unfinished novel . . . will be a thrill for Andrews's fans."

—*Booklist*

"Combining a novelist's eye for detail with personal knowledge gleaned from his years as V.C. Andrews's ghostwriter, Neiderman (*The Devil's Advocate*) unpacks the famed gothic writer's notoriously private life. . . . [H]e scrupulously unravels . . . mysteries still swirling around the novelist's life today. . . . Fans will be transfixed."

—*Publishers Weekly*

"Mr. Neiderman seems well-placed to assess Andrews's motivations, having ghostwritten scores of books in her name for over three decades. . . . This material plugs many large holes in our understanding of this fiercely private writer. . . . [T]he woman who emerges from these pages is as riveting as her books."

—*The Wall Street Journal*

ALSO BY ANDREW NEIDERMAN

The Woman Beyond the Attic

· THE V.C. ANDREWS STORY ·

ANDREW NEIDERMAN

G

Gallery Books

New York   London   Toronto   Sydney   New Delhi

G

Gallery Books
An Imprint of Simon & Schuster, Inc.
1230 Avenue of the Americas
New York, NY 10020

First Gallery Books trade paperback edition June 2023

GALLERY BOOKS and colophon are registered trademarks of Simon & Schuster, Inc.

For information about special discounts for bulk purchases, please contact Simon & Schuster Special Sales at 1-866-506-1949 or business@simonandschuster.com.

The Simon & Schuster Speakers Bureau can bring authors to your live event. For more information or to book an event, contact the Simon & Schuster Speakers Bureau at 1-866-248-3049 or visit our website at www.simonspeakers.com.

Interior design by Erika R. Genova

Manufactured in the United States of America

1   3   5   7   9   10   8   6   4   2

The Library of Congress has cataloged the hardcover edition as follows:

Names: Neiderman, Andrew, author.
Title: The woman beyond the attic : the Virginia Andrews story / Andrew Neiderman.
Description: First Gallery Books hardcover edition. | New York : Gallery Books, 2022. | Includes bibliographical references and index.
Identifiers: LCCN 2021045634 (print) | LCCN 2021045635 (ebook) | ISBN 9781982182632 (hardcover) | ISBN 9781982182656 (ebook)
Subjects: LCSH: Andrews, V. C. (Virginia C.) | Authors, American—20th century—Biography. | Women novelists, American—Biography. | Authors with disabilities—Biography.
Classification: LCC PS3551.N454 Z73 2022 (print) | LCC PS3551.N454 (ebook) | DDC 813/.54—dc23/eng/20211027
LC record available at https://lccn.loc.gov/2021045634
LC ebook record available at https://lccn.loc.gov/2021045635

ISBN 978-1-9821-8263-2
ISBN 978-1-9821-8264-9 (pbk)
ISBN 978-1-9821-8265-6 (ebook)

For my daughter, Melissa,
without whose assistance
I could not have done this

Ah Death
How pathetic you look enjoying your moments of power
And then retreating to that darkness where you curl up
Friendless and despised.
How frustrated you must be
Watching my continual resurrection
With every new reader
Turning my pages.

—*Andrew Neiderman*

contents

Preface ....*xi*

Chapter One. First Steps...1
Chapter Two. Moving up the Stairway...23
Chapter Three. Nearly at the Last Step...41
Chapter Four. To the Attic 57
Chapter Five. Opening the Attic Door...73
Chapter Six. Into the Attic...93
Chapter Seven. Living Life in the Attic 109
Chapter Eight. Leaving the Attic 123
Chapter Nine. Leaving Foxworth Hall..139
Epilogue. Color Hope Yellow: The Author Envisions 147

Note to the Reader 149
The Obsessed 151
The Do-It-Yourself Romance: "Love's Savage Desire" 243
Two Poems by Virginia Andrews: "Golden Things" and "Regretting".........247

Acknowledgments...249
Bibliography 251
Index 253

preface

OVER THIRTY-FIVE YEARS AGO, I was at a business lunch in New York City with my then literary agent, Anita Diamant. Before we were too deep into a discussion of my own latest published thriller, she paused and said, "I think we're going to ask you to complete a V.C. Andrews novel."

Anita went on to describe the book as the prequel to *Flowers in the Attic* and explained that the latest medical reports concerning Virginia Andrews were not promising.

Needless to say, I was quite surprised. However, after digesting the information and the lunch, I drove back to my home in the village of South Fallsburg in the Catskill Mountains and told my wife what my agent had suggested. My wife, Diane, was a big fan of the Dollanganger family series, especially *Flowers in the Attic*, which I had not yet read. She had been talking about the book to the point of it haunting me. I had intended to find out what it was, and then came this proposal.

Diane was even more excited about it than I was. To me, the possibility of continuing such a massive presence in the publishing world was daunting. At the time I began, there were approximately 26 million copies of V.C. Andrews novels in print. Currently, there are over 107 million, and that number continues to grow.

Anita had thought of me for this task because through her agency, I had published a number of thrillers involving family intrigue and relationships, as well as young characters. The first novel I had ever published, *Sisters*, was a thriller told from the point of view of the older sister. Six out of the seven V.C. Andrews novels published by that point featured a female narrator. Whenever I'm asked how a male can capture the point of view of a female, I give the famous answer for all creativity, expressed in the movie *Shakespeare in Love*: "It's a mystery."

Another reason Anita turned to me was the fact that while I was publishing, I was still teaching, and one of the courses I taught was creative writing. That experience enabled me to study style and thus potentially capture someone else's. Virginia's style, her development of family crises and intrigue, and her attention to settings remain a source of pleasure and interest for innumerable readers.

Now, after well over forty years of V.C. Andrews novels published worldwide and over a dozen film adaptations of the works, with many more on the horizon, it felt like time to present Virginia Andrews's biography, especially because there was so much misinformation about her and her career, as well as so many conjectures concerning the origins of her stories and the basis for her characters. Literally millions of fans worldwide continuously debate and wonder about the details of her life because she was so private.

How disabled was she? How was it possible for her not only to write the novels but also to promote them? Were her books based on her life or her family? She was living alone with her mother? Did she use her mother as an audience ever? Was there someone outside the family who encouraged her, perhaps a boyfriend? Why didn't she publish earlier? When had she actually started to write? What did she think of other writers?

We can immediately say that by Virginia's own admission, part of what made her so private and seemingly reticent about what she would reveal about herself, especially later in life, is seen in her personal letters, her interviews, and the testimony of her family. Although she rarely revealed it in public, nothing better illustrated how much she hated being viewed as different, someone to pity, than her reaction to the *People* magazine interviewer and article. She thought the piece capitalized on her disability and portrayed her as an eccentric recluse. This particular interview in *People* in 1980, in her opinion, had been constructed in such a way as to make her look unattractive and even, in her mind, horrifying. She was especially sensitive to the question of her age; by the time *Flowers in the Attic* was published on November 15, 1979, Virginia had celebrated her fifty-sixth birthday. The late '70s was not a time that celebrated late-life accomplishments—especially for women —in a way that might be more common nowadays.

Writer and horror critic Douglas E. Winter, in his collection of interviews titled *Faces of Fear*, excavated from Virginia one of her best and most honest comments about this: "When I was young, I made some new friends and they liked me a lot. They asked me my age, and when I said nineteen, they seemed disappointed I wasn't sixteen. I decided then that I was never going to tell my age again. People judge you by your age. If you are young, you're immature or impulsive, and if you are old, you must be senile and dotty." She went on to admit, "I get older and younger as I want. It bothers me that people dig so much into your life for all the wrong reasons."

She explained to Winter that when the *People* reporters found someone who claimed she was a lot older than she was at the time and then confronted her with it, Virginia told the interviewer, "You must have found an enemy." She told Winter, "[T]hey told me quite frankly, that they come to get dirt. . . . And when they don't find any, they make up things."

She especially hated the photographs in the article and told her cousin Pat Mock in a letter, "They were awful! I don't look like that old woman peeking out of the window! I hated the shot of me in the chair! I refuse to allow pictures of me sitting in that thing—but [they] sneaked in one."

Privately, she had even harsher words for the article than those, and as a result of the experience, she retreated from similar media exposure. However, by not contradicting them or the statements in other articles, she unfortunately, and unintentionally, supported the false accusations and unattractive descriptions of her. And so a primary aim of this biography is to finally reveal the truth around some of these misconceptions and establish Virginia's rightful place in the history of American publishing.

That given, one wonders, then how did Douglas E. Winter get her to do such an in-depth, personal interview after this dramatically hurtful experience? Intrigued, I asked him to explain.

"I knew about, and probably saw, the *People* interview," Winter says, "but I've never paid much attention to pop magazine interviews. They're superficial confections, compressing lives into a few nimble quotations interspersed with logline descriptions of the subject's latest role, album, book, or other event of the moment, with some emotional hook—inevitably, some tragedy, preferably one that's been overcome.

"I knew Virginia had decided never to be interviewed again, and I was warned that it would be futile to try to contact her; but I also knew she deserved—indeed, needed—to be part of *Faces of Fear* if I was to realize my ambition for the book. My persuasiveness, I believe, was the result of two simple things: honesty and context. I'd been fortunate, early in my writing career, to have befriended several major writers. Others knew me as the voice in what, at that time, was a wilderness: a critic writing about the fiction of fear for leading newspapers and magazines.

"As the book neared completion, I was working hard to include the writers I wanted who were not friends or acquaintances. And I offered Virginia a straightforward and sincere proposition. This book would provide an oral history of the fiction of fear, as told by its creators, with my own critical observations. I was inviting her into a 'hall of fame' of the writers who were crucial to the renaissance of this fiction, along with other, lesser-known writers who were crucial voices or who could offer insights into the other side of the street—the realities of commercial publishing, the perilous economics of the writing life, the honey trap of genre.

"I wanted to meet her, as I'd met the other interviewees, at home. The interview would be extensive and biographical. She could review my final draft of the chapter devoted to her, and she would have full approval over its content. (She did, and she didn't change a word—and, in fact, expanded one of her answers in a beautiful way.) And—although I didn't know the underpinning of her dismay at the *People* interview—I said she could provide the photograph that would accompany the chapter.

"I wrote to her and held my breath. And she soon sent a lovely invitation to her home. Which led to an amazing day, and one of the most delightful interviews in the book."

While she participated in some newspaper interviews, particularly around the launch of a new novel, she didn't do anything as in-depth as what she did for *Faces of Fear*. As a consequence, there are many little mysteries about Virginia Andrews for us to explore.

Her name, for example—one of the most basic aspects of a person's identity. Yet for Virginia, even that twisted and changed. On her passport she is listed as Cleo Virginia Andrews, but everyone knew her as Virginia Andrews. A social security card has her name as Virginia Cleo. And yet on her book jackets, she is identified as V.C. Andrews in America and some other countries but as Virginia Andrews in the United Kingdom and elsewhere.

Why was her name so puzzling? Her personal letters will give us insight into her reactions to her pseudonym. And the opinions of early readers will be amusing and interesting, too. We'll even find a reference to the reason for a pseudonym in *Flowers in the Attic*. According to her personal letters to family, the name V.C. Andrews was not her choice. As with so many other personal decisions that were made for her once she became disabled, disentangling what was truly her choice and what was decided for her can be difficult. How do we arrive at the answers, often having to read between the lines in her letters and her answers in interviews?

During the course of my own journey reproducing her style, her characters, and her views of family and love, my wife and I became so closely involved with the Andrewses that they literally became our second family. Having trusted me with Virginia's legacy, they trusted me with the details of her life, her relationships, and her struggles, as well as her personal papers.

Even after having written V.C. Andrews novels for decades and hearing stories about her from her family, uncovering these never seen or published letters and engaging in deeper interviews with her family brought Virginia even more to life for me, as I had never had the opportunity to meet her.

From the outset, one fact became instantly clear. Few bestselling authors are as intimately connected and as well-known internationally with just a single one of their works as V.C. Andrews is with *Flowers in the Attic*. When even frequent readers of novels are asked if they know who V.C. Andrews is, they often have a blank look until you say, "*Flowers in the Attic*." Then their eyes light up, and they might say, "I read that in high school" or "I was forbidden to read it in high school, even while I was home and in the privacy of my own room, so my parents wouldn't be embarrassed I was reading it!"

When I began writing V.C. Andrews novels, I was surprised to discover that *Flowers* was banned in many places from the first days of its release—and for quite a while thereafter. For example, the entire *Flowers in the Attic* series at the time (also now called the Dollanganger family series) was banned in Oconee County, Georgia, shortly after *Flowers in the Attic* was published in 1979. The county's board of education had decided to remove all school curriculum materials and library books deemed to have "profanity" and "pornography," concepts that were both ill-defined. The tremendous public outcry made the board backtrack and resolve to review its selection policy. However, even after this conciliatory decision, and with the review process still inching along, most of the Dollanganger books were removed from the high school library for "pornographic" content.

This was not an isolated incident. Despite the popularity of Virginia's debut, there were other libraries and bookstore owners who refused to carry it or any other V.C. Andrews novel, even if it meant losing out on sales. I can recall one of my early experiences of researching to understand and capture the essence of V.C. Andrews as a writer. I went into a bookstore in California, asked if they carried any V.C. Andrews novels, and received a firm, even angry, reply of "No. The author exploits women."

This I found amusing, considering there were copies of *Playboy* and *Penthouse* magazines on sale despite the fact that the store was owned and managed by women. But then I gave it deeper thought and concluded that if revealing the secret abuse of children and exploring and revealing the female psyche so compassionately and, from what most readers say, so accurately, especially during the adolescent years, was exploiting, then onward with exploitation.

Virginia explored these themes from her very first novel. And clearly, she had considered them for a long time, given her age (fifty-five) when she wrote the final draft of *Flowers in the Attic*. How many people do you know who set a goal for their life when they were in their twenties—something they had dreamed about since they were children—and did not give up on that goal for over thirty years despite a host of physical impediments and continued rejection?

Because of physical circumstances that we will explore in more detail, Virginia often had to stand up to type her stories, which she did for hours and hours. Her sister-in-law Joan Andrews claims, "She told me she even wore out the soles of her shoes," standing and typing on her new IBM. When she first became serious about writing, she described writing thirty to forty pages a night.

Conversely, sitting for long periods was also a challenge, and when she did, she sat tilted back at roughly a forty-five-degree angle. Virginia would sometimes type while boosted into a sitting position in bed. She revealed that she occasionally would mount a mirror behind her typewriter so that she could watch herself as she composed in order to "project better." What she was seeing in herself she could imbue her characters with, especially the blond girls who resembled her. There was no sister to confide in, no other young female near her age with whom she could share her changing emotions and feelings. Virginia searched everywhere she could for inspiration and understanding, including within herself.

We will explore ways in which she did this and point specifically to her works to illustrate the results. From the day *Flowers in the Attic* was published until now, readers have continually conjectured about how much of Virginia herself is in what her characters say, do, and think. She would get these questions from readers while she lived, and the same questions persist on various V.C. Andrews fan pages. Did she envision her mother as one of the characters in her books? Did she envision herself or some other member of her family?

My goal is to provide biographical illustrations and insights to help you reach your own conclusions about these questions and many others. Virginia's own words, printed and spoken to her family and to reporters, are invaluable, but I cannot promise some mystery won't still remain.

Beyond family, looking at Virginia's physical challenges—a constant that she would not always readily admit to and certainly not something to which she would surrender—will give us a sense of her as an artist and a person. For Virginia, there would be no retreating behind drawn window shades in dimly lit rooms, curled up with self-pity, mourning lost femininity, like some gothic heroine without agency. She would be heard at all costs.

It is helpful to keep in mind that Virginia struggled to make her artistic voice heard years before rights for the disabled became enshrined in law and at a time when wheelchairs still made most people a little uncomfortable. My sense of that period is that many people would avert their gaze from someone in a wheelchair and try to avoid conversations with them.

Strides have been made in improving the social lot of people who use wheelchairs since then, but many today still suffer certain isolation as Virginia did. As she illustrates often in her letters, if anyone was well tuned in to patronization, it was she. Virginia knew empty words when she heard them and was not afraid to point this out to her family, even when they were the ones who were guilty of it.

But as you will see, from the testimonies of those who met her in public and family members, people could be so taken with Virginia's energy and enthusiasm for her work that they rarely noted her disability, even when she was sitting at a limited forty-five-degree angle to greet fans and sign autographs. Visitors whom Lillian Andrews, Virginia's mother, permitted to see Virginia after her surge to fame heard no invectives or self-pity. Her niece and nephews loved to visit her because she was so cheerful and fun to be with, as we will see when we read her niece Suzanne's memories as a child and as a young woman.

In her personal letters, we shall see how she chafed at someone interviewing her and making her feel incapable, unfortunate, and pathetic. She despised being called "paralyzed" and made it a point in interviews to make sure the reporter understood that. Virginia Andrews was particular about the impressions she made on her fans especially.

As we can easily conclude from pictures taken of her in public or just with family, included in this volume, Virginia Andrews cared just as deeply about her feminine appearance, maybe even more so because of her limited social encounters. Her clothes, her hair, her cosmetics—all of it was certainly important to her even if she wasn't going to attend any sort of public event. When a book promotion was the reason for a photograph, she took special care. As pictures taken with fans and family included here will show, she is beaming, flourishing, and joyfully having the experience of interacting and discussing her work and her art.

According to her niece Suzanne, "Virginia loved pink rose and seafoam green colors. Some of the dresses she herself had sewn. One of my favorites was a rose chiffon, mid-sleeve, with a jewel-embellished burgundy velvet cinch at the waist. She looked like a princess. Her hair at the time was a strawberry blond, shiny, with soft curls."

Keep in mind that this was Virginia long before she became quite famous and was very aware of her appearance before her fans and the press. Suspected bone spurs and her surgeries to correct her physical issues did not steal away her womanliness and especially did not stop her meteoric rise when fame came knocking on the door of the house where she lived with only her mother.

After reading this biography, I hope fans will appreciate the complexities of describing Virginia's diminutive, hard-crusted mother—someone who never expected, and was not prepared, to become a caretaker for a daughter so beautiful and talented. Her mother, according to the testimony of family, was often in denial about Virginia's disability, often looking for an escape from this difficult reality. We might conclude that in a real sense, Virginia felt trapped in an attic of sorts. Her mother was the woman who eventually ended up opening the front door to learn that her disabled daughter, who worked at all hours of the day and night, had been heard by some of the biggest names in publishing and who had turned her into one of the most successful commercial authors of the time.

All children's parents make major choices for them, but how many adult decisions did Virginia's mother make for her after her affliction began, after her unsuccessful surgeries, after the body cast stole her teenage years when a young girl's self-image is so vulnerable? Did Virginia crystallize this question herself in *Flowers in the Attic* when Chris says, "I believe, though I'm not sure, once you are an adult, and come back to the home of your parents to live, for some odd reason, you're reduced to being a child again, and dependent"?

Certainly because Virginia needed crutches and was confined to a wheelchair for most of her adult life, her mother cared for her, and more vigorously after her father's passing in 1957. But were some people right to characterize her mother as Bette Davis in *What Ever Happened to Baby Jane?*—dominating, confining, judgmental—instead of a mother who tried her best to be protective of her fragile, beautiful daughter?

If the rumors and, in some cases, written comments about how tightly and sometimes harshly her mother controlled her were true, why did Virginia dedicate *Flowers in the Attic* to the woman? And why then, during the early days of Virginia's struggle with cancer, did she legally ensure that her mother would be well cared for? Did she feel she *had* to? Was there the push-pull of a love-hate relationship?

We have personal letters that will help us understand these apparent paradoxes that have lingered for decades and others that will reveal some hitherto unknown facts about Virginia's romantic life and her family relationships. At one point, we might easily conclude that her life was directly affected by these apparent contradictions and found voice in her novels, sometimes verbatim.

The Andrews family had no experience with fame, much less worldwide fame. They were hardworking Southern folk whose women could easily be imagined behind a protective colorful fan, smiling shyly, sipping mint juleps, and listening to their men argue about politics, their jobs, and the economy. Hearing the way the surviving members describe family functions, we sometimes feel as if we've stepped into *Gone with the Wind*—only our Scarlett O'Hara would find herself on bestseller lists, not dance cards. And she was almost as active as Scarlett as a result.

In particular, many to this day don't realize that after the success of *Flowers in the Attic*, Virginia participated in several book conferences, attended the national ABA convention in Chicago in June 1980 after the publication of the sequel *Petals on the Wind*, and spoke there at a session featuring her. She contributed to and attended publishers' publicity events, even overseas, and did book signings with a joy and delight that rivaled that of any other successful contemporary author. And, like other successful authors, she was eager to describe her craft to those dreaming of similar success.

A clear example of how she refused to hide behind any infirmity was the way she seized upon the opportunity to play a cameo role in the first film adaptation of *Flowers in the Attic*. She would not be a shy wallflower. Virginia's letters will tell us what she appreciated and didn't appreciate about the first film version of *Flowers in the Attic*, as well as why it took so long to make. These include some of the cast's reactions to her and her reactions to the first screenplay. Most exciting, perhaps, is her detailed description of her first visit to Hollywood—whom she met, the celebrities she saw there, and how she was wined and dined.

We will also have a box seat for her first and only transatlantic trip to promote her work, meet her fans, and enjoy just being a tourist. We have the press's reactions to her and her bitter reactions to their coverage, all revealed through her letters to family members and their testimonies.

However, aside from how much of her material was drawn from real life, perhaps nothing is more central to the mystery of V.C. Andrews than arriving at the truth concerning her disability. Was it the result of an accident, blundering medical attention, or a chronic condition exacerbated? Just as important is how it affected her social life, her family life, and especially her work. Perhaps one of the most exciting revelations of all is how one of these medical experiences provided the foundation for Virginia's remarkable writing career, *Flowers in the Attic*. In analyzing the novel from this perspective, we will examine theories regarding how Virginia applied her own life experiences and personal decisions to her characters' lives.

Virginia did not set out at first to be a writer. In her youth, she hoped to be an actress, for practically the same reasons she wanted to become a writer. Her medical event ended that pursuit, but she didn't settle on an ambition to be a successful writer immediately. Rather, she developed a respectable career in commercial art, somewhat necessitated by her father's unexpected death and the family's need for income to supplement his Navy pension and her disability payments. Her artistic talent was there from an almost incredibly early age. Teachers recognized it. Her classmates were intrigued with it, and her family was amazed. Where it took her educationally would be just as surprising.

So, then, if she was so successful at it, why did she give up art and turn all her energy to writing? And when she began to dedicate herself to writing, she was not an immediate success. By her own admission, she had written nine novels before she wrote *Flowers in the Attic*, none of them attracting an agent, much less a publisher. Why didn't she give up writing novels and stories and return to art, through which she had proven income?

Could it have had something to do with a self-proclaimed ability to see the future, a future she saw filled with success, and her belief in reincarnation? Would it surprise you to know that Virginia was convinced she was gifted with ESP and thought this gift prepared her to confront the challenges presented by chronic pain and limited mobility? Did "psychic" experiences strengthen her faith in her eventual writing success? From her letters included here, it is almost eerie to see how confident and determined she was.

What does triumph look like for a successful author as opposed to, say, a business entrepreneur? Authors, all authors, find success with their work when they create an intimate connection with their readers. These authors succeed in going beneath the surface of romance and love, hate and envy, dreams and pain, to touch what is true not only for themselves but for humanity in general. It's this achievement, especially the fears and challenges of adolescence and the betrayal within families, that allows some authors, like V.C. Andrews, to become international successes.

At the time of this writing, there is a V.C. Andrews title in just about every country that has a publisher, including, as of relatively recently, mainland China. What is it about this author, her characters, and her stories that touches the hearts and minds of people regardless of their nationality, language, and socioeconomic development? What makes her universal? And especially, what makes *Flowers in the Attic* and all its sequels so popular in all these countries, a popularity that truly seems immortal?

Virginia's books continue to sell in significant numbers. Most dramatically, adaptations of V.C. Andrews novels have been featured so often on the Lifetime channel that the channel is claiming the author as part of its cachet. To this date, Lifetime has done fourteen movies, each garnering some of the best ratings among all its movies. This clearly disproves the idea that these stories were for a past generation and are not timeless. There is a constant influx of new readers, of young girls and young women discovering them—and let's not forget the new male readers, despite the common perception of V.C. Andrews as for women only. In fact, her first fan letter, as we will see, came from a man.

Indeed, Virginia's works are timeless and universal. What makes them so? Is it the successful way she captured the development, subtle at times, from childhood to adolescence, adolescence to adulthood? She admitted to reading and studying psychology at the time, but she also admitted that she couldn't live without fantasy. Fantasy led her to creative writing, to fiction, in which an author could take the omniscient point of view and, in a sense, play God.

Most writers do that, play God, though perhaps not as purposefully as someone like Virginia, who lived within narrow borders for most of her life. Looking down on her cast of characters, she, like all writers, designated where they would go and how. To be a successful writer, you have to sublimate yourself and see the world through the eyes of those you have created. You sift your personal likes and dislikes, dreams, and ambitions through a very fine sieve constructed from the characters you've created. Novels, after all, are not meant to be autobiographies.

But, as we will discover through her own comments and clear analogies to her own experiences, for Virginia, any rule about novels being pure fiction was not so strictly observed. Indeed, if your characters are providing you with a freedom of movement that life has denied you, you want them imbued with much of who you are. You want to slip into them and do what they do, go where they go, whether that is to a dance, to a party, or on a simple walk in the park, even an exploratory walk like the one Audrina takes in *My Sweet Audrina*.

And yet how far can one go with this theory? Do we apply it specifically to a novel like *Flowers in the Attic*, every major story beat? Certainly no one wants to be locked in a small bedroom and an attic for over three years during their adolescence. But can't the argument be made that Virginia was indeed locked up in a *medical* attic following her surgeries and body cast? At one point, we will see how she admits to the analogy.

The point is clearly illustrated in a letter she wrote to her nephew Brad Andrews: "No one knows more about depression than I . . . it is my daily battle to fight and to win. I live in the tightest cage of all, my own body." Although the analogy isn't exact, trapped and caged is how she had envisioned the Dollanganger children in *Flowers*. Can we understand how sympathetic she would be and how important it was to her for her readers to feel the restrictions?

Readers are always interested in hearing about what real person some character is based on. And theories run especially rampant regarding *Flowers in the Attic*. This biography will describe some significant revelations regarding them. How much will Virginia Andrews finally admit to? How much of herself did she inject into the fictional Cathy Dollanganger?

Most commentators and reviewers searching for answers have been frustrated by Virginia's contradictory statements about herself—some deliberately so—and by her avoidance of penetrating interviews. In *Faces of Fear*, she reveals, "I'm a Gemini, and I've got a tremendous need for secrecy. I don't want to tell people all about myself. I decided that I would put bits and pieces of me in my novels, and they won't know which parts are really me."

Apparently, she deliberately sought to be mysterious. What did she fear about being more truthful? Where can we go to find the truths she never revealed to the public?

Because of the surviving family's cooperation, we have not only historical family details in documents but also family photographs never before seen and Virginia's own letters, most of which have never been read by the public, filled with her thoughts and opinions about herself and the world around her. Much of the information in this biography also has come from interviews with Virginia's closest relatives, who lived with her and her mother at times and thus witnessed Virginia's life-changing events themselves. These are the recollections of her contemporaries. Much is taken from their personal discussions with her and what they themselves gleaned from those interactions. (This includes an aunt who at the time of this writing is 103 years old and in possession of a vivid memory.)

Because of all this, while we can never really know a person in full, I am confident that we can begin to understand what forces conspired to create the writer V.C. Andrews became.

From the way her family describes it, it did seem as if someone had waved a magic wand, just like the good fairies in her fantasies. One day she was a much-protected and quite isolated young woman not really known by the people of Portsmouth, Virginia, and then, although it took almost all her adult life, suddenly, surely overnight to them, she became one of the city's most famous people. Awards would come her way, one from the governor of Virginia, another from the city of Norfolk, in their celebration of local notables. The media would pursue her, and a major publishing company would wine and dine her, arranging for her to meet fans at book conventions and autograph sessions. There was talk of a Broadway play based on *Flowers in the Attic*. Movie producers would seek rights to her big achievement. Almost as if the wind had picked up her identity and carried it across the ocean, her fame would fly to international capitals.

One of the most important and perhaps most fascinating questions is how—after she had been diagnosed with cancer at age sixty-one, four years after the publication of *Flowers in the Attic*—did knowing she was in a losing struggle with cancer impact her work and her relationship to her family and fans? Almost as soon as she got to enjoy the accolades, the financial success, and the self-satisfaction of seeing her dreams materialize, it was all being snatched away from her.

How natural it would be for such a person to be bitter and angry toward the end, but was Virginia Andrews? She wasn't leaving behind children or a husband, but she knew she was leaving behind books that would go on. Indeed, she wrote again to her nephew Brad after she had experienced having her books become bestsellers and told him, "I have never felt the need to be a mother. I consider my books my children, children that will never die from what my public and publishers tell me."

She was right about that.

And so, as with any biography, but perhaps more so here because Virginia Andrews herself was quite private, we have the main question we must try to answer: Who was she?

We'll get to know Virginia Andrews through what she tells us in her letters, in her interviews, and in what she said to her family and how she related to them. Alongside this, we'll wonder, what gave her the courage to come out of her undesired—as she herself said—"cage" to greet her overwhelming success and then gracefully, tragically, watch her life slip away?

chapter one
First Steps

A COOL BREEZE SKATES over the Elizabeth River and combs through the grass around the tombs and monuments in the Olive Branch Cemetery on Cpl J M Williams Avenue in Portsmouth, Virginia.

Despite the passage of decades, or perhaps because time has cemented her name in literary history, reverent admirers enter the Olive Branch Cemetery to pay their respects to an author who has deeply touched their lives and the lives of millions of readers worldwide. Looking down at her footstone, they see she is simply described as *Author*, but when her admirers look at her monument behind it, they first see an inscription bearing the titles of the books that gave her domestic and international fame, headed by the title that most likely has brought them here: *Flowers in the Attic*.

Walking around to the rear of the monument, they see that Virginia Andrews had these thoughts inscribed, a farewell letter to her fans:

Books opened doors I hadn't even realized were there. They took me up and out of myself, back into the past, forward into the future, put me on the moon, placed me in palaces, in jungles, everywhere. When finally I did reach London and Paris—I'd been there before. When books fail to give me what I need, dreams supply the rest. A long time ago I dreamed I was rich and famous—and I saw flowers growing in the attic. Dreams can come true, no matter what obstacles fate chooses to place as obstacles to hurdle, crawl under, or go around. Somehow I always manage to reach the far side.

What else can I say? To have a goal and achieve it, despite everything, is my only accomplishment. If I give a few million readers pleasure and escape along the way, I do the same for myself.

—Yours, Virginia C. Andrews

Cleo Virginia Andrews, who went by Virginia Andrews (her mother's preference, because she loved the state of Virginia), was born in Portsmouth, Virginia, on June 6, 1923, the second child of William Henry Andrews and Lillian Lilnora Parker, who had married on May 8, 1920. This was the year the Nineteenth Amendment was ratified and women could vote. Lillian Andrews was only eighteen and still couldn't vote—it wasn't until 1970 when the voting age was reduced from twenty-one to eighteen—but even so, she was certainly one with a strong presence in this marriage. In fact, William's close friends called him "Bid" because he never knew when to bid when playing bridge and waited for Lillian to tell him what to do, a small but telling sign of her forceful personality and his reliance on her thoughts and opinions.

Did she, like many wives, tell her husband how to vote? When to make a change in their lives? Where to live? What work he should do? The evidence seems to support a big yes. Words used by surviving relatives to describe her ranged from "determined" to "controlling." These personality qualities will have great meaning and importance for us to understand once the family of five essentially becomes a family of two: Lillian and her daughter, Virginia.

William enlisted in the US Navy and would send home money for his young family when he was away. In one postcard he wrote from Cuba, he said, "I will always send you money and I will always be faithful to you."

Not formally educated, Lillian worked as a telephone operator. Affectionately known as "Hello Girls," these women had the tedious job of connecting calls via cables and jacks at the telephone exchange. According to Virginia's aunt Eleanor Parker—whom the family called "Baby Sis" because she was the youngest of the Parker sisters and who is now 103 years old—Lillian was headstrong, a wild child who had been sneaking out of her house at night to attend the dances at the navy yard.

From what Virginia's cousin Pat Mock recalls, Lillian's father was a very conservative man who strongly disapproved of his daughter's nocturnal adventures. She even recalls hearing he had occasionally gone after Lillian and dragged her back from the streets, "and not gently." This will prove to be quite a contrary view of the woman who later ruled her family with almost as much conservatism as her father had once ruled her with.

However, it was at these navy yard dances where Lillian met William, who Baby Sis said was a handsome man who was always impeccably dressed, and whom everyone seemed to love. "From what everyone told me about their romance, everyone in the family was pleased with the choice Lillian had made," said Mary Andrews, the wife of Virginia's brother Eugene.

The Andrewses' first child, William "Bill" Andrews Jr., was born on May 24, 1921. The young family struggled on William Sr.'s naval pay and were as yet unable to afford a home of their own. They lived with Lillian's parents and her five siblings in a large four-bedroom home in Portsmouth. Pat Mock recalls that Lillian's father was a successful businessman and had one of the biggest brick houses in the area.

Two years later, Lillian gave birth to Virginia. For an additional two years, they remained a naval family, with William often away from home and Lillian sharing the household duties with her mother.

William Sr. was a veteran of World War I and was used to Navy life. Some of the Andrews descendants suggest that Lillian insisted her husband finally leave the service. They often heard her say he should "get a decent job to support his family," and she finally convinced him that his romantic Navy life had to come to an end. There were two children to support now. She wanted her family to be secure; she wanted her children to be protected, and all her living relatives remember she was not shy when it came to her opinions. This was surely a telling example of her firm, no-nonsense personality.

In 1927, the circle of life would take young Virginia and her older brother, Bill, and their parents first to Rochester, New York, where William Sr. had been born and raised. His parents were still alive, as were his three brothers, Arthur, Roy, and Wallace. The Andrews family had a big dairy farm outside the city, but only Arthur helped his father run it. William Sr. had taken his young family back to his birthplace not to work the family farm but because he had the opportunity to work for Bausch & Lomb, one of the earliest and most successful optical companies, famous for developing groundbreaking sunglasses for the military in World War I, which had been founded in Rochester.

Soon after they arrived in Rochester, William Sr. bought a relatively new house that his brother Wallace, a builder, had constructed not far from his own house at 25 Wetmore Park, in a quiet residential part of the city. Virginia and her family lived in Rochester from when she was four until she was nine.

Although far from wealthy in the 1920s, Virginia's family was living during a period of economic boom that drove more and more people from the rural world to the cities, aided by improvements in indoor plumbing and modern sewer systems.

The comparatively undeveloped Portsmouth where she had lived previously would be a dramatic contrast to the city of Rochester, even for one as young as Virginia. Rochester was bursting with urban energy. In the late eighteenth century, Rochester had flourished with the opening of the Erie Canal and became a major manufacturing center, bustling with a growing population and five freight and passenger railroads.

It will surely be of interest to her fans to know that young Virginia's startling impressions of a rapidly modernizing urban world came from a deep-seated belief, even at so young an age, that she had lived in this very place during an earlier time. Virginia seriously believed in reincarnation. According to her sister-in-law Mary, she called herself "an old soul" and her mother "a new soul."

"When I was a little girl," Virginia told Douglas E. Winter in *Faces of Fear*, "particularly when I was very young—three or four—I would look at things like automobiles and skyscrapers, and I would say, 'They didn't have those when I was here before.' I was sort of expecting horses and carriages. And then I would feel strange thinking this."

She claimed she would get flashes of other lives when she was a child. Adults would shake their heads and smile as adults do at children's imaginations. So, according to what she told others later in her life, she began to "shovel it all under" and didn't think about the subject for a while and later tried to stop the sensation from happening so much.

Despite the effort to keep it to herself, her belief in her psychic visions would remain with her through most of her life. She would use the concept in *Flowers in the Attic*, where Cathy has a premonition that she will fall in love with the first man she meets, although it won't be just any man. Like a young Virginia, Cathy had visions, detailed visions. "If I had a dream that the airplane I was taking was going to crash," Virginia said, "I wouldn't take it. So before I take a flight, I try to remember what I dreamed." Perhaps one of the most notable of Virginia's visions was, "When I sent *Flowers in the Attic* off to my agent, I had a big house dream."

Transferring the visionary power to Cathy in *Flowers in the Attic*, she wrote: "And somewhere in that crimson-colored never-never land where I pirouetted madly, in a wild and crazy effort to exhaust myself into insensibility, I saw that man, shadowy and distant, half-hidden behind towering white columns that rose clear up to a purple sky. In a passionate pas de deux he danced with me, forever apart, no matter how hard I sought to draw nearer and leap into his arms, where I could feel them protective about me, supporting me . . . and with him I'd find, at last, a safe place to live and love."

And this is precisely what happens when Cathy meets Julian Marquet, the dancer who had been pursuing her since the day they met. Was he the dancer she envisioned in the attic? She marries him impulsively in *Petals on the Wind*, the sequel to *Flowers in the Attic*. Visions and prophecies run dramatically through all the novels Virginia wrote. What she believed for herself she was sure to have her characters believe. This was no mere literary device for Virginia.

Eventually, this fascination with clairvoyance would come out in the more in-depth interviews after her success with *Flowers in the Attic*. Virginia even claimed to have foreseen her father's death two weeks before he died of heart failure in the hospital.

Elaborating in *Faces of Fear*, she said, "I woke up and I was crying and I told my mother, and she said, 'Don't tell me. I don't want to hear it.'"

According to Virginia's niece Suzanne, Lillian would get frightened whenever she saw Virginia make a prediction, no matter how silly or insignificant it might seem.

"When I lived with my grandmother and Virginia for a month, I saw her tell Virginia to 'stop that' whenever she predicted this or that, especially if it involved members of the family or neighbors. I had the impression my aunt took a little pleasure in teasing my grandmother with her sudden predictions, made up or not, when she was younger."

Everyone remembered that young Virginia had a jovial personality, was more like her father, and could be a little impish. However, there was nothing jocund or blithe about what she had envisioned for her father. Their relationship was close, their love quite strong. He had inspired her in many ways, especially when it came to literature.

The seriousness with which she took clairvoyance never waned, despite how her mother forbade it. She tied it closely to her dreams. At one point during her writing career, she would express a desire to write a novel about someone with psychic abilities. She would think a character who was living what she would often call an otherwise dull, ordinary existence fascinated her. There was no doubt she saw herself as such a person. Late in her teenage years, mainly because of the restriction her disability and consequently her mother had placed on her, she didn't have friends or a boyfriend. Adventurous journeys were limited to the front porch.

Perhaps visions and dreams were another reason Virginia would eventually be drawn to writing fiction. In a real sense, the author of a novel must see the future for his or her characters. Once she had a plot premise and a main character, Virginia could begin to envision where the events unfolding in her imagination would take her protagonist. This is also why forming the character is so essential, because his or her personality, ambitions, and likes and dislikes will determine the plot. Simply put, if characters are vivid enough, they will naturally lead the writer down a path. For Virginia especially, it was another exercise in clairvoyance and clearly the door to escape the confinement her illness had imposed. Thus, her developing imagination encouraged her to explore, and as time went by, that drive only intensified.

"I step into a universe of my own making," she was quoted as saying in the *Virginian-Pilot* and the *Ledger-Star* in 1986, "and I am the god. What a sense of power! Nobody can exist unless I let them."

Creative and imaginative people hunger for a means of expression, even at a very young age. But it is one thing to be imaginative and pretend, to be part of the make-believe games you might play with others your age, and quite another thing to be innovative and creative enough to produce something of value, which Virginia did first with her visual art.

One of the earliest examples of her imaginative artistic skill came when the famous architect Frank Lloyd Wright arrived at her elementary school to speak to her second-grade class in Rochester, four years after her family had moved there.

Much later in life, when she was talking about her art experiences, Virginia related her vivid memory of Wright pausing at her second-grade desk, standing behind her, looking over her shoulder, and asking, "Why did you draw a round house with all glass?"

She recalled her teacher standing by with a small smile of pride and curiosity. From what Virginia described, one of the world's most famous architects did not intimidate her seven-year-old self. To her, the answer was plain and simple.

"Well, it's my mother," she replied. "She always complains that she never seems to have enough windows."

Virginia had a clear recollection of the encounter, the classroom situation, and Wright's reaction. As noted in a Simon & Schuster press release after *Flowers in the Attic*'s publication (a release that Virginia helped create), Wright told her teacher, "A child like that scares the hell out of me."

The fury with which she would imagine and then create her artistic images was already overwhelming in grade school. Her memories of this period were vivid and expressed in a number of interviews. Her second-grade teacher gave Virginia an easel and placed it at the back of the class because she would finish her work quickly and otherwise become a distraction to the other kids. Moving her to the rear didn't solve the problem, however, as her classmates would turn around to see what she was drawing or painting, and the teacher lost their attention anyway.

One temporary solution to fill Virginia's spare time in class was to send her to help in the principal's office, to be kept busy copying information about student attendance and school repairs. Years later, as an adult, she felt that the experience was one of the first to urge her into writing. In *Faces of Fear*, she related, "He [the principal] said, 'Remember, you've got the talent to do anything you want to do as long as you stick to that one branch . . .' and every time I would falter in my writing, I would think of him."

Eventually, Virginia's second-grade teacher took a closer look at her work and realized that she really did have a prodigy on her hands, something Virginia called herself many times in conversations, letters, and interviews.

Virginia explained it to Winter this way: "Well, we had a house that had an interesting design, and I knew you couldn't see it if I did it head-on, so I drew it three-quarters and in perspective. My people had necks and arms and waists. Any of my teachers who looked at my work were stunned because 7-year-olds don't know to see perspective and how to go to a vanishing point."

Virginia's teacher was frustrated but also excited. She showed Virginia's drawings to the principal, but he was skeptical. He was, after all, looking at the work of a seven-year-old. This wasn't childish doodling.

"You saw her draw these?" was the response Virginia recalled and often bragged about when she related the story to her sister-in-law Mary. Her teacher confirmed it, and the principal was astonished.

Here was a wunderkind in 1930—what could a grade school offer her? Her teacher couldn't ignore the rest of her pupils and concentrate more on Virginia, and yet the principal might have felt guilty letting this budding talent die on the vine. Amazingly, the powers that be doubted that even a high school art class could further develop this nascent talent. They had a solution that was far ahead of its time: they sent the diminutive seven-year-old child to junior college art classes.

Virginia remembered sitting on a big dictionary to see the front of the classroom at the junior college. In *Faces of Fear*, she described the experience: "I think my nose just used to clear the desk and I would draw with all these great big kids."

Can we imagine what it was like for eighteen-, nineteen-, and twenty-year-olds to see a bright and inquisitive little seven-year-old girl listen to and follow the instructions that perhaps challenged even them? Would the older students feel resentful? Maybe. After all, what they were being asked to do was something that even a grade-school child could do. Perhaps their skepticism would have abated when they saw what Virginia could accomplish.

Virginia, on the other hand, was not intimidated sitting among older and bigger kids. What did they have to do with the art that became her passion? According to her, the development of her talent was unstoppable. She took her vision and her art with her everywhere. She claimed she would draw on all her books, illustrate everything she read. She admitted to defacing library books by drawing on them. She said she used to color the black-and-white funny papers because she wanted them to be in color; she even tried to color the bedroom wallpaper because she thought it wasn't lively. There was an excitement in her life that few seven-year-olds enjoyed. Most were temporarily amused with a coloring book or when given a blank pad and a pencil, especially with multicolored pencils, but Virginia was more than amused. She was challenged, and after mining her imagination, she skillfully created pictures adults admired.

She was never far from her love of art and what she had learned about colors, shades, and tints, even when she wrote *Flowers in the Attic*. The novel opens with Cathy Dollanganger telling us, "It's so appropriate to color hope yellow." She was, of course, relating it to sunshine, brightness, symbols of hope that would exist outside the attic.

Later, perhaps employing what she had learned in her advanced art lessons, Virginia speaks through Cathy: "Momma bought us art instruction books by the dozens. The first of these books taught us to reduce all complicated designs into basic spheres, cylinders, cones, rectangles and cubes. A chair was just a cube—I hadn't known that before. A Christmas tree was just an inverted ice-cream cone—I hadn't known that before, either. People were just combinations of all those basic forms: spheres for heads; arms, necks, legs, torso, upper and lower, were only rectangular cubes or cylinders, and triangles made for feet. And believe it or not, using this basic method with just a few simple additions, we soon had rabbits, squirrels, birds, and other small friendly creatures—all made by our very own hands."

This description of what Cathy did with the animals clearly reflects some of Virginia's designs and needlework created years earlier as well. Describing her own work in a letter, Virginia wrote: "I decorated mine with polka-dots, gingham checks, plaids, and put lace-edged pockets on the laying hens." Drawing from the details of artwork she did during her medical confinement in her teenage years after dropping out of school for health reasons, Virginia refers to Corrine bringing Cathy sewing notions like "lace, cords of all colors, buttons, sequins, felt, pebbles and other decorative materials."

Cathy's fictional biography in *Flowers* often bears a resemblance to Virginia's actual life. While drawing exact equivalences can lead to error, in some places, as with discussions of art, there is a true mirroring.

A second area of similarity: Cathy's family, prior to the father's accident, existed in an atmosphere of happiness and security, one Virginia surely related to.

Virginia's childhood was a time when her family, like so many middle-class families during the late Roaring Twenties, would enjoy some measure of financial security. Her father was gainfully employed, they had a relatively new house, and their family was growing. Lillian gave birth to Virginia's younger brother Eugene five years and ten months after Virginia was born and nearly eight years after Bill Jr. Virginia and Bill Jr. were often looking after baby Eugene, especially when their mother went shopping. Contemporary relatives say they both enjoyed and welcomed adult responsibility.

Did this childhood parental experience find life in *Flowers in the Attic*? Was motherhood something Virginia longed for later in life, despite at least one disclaimer to the contrary to her nephew?

It was always something looming out there. She did say she had planned to be married by age thirty. "I never wanted to be an ordinary housewife," she told Stephen Rubin in the September 1981 *Washington Post* article "Blooms of Darkness." "I had no intentions of getting married till after thirty, but life kinda threw me a curve. I think if I had failed at writing maybe I would be bitter now. I always wanted to be somebody exceptional, somebody different, who did something on her own."

Perhaps she expressed her frustration at never being able to become a wife and mother best in *Flowers*, when Cathy tells her twin siblings, "Why can't you pretend I'm Momma? I'll do everything for you that she would. I'll hold you on my lap, and rock you to sleep while I sing you a lullaby."

When one learns more about Virginia's confinements and social restrictions, one can easily envision the writer imagining how she would be with her own children, were she to have them. .

And yet at the start, none of this dark future, despite her prophecies, weighed heavily on her. Not yet, not in this childhood. A new younger brother, accolades for her artwork, her father's family nearby, and a blossoming, exciting urban world around her all provided Virginia with great childhood happiness, that magical "summer day" Cathy saw in *Flowers*. Relatives recall that her parents were often complimented regarding Virginia's beauty and intelligence. The future was full of promise for the Andrews family, as well as for so many others in the growing middle class.

These years of comfort and happiness were starting to tremble, however. Lillian had given birth to Eugene just as another birth was occurring, forces that would shorten the idyllic middle-class existence for so many families. The threads of this coming devastation were insidiously at work weaving through the nation, and indeed the world. The economy was set to collapse like a house of cards.

Like so many veterans of the Great Depression, Virginia would have a more intense fear of what it would mean to lose her wealth and material possessions when she began to accumulate them. She could certainly refer to her family's experiences with financial pressure during the Great Depression and what she had witnessed around her when she described the plight of Corrine and her children after Christopher Sr. was killed and left the family destitute at the start of *Flowers in the Attic*.

Millions of people everywhere suffered similar financial panic in the 1930s. Experiencing the Depression and later the loss of her father, Virginia would have no trouble envisioning a newly widowed woman so desperate to survive that she would appeal to the mother she had fled, asking someone she had once run from to help her and her children. Just from the experiences of the women in her own family, she would see the glass ceilings everywhere.

Flowers in the Attic is set in the 1950s. In 1957, 70 percent of working women had clerical positions, worked on assembly lines, or had service jobs—nothing a woman like Corrine would do. Only 12 percent had a profession, and 6 percent had management positions. Again, nothing we could envision Corrine being capable of doing. She had no skills or business acumen, had never attended college or had a job. Regardless of the period, the Corrine created by Virginia in *Flowers* was burdened with four children; her chances of gainful employment were next to nil.

Like so many who had lived through the Depression and its aftermath, Virginia was always keenly aware of the value of things, down to the very penny. In many letters to her family, she often referred to expenses. Even after *Flowers* was placed with a publisher and she was writing a sequel, she wrote to her brother Eugene, his wife, Mary, and their children: "And so far I am not one cent richer, only poorer. I keep buying IBM ribbons like peanuts for elephants to eat, and boxes of 20 lb. bond, costing 9.75 per box, and second sheets of four colors, 6.75 per box—(ream) . . . and I'm not earning a cent. If I don't make it big with this book, I'll be worse off than when I started, for the IRS will be after me, plus the Social Security people."

Although it's somewhat amusing for us to see Virginia's dollars-and-cents concerns—knowing what we now know of how impressive her success would be—she was right to worry at that point. Most published authors don't make more than their advances, and she had only received a $7,500 advance for *Flowers in the Attic*. Her concern was related to her understanding of the government benefits she was receiving as a disabled person. She told her family in the same letter: "You may not have thought this, but accepting the advance will take me off of Social Security, and the health benefits I receive." (In order to receive such benefits, she wasn't permitted to earn more than $3,300 per year.)

Moreover, the future millionaire was already thinking like her own accountant. She told her family: "But my royalty advance is more than double that amount . . . and therefore, this year I will have to pay income taxes, too."

However, she wasn't raised by particularly frugal parents. After 1941, despite their having navigated through the Great Depression, Virginia's parents were very proud of her and wanted to spoil her. Her cousin Pat writes: "My mom frequently said they always gave Virginia beautiful things. When rubber bathing suits were the rage, Virginia had one in every color. When it came to Virginia, nothing was too good for her. Forty-dollar blankets were casually purchased when 40 dollars was a fortune in the 1940s. In that respect, Virginia's mother Lillian was very generous."

Let us not forget that these were war years, too. So much of what had been taken for granted, the basics of life, even during the Depression, had become more valuable than ever. During these years, the war years, William Andrews Sr. continued to make a good living, support his family, and maintain his home.

The roller coaster of emotions Virginia put her characters

through in her novels was happening and did happen to her. If her biography, her life, could be described as anything, it would certainly be a car ride taking her up and then down hills before finally taking her very high and then tragically dropping her precipitously just as she finally felt the wind in her beautiful hair.

But what about the other influences on her work, the ones that would take her up the stairway to open the door to what would be one of the most famous attics in all of literature? Psychiatrists, psychologists, and sociologists largely agree that the major aspects of someone's personality are formed during the first five years of childhood. Examining more of Virginia's early life, we find this to be quite true, from her father's influence on her reading to the accolades she received for her art.

Because so much of Virginia's work revolves around family dysfunction, one would anticipate finding dysfunction in her family. However, relatives have vivid memories of the William Henry Andrews family being stable and loving. Despite the dark worlds of parent-and-child relationships that Virginia depicted in her novels, familial recollections and known familial history seem to indicate that she did not tunnel down into her own childhood to mine the specific cruelties and betrayals that we find so vividly drawn in her stories and characters.

In all of her letters in which she discussed her childhood, Virginia recalled happy times and a close, loving family. In *Faces of Fear*, she said, "I didn't have a terrible childhood. The most terrible things about my childhood probably were those that I created in my mind, because my childhood was so ordinary, and I wanted it to be more exciting. But it wasn't exciting. A lot of people think I was tortured, but my parents didn't do anything. They didn't beat me. They didn't whip me. They didn't lock me away. I didn't go hungry. And I had a lot of pretty clothes. . . . I don't know how I suffered, except that I wanted a life much more adventuresome, and I didn't think it was, so I used to play exciting games with my friends. They told me I was the best instigator of the plots for our games."

A major question for us while we travel through Virginia's life then is, from where did she draw these psychologically grotesque figures? Few of them are physically ugly. There are no Freddy Kruegers in her novels, although the nightmares of the children tormented in her novels aren't remarkably different from the experiences of children victimized in graphic horror stories. Virginia gave us a whole new definition of frightening when she wrote *Flowers in the Attic*, but perhaps what she envisioned was not so much invented as it was uncovered. The fears she wrote of, as we will see, were somewhere in everyone, something many readers were unwilling to confess.

Books were a big part of Virginia's early life. In the *Virginian-Pilot* interview, she described her father taking her to the public library and signing her up for her own library card. She claimed he was a reader and said that on that first day at the library, he went home with two books and she with nine.

Virginia wrote that her father kept only three books in the house: the Bible, *The Navy Man's Journal*, and *Tarzan and the Jewels of Opar*. She said *Tarzan* piqued her interest in storytelling and claimed to have read "most of the classics" by the age of twelve.

Virginia never explained to any interviewer or member of her extended family why her immediate family owned so few books despite her father's emphasis on them. Most quickly realized that a gift of a book was the thing Virginia would appreciate the most. Virginia recalled her mother objecting to the cost of new books and telling her there was always the library. And truly, the library was a place she often frequented until she could afford to buy the books she wanted.

In 1973, when she moved back to Portsmouth after having lived in Missouri and Arizona, Virginia told her aunt Baby Sis in a letter: "For me, the trial is doing the proper research. Even in fiction you have to be accurate. I can't go to the library when I need to. Libraries are reluctant to rent out their reference books. But, fortunately, there is a school across the street quite willing to let me borrow any book they have, and I might need. Unfortunately, their books are written for children, and they skim lightly over every subject. In the end, I'm forced to buy many expensive books, and now, I have a formidable library of my own. Every time a new book comes into the house, Mother voices objections! 'Stop!' she cries. 'When we move, it will cost thousands just to transport your damn books!'"

In her teens, Virginia discovered the novels of Charles Dickens, and because they became her favorites, she admitted going through a period of trying to duplicate Dickens's style. In the prologue of *Flowers in the Attic*—again giving more evidence of how much of herself Virginia put into her young protagonist—Cathy tells us, "Charles Dickens would often start his novels with the birth of the protagonist and, being a favorite author of both mine and Chris's, I would duplicate his style—if I could."

Virginia took delight in describing the library in Foxworth Hall and the shelves that went all the way up to the ceiling, the source for all the books Corrine brought Cathy in the attic. Books were always seen as windows and doors to the worlds beyond Virginia's reach and were the same for Cathy. In the novel, Cathy reads *Wuthering Heights*, one of Virginia's own favorites, and Cathy tells us, "I loved reading Shakespeare and Eugene O'Neill, and anything that was dramatic, fanciful and fraught with tempestuous emotions."

Corrine brings them the same books they've read and enjoyed before: *Little Men*, *Jane Eyre*, and the fairy tales of the Brothers Grimm and Hans Christian Andersen—more classics that Virginia herself would have devoured.

The only thing that compared to this form of escape from a real locked-up attic and a confined life were Virginia's dreams, dreams she claimed roused her imagination.

Referring back to herself at seven years old, she said in the *Virginian-Pilot* and *Ledger-Star* interviews after the book's publication that she used to have "these fabulous dreams and I thought what fabulous books those dreams would make. A lot of my books are based on dreams. When I get stuck, dreams help me out."

It is not unusual when exploring the minds and creative impulses of very successful novelists to find them referring to dreams for their inspiration. Mary Shelley claimed that at eighteen, she had a dream that would change her life, and we all know what that dream became: *Frankenstein*. As highlighted by Harriet Hall in her 2018 article "Who Was Mary Shelley and What Inspired Frankenstein?" Shelley wrote her thoughts through the voice of her protagonist: "My dreams were all my own; I accounted for them to nobody; they were my refuge when annoyed—my deepest pleasure when free."

Both Shelley and Virginia mention the importance of their dreams to their writing. Also like Virginia, Shelley taught herself, between homeschooling and being an avid reader. And, amazingly, like Shelley, Virginia was and is credited with creating a new genre. Shelley created science fiction because her work couldn't be assigned to a genre at the time *Frankenstein* was published. There was nothing like it. And Virginia couldn't be assigned a typical genre early on, either. There is too little development of serious romance in her novels to place them comfortably on the same racks as Harlequin titles or the like; perhaps this lack could be directly attributed to what she missed experiencing in her own life.

V.C. Andrews novels are certainly too slow-paced to qualify as thrillers. Dynamic or violent action is quite restrained. And yet there are surges of love and affection. Sex is never graphic, but it's there. And goodness knows, characters are pushed down stairways and/or poisoned. Many booksellers shelve V.C. Andrews novels in the horror section, but Andrews's concerns with family, emotion, and relationships put her books firmly outside that genre, as Winter examined in his words about *Flowers in the Attic*: "The story is animated by nightmarish passions of greed, cruelty, and incest, told in romantic, fairytale tones, producing some of the most highly individualistic tales of terror of this generation."

There is and was a strong tendency to think of V.C. Andrews as a young adult (YA) novelist. In recent decades, that category has certainly expanded and taken turns of plot that we would never have expected in a Nancy Drew story. Despite the reach of Andrews's novels beyond young girls, we might sometimes still find her in the YA section simply because of the ages of her protagonists and the genre convention that such protagonists suffer challenges and problems usually experienced by older people—they are thrust into adulthood too soon.

Regardless of genre, that early push into adulthood would happen to Virginia herself, albeit in a different way from the characters in her novels. She was experiencing a normal childhood, excelling in grade school, performing in a high school play, and building friendships. However, her experiences with illness and physical disability both rushed her maturity and restrained it.

Obviously, the times and events, both historical and social, have their impact on everyone's childhood, too. Writers consciously or subconsciously record their experiences and find ways to bring them back through their work, sometimes greatly surprising themselves. Perhaps it's not inaccurate to say that writers especially work under the spell of their subconscious thoughts and feelings. In *Faces of Fear*, Virginia said, "I live all my books. When I go into my office, I lose touch with my conscious; I come in tune with my subconscious and it turns on like magic. So as I begin to push the buttons on my computer, I am also programming myself."

As a result of the economic tsunami, William Andrews packed his family in his Chevy and drove back to Portsmouth, Virginia, in 1930. As young as she was, did Virginia recall the same fear and panic as she described for Corrine and her four children fleeing their happy home, destitute, when her husband, Christopher, is killed at the start of *Flowers in the Attic*? "Now all our beautiful things would be taken away."

Before they left Rochester, how many children and families did Virginia see evicted from their homes, staring at the abyss? Darkness was seeping in all around. Boys and girls her age and younger were clinging to their mothers' skirts, their eyes big and filled with fear, perhaps the same fear the Dollanganger children saw as they rode on the train and as they walked through the darkness toward this looming house that seemed to peer down on the rest of the world. Frightened as they were, they were filled with the hope that their mother's promise would be fulfilled.

What did this cheerful, artistic, and imaginative young girl, fleeing Rochester with her family, cling to in order to see the same hope lying ahead in their return to Portsmouth? Surely some of that was waiting in the embrace of family. But perhaps she instinctively knew that the one thing the economic free fall in the country could not take from her was her talent and imagination.

She had reason to have confidence in her talent, even in a world where so many adults as well as their children looked lost. Again, revealing a deeply held sense of pride, she repeated what the principal had told her when she spoke to Winter for his *Faces of Fear* interview: "Remember, you've got the talent to do anything you want to do as long as you stick to that one branch. Decide which one you want to follow, and lop the other ones off." At one point in her life, she lopped off visual art and turned to creative writing. However, she claimed that every time she would falter in her writing, she would think of the school principal. After so much rejection in her earlier years, she must have wondered if it was time to chop off that branch, too. Thankfully, she did not.

When the Andrews family arrived in Portsmouth, they confronted a much less-developed urban world than the Rochester they had just spent years living in. It wouldn't be until 1935 that Portsmouth would get motor buses, whereas Rochester already had subways, with the street railways that had morphed into buses. There wasn't half the hustle and bustle in Portsmouth that Virginia had known in Rochester.

The family moved back in with Lillian's parents, the Parkers. Besides the stock-market crash of 1929 and bank failures, the drought contributed to these years of poverty and struggle that would last until 1941, with 1933–34 being the worst of the hard times for most average Americans.

Interestingly, the state of Virginia had experienced a delayed reaction to the Great Depression. Because of the nature of its economy, the high rate of subsistence-level farming, and the support of federal money in the Washington, D.C., and Norfolk areas, the population was resistant to the initial effects of the crisis. Nevertheless, the state was hardly Depression-proof. Unemployment began to rise more rapidly in 1931, farm prices plummeted, the state government cut spending to maintain a balanced budget, and relief rolls rose sharply. By the time the Andrews family arrived in Portsmouth in 1932, Norfolk and Portsmouth had fired teachers, imposed salary cuts, and closed city kindergartens. Almost two-thirds of the state of Virginia's counties reduced school terms to less than eight months. In Portsmouth, one church was feeding a hundred people a day with leftovers collected from the Norfolk naval base.

Fortunately, William Andrews's father-in-law found him work at the Navy shipyard. As most families were doing, the Andrewses garaged their car to eliminate the expense of gas and maintenance. They saved newspapers and old rags, and they repaired clothes. Virginia's ability to sew and create her own clothes later surely found some of its origin here. After a few years, William would leave the shipyard and put his skills to work at a tool-and-die company. Amiable and always ambitious and optimistic, Virginia's father would never stop finding ways to provide for and support his growing family.

Virginia continued her schooling at the Robert E. Lee grade school, skipping third grade and then being promoted to sixth grade after fourth. How this was effected is unclear, but typically, this sort of advancement was based on an exam a teacher would administer. Considering her early school achievements, her study habits, and all the reading she had done and continued to do, her advancements through grade school were not surprising.

And then, as if lifted by a wind blown from destiny, that journey took a devastating turn. As would be echoed in her novels, it was a turn occurring on a familiar place: a stairway.

The stairway is especially prominent in *My Sweet Audrina*. But in describing Virginia's descent, we are facing something much less gothic in nature: a high school staircase. Virginia's plunge would begin with a figuratively and literally twisted fall. It was almost a free fall, with at first nothing tangible to seize to stop it. She grabbed a banister and injured herself with a painful twist carrying out the instinctive action. It was an accident that we will see had so many ramifications that it would have understandably stopped most people from doing anything more with their lives.

But Virginia's imagination was relentless, and through it and through what she could create, she would rise again. Perhaps she didn't stand up as easily as everyone else, but she was certainly ready to confront destiny face-to-face, a true phoenix rising from the ashes.

But what had life been like in her late childhood years leading up to her crisis? How different did it become, and how did she and her brothers adjust to their new home and the dramatically new times? In order to understand the devastating effect her disability had on her young life, it's important that we contrast her later life with the almost idyllic days before, related to us by Virginia herself in her interviews and in the words of her closest brother, Eugene.

chapter two
Moving up the Stairway

VIRGINIA ANDREWS FACED GREAT challenges throughout her life. In letters to her family and in intimate conversations with her niece Suzanne, Virginia admitted to having especially great difficulties in her adolescence, whether it was sharing her changing emotions with girlfriends or responding to the interest of a boy. She had come through a happy childhood, but confronting her own sexuality was further complicated by her physical degeneration after her accident.

As elegant and interesting a teenager as Virginia was becoming, she couldn't hide the pain and the awkwardness she endured from what would turn out to be a form of premature arthritis that grew worse over time. However, even before this, she blamed adolescence itself for being a most confusing time.

It's important to keep all this in perspective: Virginia's adolescence occurred in an age of far more innocence, the 1930s. Mothers, especially ones like Lillian Andrews, were not fond of discussing intimate subjects. Sex was almost a profane word in and of itself. Cousin Pat recalls that Lillian was the only one in the family who had a negative reaction to the incest in *Flowers in the Attic*: "She was outraged and said she would never read another word Virginia wrote."

Despite the way Lillian's younger sister Baby Sis depicts her in comments describing her disobedience, which included staying out past curfews and hanging out on street corners with her friends to her father's dismay, those "wild" days did not result in a liberal-minded parent. We will see Lillian's prudish, conservative ways even more vividly illustrated when men try to court a mature Virginia, a woman her mother thought vulnerable because of her disability. Time and time again, Virginia's personal experiences find a voice in her writing, and feelings of budding sexuality perhaps the most vividly. Sheltered and isolated during her teenage years, Virginia lacked the social relationships that would help her mature into adulthood.

Similarly, consider how Cathy in *Flowers* had to rely on her brother for knowledge and understanding of her own maturing sexuality. He hid his embarrassment by remaining as objective and scientific about it as he could. It was only when he couldn't look the other way that things began to change. It was an easy identification for author Andrews to make.

Virginia's medical problems occurred at the height of her adolescence. She was experiencing them at the doorway of her teenage life, and they exploded in her mid-teens. However, the way she ignored the hold that the crippling arthritic condition had on her throughout her life so she could create her world-famous novels gave her a heroic, almost mythical status.

The childhood happiness that Virginia referred to in her interviews occurred at a time of tragic and painful suffering in the country. When the Andrews family moved to Portsmouth, Virginia, for a second time, moving in with Lillian's parents once again, everyone in the household was navigating the rough waters of the Great

Depression. At least William Andrews's work at the navy yard was consistent through the hard times, and surely this stability helped provide happier childhoods for Eugene, Bill Jr., and Virginia. Virginia entered the Robert E. Lee grade school and eventually began Woodrow Wilson High School at almost thirteen, the age most would be in seventh or eighth grade.

There is no doubt that William Sr.'s having solid employment took away much of the pressure and turmoil that plagued most families during the economic turndown. How bad was it around the Andrews family? By 1940, upward of 1.5 million wives and children were living apart from their husbands and fathers, and there were more than two hundred thousand vagrant children wandering the country because of the breakups of families. Yet the Andrewses, because of their ingenuity, not only survived but seemed to be living in an alternate universe, closer to what was in store for the country in the prosperous postwar years to come. In her letters, Virginia recalled the excitement she and other fortunate children enjoyed on summer days when the horse-drawn ice cream wagon came down the street. In most communities, such an indulgence didn't exist during the Great Depression, and even where it did, children didn't have the money for it.

The year the Andrews family moved back to Portsmouth has been described as the bleakest point of the Great Depression. About a quarter of the US workforce was unemployed. Those who still had jobs had their wages cut or their work reduced to part-time. Even upper-middle-class professionals, such as doctors and lawyers, saw their incomes drop by as much as 40 percent. The motto was, "Use it up, wear it out, make it do, or do without."

The Andrewses held on to their family pride and united in their efforts to "get through it." Virginia vividly remembered herself and her brother Bill Jr. helping their father in the "Depression vegetable garden." Survival was a family project. Everyone worked for it, however young. Depression-era homemakers like Virginia's grandmother

Lucy and her mother, Lillian, learned how to stretch their food budgets with casseroles and one-pot meals.

Virginia and Bill Jr. enjoyed the church hayrides in horse-drawn wagons, riding the picnic train that stopped on Randolph Street and Atlanta Avenue. Sometimes they drove twenty miles to Virginia Beach for the day. Virginia's younger brother, Eugene, recalled their father driving them in his '35 Chevy, "the laundry basket filled with fried chicken, potato salad, deviled eggs, big thermos jugs of iced tea, and a huge tablecloth to fit over one of the dozens of wooden picnic tables lined up under the pavilion. The pavilion joined a long frame tunneled arcade where all the concessions were. The penny arcade, fun house, etc., that sort of thing. I usually tagged along with Virginia and one or two of her friends while Bill Jr. took off with one or two of his friends.

"I remember the times when three or four cars filled with our family and Mom's would take off to Nags Head and Kitty Hawk, North Carolina, seeing the Wright Brothers Monument with Virginia and other family members. Virginia was about twelve or thirteen. The three of us played on the hillside around the monument, picked and ate scuppernong grapes, and rolled around the tall grass. There were church lawn parties, where something called potlucks occurred, a popular way to share food and a cheap form of social entertainment."

There were ten-cent westerns to attend—a special thrill for Eugene and Virginia—even though more than one-third of the cinemas in America had closed between 1929 and 1934.

Eugene recalled Virginia taking him to the movies when he was old enough. In particular, he remembered going to see *Pinocchio* and *Snow White*. In his attempt to write of his life with his sister, a project he has never completed, he vividly describes walking home after the movie: "After *Snow White*, Virginia insisted we walk. All I could think of was that terrible witch and so we ran most of the way home."

These were the "happy Depression" days, the family days. Eugene wrote, "Once school was out, Virginia seemed like any other little girl. She loved to run and play and do all the things little girls like to do."

He meant that her higher level of intelligence and artistic talent didn't make her seem so different that other children her age would avoid her, or she them. This love of the simple things while craving something different, fantasizing, and creating made her even more exceptional. Enjoying holidays and visits with her niece and nephews, aunts, and cousins illustrated her love of family, of friendship and belonging. In less than a decade, most of this carefree lifestyle would be lost to her. But for the present, despite the economic storm raging throughout the country, Virginia and her brothers were still in the idyllic world that most children craved.

The beginning of *Flowers in the Attic* has such a personal tone reflecting this period of happiness in Cathy's life that it could have been the beginning of Virginia's autobiography. (She did try to write one when she was older but was so depressed by it that she tore it up.) But if we look carefully at Virginia's work, we can discern some of her story despite how well and insistently she denied most such associations. For example, knowing what her childhood in Rochester and later in Portsmouth was like, just substitute "the Thirties" for "the Fifties" in the first chapter of *Flowers in the Attic*.

"Truly, when I was very young, way back in the Fifties, I believed all of life would be like one long and perfect summer day. After all, it did start out that way. There's not much I can say about our earliest childhood except that it was very good, and for that, I should be everlastingly grateful. We weren't rich, we weren't poor. If we lacked some necessity, I couldn't name it; if we had luxuries, I couldn't name those, either, without comparing what we had to what others had, and nobody had more or less in our middle-class neighborhood. In other words, short and simple, we were just ordinary, run-of-the-mill children."

This is not to say there wasn't a great deal personally to overcome during these seemingly idyllic early years. Just about three years after the Andrews family arrived in Portsmouth, when Virginia was twelve, the family experienced a true tragedy when Virginia's grandfather was caught between his large boat and the seawall and crushed to death. Pat Mock recalls the mortal injury being a crushed spleen, for which there were apparently no good treatments at the time.

After his father-in-law's fatal accident, William Sr. moved his family quickly when a new home came up for sale at 1729 Atlanta Avenue in Portsmouth. The house had the minimal traditional architecture popular in the United States from 1900 to 1950. He renovated it over time to be more like the ranch-style homes in the neighborhood, including the refinished brick masonry. It would be known as a cross-gabled house because of the roof structure. It was a modest home, with three bedrooms, one bathroom, and a dining room, living room, and kitchen. There was a separate garage at the end, with a split driveway, which was also utilized as the laundry center. It had a double sink and a wringer washer. Some of these details are mirrored in the small towns in V.C. Andrews's Landry series.

The move was essential, making it more convenient for Virginia's aunt Iris and her husband to return to the Parker home to take care of grandmother Lucy, who could not drive, nor could she read or write.

The struggles of her grandparents had a major impact on Virginia, who, in referring to her early family life, recalled not only the tragic death of her grandfather but also her grandmother's disadvantages from being illiterate. It was especially notable for Virginia, who recalled reading an entire newspaper in Rochester when she was only in the first grade. When Virginia was older, she recalled how her father used to read the Rochester paper aloud to her when they lived there, skipping over certain things to keep the daily news age-appropriate. She was only in the third grade, but she liked to brag that later she would sneak back to the paper and read it all, even the parts he had skipped.

Of course, one has to recognize the unfairness of women's lack of access to, and even dissuasion from, a robust education at the time Virginia was in school. The basic belief in the 1930s was that women should marry as their first priority. The predominant theory was that college-educated women were less likely to marry simply because they waited too long or sought equal status with their husbands at home. The unwritten warning was there: if you want a husband and a family, don't pursue a formal education. For Virginia's grandmother, growing up in the rural nineteenth century didn't include reading and writing, and she, of course, managed to marry without those skills.

Virginia became aware of all this and surely reflected on the status of women in her writing. Although Cathy's mother, Corrine, is literate in *Flowers in the Attic*, she lacks the education and knowledge to find any means of employment. Was it simply that this was expected of women who came from wealthy families? Were they doomed to marry someone of stature who would naturally be in control? Although far from domineering, Corrine's husband, Christopher, kept her from knowing and understanding the details of their financial plight. She is described as not knowing about any of their debt or even what money they had. She is obliviously satisfied with not having to deal with such details as paying for what she has bought.

When Corrine becomes widowed, it is clear there is little she can do about it but throw herself on the mercy of her mother. Such a character made sense to Virginia simply because of what she had seen in her own family and the families around them. While Corrine was treated more like a princess and spoiled, and lacked responsibility, even during her early days at Foxworth, the women Virginia saw as she was growing up weren't given the opportunity to take on more responsibility—clear differences with similar results.

On the other hand, Olivia, the famous grandmother in *Flowers* who rules over the children in the attic, is definitely an exception to the image of women in her day. Her intelligence, especially when it comes to helping her father in his business, is quite well portrayed in *Flowers* and expanded upon in *Garden of Shadows*, the series prequel.

Malcolm Foxworth is actually threatened by it. I often wonder how much of Virginia's disapproval of and intolerance for the belittling attitude toward women she was able to vicariously express through Olivia's dominance and intelligence.

Say what you like about her religious fanaticism and cruelty, but in the novel, Olivia is quite capable of running the Foxworth manor and business empire when Malcolm is incapacitated. Of course, one wonders if there was someone specific Virginia was depicting. There were undeniably successful businesswomen who served as models for emerging women and for those who had emerged by the 1970s. Virginia was on solid ground depicting Olivia as one so capable of evaluating investments and balancing books that her father treats her as a business partner in *Garden of Shadows*. After the publication of *Flowers in the Attic* and the sequels, Virginia was especially proud of her own financial acumen, aware of expenses and hands-on with issues of taxes and living costs. This was someone who, before her success, had never been involved in the simplest of financial arrangements—never buying clothes for herself, let alone cars and houses.

"Already I have filled out my income tax forms, and was horrified at the amount of taxes I have to pay on what I call a trifling amount of income—and just wait until next year," she wrote to Mary and Eugene Andrews. "My living expenses have taken a tremendous jump since buying this house. We still own the other one, too. The real estate business is just about dead. If we don't sell soon, we will have to rent as our electricity, gas, and etc. is still going on."

Aware of what her financial responsibilities could become, she expressed a deeply felt fear: "When Mother is gone, if I should live that long, I will have to pay for every service performed. I have to save for that day." Conversely, the money allowed her to express more of her independence, about which she noted: "But I do have more control, due to that money you make . . ."

All this informs us continually that history and environment, especially family situations, affected Virginia's work as much as, if not more than, they would for any fiction writer, even slipping into fantasy. As was pointed out, despite all these obvious connections to her fiction, Virginia constantly resisted her personal life being tied too tightly to her work. She was aware of how ugly it could make her mother-daughter relationship appear, a concern she expressed to her family in letters.

Nevertheless, she wrote about things she was sure her mother wouldn't want her to confront. She wrote behind closed doors and never shared her work with Lillian. Eventually, she realized that to free up her imagination and get to that place where her work would be interesting and original for her, she had to write about these subjects. She knew her mother would be sensitive to what people said about them, especially about Virginia. How much of Virginia's mother was in the character of Olivia? That question was constantly pursued, starting almost immediately upon the publication of *Flowers in the Attic*, but Virginia always tried to disassociate her personal life from the lives of her characters.

Although she told a reporter from a Portsmouth newspaper, *Currents*, in 1980 that she preferred to have a character tell a story in first person because "you can really get inside a character," she went on to say, "A lot of people think it's me I'm writing about, but it isn't. All fiction, I think, has some substance of truth, but then the imagination takes over in developing a plot. If people want to think I'm writing about myself, let them."

How could she have it both ways?

She was very good at playing this cat-and-mouse game. In fact, she clearly enjoyed it, especially later in her life, when so many were pursuing her for revelations about herself and her work. Perhaps another strong reason for the denials was that she placed so much weight on the power of her imagination, the fantasy, and slipping into her own world. Why damage it with "reality"?

Yet Virginia Andrews did not choose to ignore the conflicts, difficulties, and cruelties she witnessed in other families. When her niece asked her what the source was for her stories, she admitted to being influenced by the terrible newspaper stories about other children. "It makes you think about the why. And from that, characters develop and stories begin to form."

She would say it many times to many different interviewers and commentators: she was in a constant pursuit to understand why people who were supposed to love each other instead hurt each other. It's the essence of her stories, especially in *Heaven* and *My Sweet Audrina*. Fathers were truly quite cruel in these novels, torturing their daughters psychologically and sometimes physically. As we have clearly seen, that dynamic did not apply to Virginia's relationship with her own father, but she wasn't going to ignore what happened to other children, even at the risk of her fans thinking it all really happened to her. Making the point and exposing the terror of children formed a central theme for her.

In fact, in the prologue to *Flowers in the Attic*, she has Cathy say, "I will hide myself away behind a false name, and live in fake places, and I will pray to God that those who should will hurt when they read what I have to say. Certainly God in his infinite mercy will see that some understanding publisher will put my words in a book, and help grind the knife that I hope to wield."

These lines demonstrate the sense of pain and the anger Virginia experienced and skillfully expressed. One can take joy in the eventual happier resolutions in her stories, but it's the journey, always the difficult journey, that she reveals in heart-wrenching detail. As we will continue to see in this biography, much of this had roots in her personal struggles with her health and the family's convoluted life. However, a strong case can be made that she was looking out of windows more than into mirrors when it came to the way some parents treated their children. She saw it in her contemporaries, especially during the Great Depression.

Virginia's quick advancement in grade school in Portsmouth already had placed her with older students, expanding her view of families and relationships. Ordinarily, peers might resent someone younger being considered their equal, just the way college art students had at first been put off by having a seven-year-old sitting beside them. Nevertheless, Virginia's elementary school life went smoothly. Her younger brother, Eugene, recalls, "Of the three of us, Virginia was always the most studious. She loved school and was always her teacher's pride. I remember when my dad enrolled me in grade school and when the school principal, Mr. McGavic, and some of the teachers, Miss Avery, Miss Ames, et cetera, would come up to my dad and tell how much they liked Virginia, 'so industrious,' they would say, 'so smart, such wonderful manners, and such a pretty girl.' I can even remember my first-grade teacher, Miss Hutchinson, saying to me when I was first enrolled in grade school, 'Oh, you're Virginia's little brother. She's so smart, the other teachers tell me. If you're just half as good as your sister, you'll be one of my best students!'"

Indeed, quite an avid reader, Virginia expanded her reading lists, claiming she found "girl" books dull and choosing stories for boys instead, favoring adventure and fantasy. She loved fairy tales. In one of her talks to writers at an event after the publication of *Flowers in the Attic*, she said there was "truth behind fairy tales."

The truth she was getting at had to do with the sort of fear you could experience by reading something like "Hansel and Gretel"— and she didn't mean the moral of the tale. Although it's not the horror of Freddy from *A Nightmare on Elm Street*, it's pretty scary when you consider that it centers on a brother and sister lost, or abandoned, in a forest, where they fall into the hands of a cannibalistic witch living in a house made of gingerbread and other sweet treats—all things that kids would love.

She recalled this concept in her interview with Winter in *Faces of Fear*: "There is an element of horror in fairy tales, so that when I would go through the woods I was always looking for something—

a witch, an ogre, something scary—and it was never there, and that was a bit disappointing. I didn't want to read a real horror like a rapist or murderer, but I wanted fairy-tale horror.

"I read Edgar Allan Poe and I was absolutely fascinated with him. I can't read him today, he's too dull. But at the time, I adored Poe because he gave me the chills, made me shudder. I liked *Frankenstein*. My uncle bought me a first edition of *Dracula* when I was twelve, and he said, 'Now this is valuable. Keep it and treasure it.' The book scared me so much I would put it in the closet and cover it up, and I would put a little piece of garlic at my windows. I even bought a crucifix to keep Dracula away from me."

Virginia certainly saw the power in fairy tales, elements that most people at first look don't realize; she relied on these "scary fairy tale and horror" elements in her novels. Although Olivia looks like a monster to the kids, she is their grandmother.

Poison on doughnuts? Kind of a "gingerbread" idea . . .

Virginia's niece Suzanne remembers her "reading Aesop's fables . . . [she] loved the fables. She also loved 'Snow White and the Seven Dwarfs.'"

As for other influences on her writing, she did tell the reporter in a 1986 *Virginian-Pilot* interview that she preferred the moody books such as *Jane Eyre* and *Wuthering Heights*, along with Russian novels with rain and stormy weather. And indeed, if you carefully study the books she wrote, you will see a constant awareness of weather and its effect on her characters and their feelings and thoughts. Early on, from her reading, she learned how to use the weather and the environment to set a mood, as she did in *Heaven*.

". . . poor Granny had led me out into that cold, wintry night so many years ago, to visit a cemetery . . ."

"And here I was, long past midnight, sitting on a cold, stony bench in a deserted rose garden, allowing the soft falling rain to drench my hair . . ."

"The air was cool and sharply pungent. . . . I stared up at the sky. It seemed to me like an inverted deep bowl of navy-blue velvet, sparkled all over with crystallized snowflakes instead of stars—or were they tears of ice that I was going to cry in the future?"

Cold and darkness, rain and clouds—all accompany sadness and introspection. Rarely do her characters mourn someone they love under a blue, warm sky.

The books, the movies, the stories about other families she had heard while in school and listening to her family talk at dinner, what she had read in newspapers, and what she overheard afterward from adults whispering gossip—all of it clearly stimulated Virginia's very active imagination, driving her more to her writing than her art. For her art, as we shall see, was used to capture beauty, fantasy, and dreams, not the terrors and mysteries of family intrigue.

One must consider, however, that her pursuit of commercial art as a means of making a living followed quickly on the heels of her debilitating medical condition. It was so logical to turn to art, because she didn't have to travel to do it, and she had been complimented so often on her artwork already. Her mother encouraged it more than she encouraged her writing and even personally pitched her fashion work to department stores. Most important of all, it's not an exaggeration to say Virginia was desperate to find something of beauty in this dark and depressing world.

And yet, it's understandable how fascinating it is that this storyteller chose to travel through her artistic imagination first, even though books and stories, and especially fantasies, surrounded her. She had a double talent. But the demons that wanted her to face darker subjects didn't prevail in her artwork. Was she trying to keep them at bay initially?

How did this decision to direct her artistic energy to the written word develop? She was definitely attracted more to plots about fantasies at the start. Like most very young writers, she was happy to be in the world of make-believe. What brought her to her dark view of family relationships?

Although many point out the fantasy-like elements in Cathy Dollanganger's imagination while she was locked away in the attic of Foxworth Hall, it was not the world of princes and princesses, dragons, and magic that would create the unique voice in Virginia's published works. She never let go of fantasy, but it fell into the background of the darkest view of family behavior and relationships.

She kept fantasy novels on the back burner while she went forward with the dark premises of *Flowers in the Attic*, its sequels, and the novels that followed: *My Sweet Audrina*, *Heaven*, and *Dark Angel*.

Her artwork, although beautiful and attractive enough to find customers, including even her dress designs sold to department stores, wasn't enough to satisfy her need to find her identity. Many times she said that the mediocre, the ordinary, was never going to be enough. Call her a dreamer, call her ambitious or even impetuous, whatever way you label her and whatever you believe drove her, you have to come back to the power of that imagination.

She tracked her development as a writer for us by describing her motivations for wanting to be an actress, then an artist, and finally a writer. She admitted to the restlessness and the hunger to expand her identity. She was fascinated, as are most writers, with submerging herself into different personalities. She thought at first that she could do this as an actress, and when that dream was sabotaged by her disabilities, because at the time there was little in the way of accommodating disabled people on movie sets or in theaters, she eventually made the transition to writing fiction.

There are so many unseen similarities between an actor and a writer. Good actors must know where they are on the stage. They must know the setting, because the setting impacts how people feel and what they do. Some dramatists rely on the genius of set designers after they provide a few simple words like "city street at night," "formal living room," or "porch of an old house."

A novelist must give his or her characters a place. The setting will affect how they feel, too. Virginia took her time with descriptions of place. For instance, in *Flowers*: "I sat up and looked around this room that was, perhaps, sixteen-by-sixteen. Large, but with two double beds, a massive highboy, a large dresser, two overstuffed chairs, a dressing table between the two front windows, with its own small chair, plus a mahogany table with four chairs, it seemed a small room. Cluttered."

This initial description of the room the four children will be contained within helps darken the hopes of Cathy and Christopher Jr. Who would lock the door to keep her four grandchildren so closeted? How will this confinement—especially of the two small, active children—affect them? What will it do to their moods, and how will it change who they are? Setting heavily influences the characters and, along with their mother and grandmother, turns them into who they become in the novel and its sequels. In fact, in some ways, the setting is everything in *Flowers*.

Did this choice to write so dramatically about confinement come from Virginia's own sense of it? To grow, to experiment with your growing personality, was something she longed for, and it's something Cathy especially longs for.

Her arthritis told her, *You can't be an actress. You can't be someone else even for a few hours on a stage or in a movie.*

But her becoming an author told her, *You can create and, while you create, become your characters and go anywhere and be anyone.*

Perhaps this was the biggest motivation for Virginia. In her novels, she could walk out of her house. She could see other places and confront other challenges. It was no wonder that she put her easel aside and began to travel through her words.

According to E. D. Huntley in *Dictionary of Literary Biography*, Virginia told Barbara Lewis of the Charm Associates school in Norfolk, "Books opened doors I hadn't even realized were there. They took me up and out of myself, back into the past, forward into the future, put me on the moon, placed me in palaces, in jungles, everywhere. When finally I did reach London and Paris—I'd been there before."

Before Virginia chose her ultimate career path, she reveled in the complexity of being a teenager. These were simpler days for teenagers and tweens. Nancy Drew stories were popular. On the radio, people were listening to the music of Jimmie Rodgers, Big Joe Williams, Roy Acuff, the Smoky Mountain Boys, and the Benny Goodman Orchestra. Despite the Great Depression and the lead-up to the war years, teenagers were living somewhat carefree, dreamy existences. There were still dances and girl talk, school plays and concerts, fairs and parties.

In talking about her youth, especially before the severity of her medical issues manifested, Virginia said she thought that the hard time she was having during her adolescence was typical. All teenagers, she believed—and as she would later portray extensively in her novels—have a hard time with their sexual identity.

What set off alarm bells in her during these early teenage years was the way older men, even the fathers of her friends, would look at her. It both frightened and intrigued her.

In the *Virginian-Pilot*, Virginia said, "I had a hard time when I was a teenager. I think all teenagers do. In those days, nobody told you about anything. You were in the dark about sex. I was a pretty girl. It wasn't so much that friends of my brothers were interested in me. Their FATHERS were interested in me. I couldn't talk about it. I wanted honesty, and no one gave it to me. Instead I was handed fairy tales. So I went to the library and got out a book."

I would have the opportunity to question her teenage niece about this. There was a strong physical resemblance. She reinforced some of the "uncomfortableness" Virginia had felt, which, as we know, only strengthened Virginia's interest in what might be called the *Lolita* syndrome.

In the famous novel by Vladimir Nabokov that lends the notion its name, a grown man is overwhelmed by his fascination with a beautiful twelve-year-old, and eventually she encourages his interest, unaware of the impact it will have on her mother. This *Lolita* syndrome was something Virginia certainly explored in *Petals on the Wind*, when young Cathy Dollanganger has an on-and-off relationship with Dr. Paul Sheffield. His housekeeper, Henrietta "Henry" Beech, a mute African American woman, had rescued the fleeing Dollanganger children and brought them to Dr. Sheffield.

It is, as we'll continue to see, Virginia's ability to utilize her experiences and imagination that positioned her to do what most successful writers do: expand on the "what if" question. What if she had been able to have a frank conversation with someone about these unwanted and inappropriate advances? Or what if she had encouraged one or more of the friends' fathers back in her teenage years? Is that what Cathy does with Dr. Sheffield?

Virginia believed that being one of the prettiest girls in school always made that person the target of the envious and jealous. She suggested that this led to her having problems with other girls early in her teenage years. She had been in high school long enough to understand the power of jealousy and competition for the attention of boys.

She put her limited experience to work in *Dark Angel*, again suggesting strongly that her ideas stemmed from her own personal experiences. The girls of Winterhaven, the private school Heaven attended, were quite jealous of her beauty and sweet personality. They looked for ways to pounce on her and belittle her: "All I had to do was make one mistake and those girls with their 'right' background would scorn me for what I was."

Although Virginia continued developing her art, the writer in her began to emerge during her early teen years. She excelled in her schoolwork and at fifteen won an award for writing a parody of Alfred, Lord Tennyson's *Idylls of the King*. (Sadly, this work has been lost.) This was to be the same year the problems developing in her hip were aggravated when she twisted herself on that high school stairway.

The ironic, almost cruel questions we are left with as the struggles and defeats followed Virginia throughout her life as a young adult and an adult are: If she hadn't been confined—trapped, if you will—by her own damaged body, would she have become the international author and star she became? If life had been smoother and her beauty and intelligence had been permitted to grow unencumbered, would she have settled into a marriage with children and only dabbled occasionally in art and creativity? This is not to say that a woman in that situation couldn't be creative. There are so many examples of ones who were and are, especially now. It is simply that a woman in the '30s and '40s and even the '50s creating an independent stream of income while in a marriage was rarer.

As we continue with Virginia through her difficult journey and see how and where her interests inevitably developed, it's reasonable to conclude that she might have found a different way into Foxworth Hall, but no matter what route Virginia might have taken, her Cathy Dollanganger would have been there. Nothing, not even normalcy, could have stopped Virginia Andrews from finding the flowers in the attic.

chapter three
Nearly at the Last Step

THERE HAS BEEN WIDESPREAD confusion over the medical battle that began for Virginia at the age of fifteen. (Although, amazingly, even to this day, some fans I've encountered and who comment on Facebook pages are surprised to discover Virginia was disabled.)

Many believe that what happened to her in high school eventually brought about her early passing at the age of sixty-three. That would be true if you could develop the argument that her arthritic condition weakened her immune system to the extent that cancer could fatally invade her body, but this would be unscientific conjecture.

The most incorrect information is that Virginia fell down a stairway in high school and suffered a trauma to her back. There was no *fall* down the stairs—and certainly nothing like the stairway fall in *My Sweet Audrina*. Yet Virginia's disability has been described that way in countless articles, in introductions to book reviews, and even by radio and television reporters. Part of the reason for the mischaracterization of her physical issues might very well lie with Virginia herself and somewhat with her mother.

Even before the 1980 *People* magazine article and its photographs that Virginia ranted about, she was tight-lipped when questioned about her medical condition. In letters to and phone conversations with her family, she railed against the reporters and commentators who wanted to create "some sort of paralyzed creature struggling to type out her fantasies." She saw herself being depicted as "The Humpback of the church of bestsellers, a creature dressed in beautiful clothes to distract the viewer from seeing the abnormalities."

Although Virginia and her mother did attempt to—and often succeeded in—putting on a pretty and happy facade, as her fame began to develop rapidly, there were more and more calls for public appearances and an accompanying desire to publicly explore her physical disabilities. Virginia resisted them all. How easily and quickly someone else seeking more attention might have seized on the opportunity to use their hardships to stress the accomplishment of doing something outstanding.

But not Virginia Andrews; she was not after a promotional gimmick to sell herself and her work.

She lived by the credo that if you didn't talk about the issue publicly, at least for the hour or so of the necessary book promotion, it was as if it didn't exist. Her disability remained a real mystery for some time, and it is misunderstood even now. Rumors love a mystery. Virginia said that mean-spirited people, even neighbors, fanned the flames of the idea that she had been beaten, severely punished. It really wasn't until years after all the medical treatments that Virginia, once in the public eye, began to address her physical condition. Often, she deliberately exaggerated to confuse reporters. Despite her malady, she had what some might call a "sick" sense of humor about it. Others might say she was trolling those who had no right to inquire about such things.

Virginia's niece Suzanne recalls how much her aunt enjoyed toying with the press: "She'd even giggle about it. It annoyed Virginia that reporters concentrated on her physical disability so much that she would confuse them about it. It was her kind of sweet revenge. To do it, she would exaggerate or even invent some treatments."

The fact is that no one in her family had ever heard of some of the things she said in Rubin's 1981 *Washington Post* article "Blooms of Darkness" describing what had happened to her—especially stories about surgeons having strokes while operating on her or predictions of many more surgeries, including a dangerous, life-threatening one supposedly on the horizon.

In that article, however, Virginia related a diagnosis that the family recognizes as closest to their understanding of the issue: "When it finally became obvious that the bone spur had thrown my spine out of alignment, it led me into a bout with arthritis, which I needn't have had if they had taken the bone spur off immediately.

"This went on for four years, starting when I was about 18. Then they began to correct the damage with operations. I had four major ones and have one more coming up."

However, then she veers into territory nobody can confirm and which most doubt: "I can have corrective surgery, but I'm a little leery of doctors because they made mistakes with me. One doctor had a small stroke while he was operating. The saw slipped and he cut off the socket of my right hip.

"I have to have a new replacement. But the operation is very serious for me, life-threatening. I'm not in pain now . . ."

How much of this was a dramatization and/or exaggeration, no one in the family can say. But most of her family knew the truth about the origins of her physical disability.

Her sister-in-law Mary remembers being told that Virginia had taken a wrong step on the stairway at Woodrow Wilson High School, which resulted in badly twisting her hip. "My husband, Gene, had found out that the doctor who had examined her after she complained of persistent pain believed the twist had been violent enough to tear a membrane on his sister's hip. Eventually, after more physicians examined her, the conclusion was she had started to develop little bone spurs.

"The family was deeply concerned. Although I didn't know her when she was very young, I knew from the way everyone spoke of her that she was thought of quite highly. She had been achieving well in school and was quite a beautiful young lady.

"But I must say that when I had first met her and times after, I didn't hear her moaning and complaining. If anything, I was moved by her avoidance of self-pity. It was and is easy for me to understand why she didn't want to dwell on it, especially later on in the newspapers and magazines when she became quite famous."

Her cousin Pat, who not only had Virginia and her mother live with her but often as a very young girl had spent time at their home, blames the confusion about the details of Virginia's accident on Virginia's mother telling people her daughter was "pushed down the stairs in high school, permanently disabling her. It was those jealous girls."

Many were willing to accept this description.

Pat conjectures that Virginia's medical condition embarrassed her mother and that was the real motivation behind her lies. She believes that at times, Lillian hid the fact that Virginia had any medical issues at all. Both she and her husband, William, were proud of Virginia's beauty and depressed about her inability to resume a normal life. Lillian's attempt to hide or ignore Virginia's disability is understandable, considering Lillian's beliefs and personality, and this might even go far to explain Virginia's own attitude about herself and how she was portrayed.

Virginia began twelfth grade, but in October of that year, the pain had continued to the point where she was unable to walk without difficulty to and from school. Both Virginia and her parents were quite aware of the struggle. According to Pat, "One event stands out regarding school and her illness. Virginia came home from school upset that the crossing guard had lost her temper with Virginia for walking across the street so slowly. She said, 'Hurry up, Gimpy' or 'Hurry up, Limpy.'"

Surviving relatives recall Lillian's anger at the way her daughter was being teased and treated by her peers as well as adults like the crossing guard. Virginia continued to endure excruciating pain, making sitting at a school desk for long periods of time difficult. It was clear that all the normal treatments for a twist or a pull on muscles and tendons weren't working.

School records show that Virginia had to leave Woodrow Wilson High School in Portsmouth in October 1940, in her senior year. The records note "Health reasons."

But what was the true medical history that followed?

Virginia claimed that although she was suffering from the pain caused by bone spurs that formed on her spine, she was unable to convince physicians during those early days that she had a problem. As she described the issue in a number of interviews and in her conversations with family, doctors told her that she walked too gracefully to actually be in so much pain. "I found out that looking too good is a terrible way to go into a doctor's office. They don't take you seriously."

We recognize in her experience a timeless problem for women. As recently as May 3, 2018, Camille Noe Pagán, in an article in the *New York Times*, related that "research on disparities between how women and men are treated in medical settings is growing—and is concerning for any woman seeking care. Research shows that both doctors and nurses prescribe less pain medication to women than men after surgery, even though women report more frequent and severe pain levels."

Cousin Pat's father, Fred Parker, recommended that the family take Virginia to Johns Hopkins for the evaluation of her problem. It resulted in her first surgery to correct the bone spurs. If anything, this surgery seemed to have made the problem worse. Virginia was then brought to another hospital, the University of Virginia Medical Center in Charlottesville, where she underwent a second operation. As far as anyone could tell, the original diagnosis was still the most likely to be true: the twist on the stairway exacerbated an arthritic condition that was resulting in a fusion of her bone structure. The second operation was an attempt to clear that up but would require Virginia to be in a body cast afterward.

Despite all this, there was a silver lining in store for Virginia. Although it wouldn't show itself until nearly forty years later, there was something that wouldn't have happened if Virginia hadn't been brought to the University of Virginia for another attempt at alleviating her condition, something that would trigger her fame and fortune years later.

According to Pat, Virginia told her that while she was at the University of Virginia hospital, she became infatuated with a handsome young doctor, who was equally infatuated with her: "They became very close while Virginia was a patient there. She told him about her endeavors and dreams of becoming a published author. Consequently, he thought he would give her a story to write, a true story. He confided in her about his strange young life. The premise, and surely the shocking revelation for Virginia, was that he and his sisters had been hidden away in one of Charlottesville's huge mansions for over six years to preserve the family's wealth. I never learned his name or the family's name. The information was, however, straight from Virginia to me."

We don't have to guess what this anecdote became, but interesting questions arise: Did the doctor specifically mention an attic? How many children were incarcerated in the true story? Were there any twins? Who imprisoned them? Was their grandmother involved?

We know, of course, that there are four children in *Flowers in the Attic*. Pat believes her own family members, absent the incest element, were possible models for the kids. She has a brother who became a doctor and two younger siblings who are twins.

What are the similarities that we do know of? The setting of the story the doctor told and the setting of *Flowers in the Attic* are both in the Charlottesville area of Virginia. The older brother wanted to become a doctor. The hiding of children to regain an inheritance matches Corrine's motivations in *Flowers in the Attic*. She hid her children because if her father knew she had children, she would be cut out of his will. One potentially similar plot point in the doctor's story is that if the trapped children no longer existed, the path to the next beneficiaries would be activated. Of course, Virginia had much more to add to this plot premise by way of the incestuous relationship between Corrine and Christopher Sr., who we eventually learn is her half brother.

However, it's fascinating to contemplate that *Flowers in the Attic* stemmed in part from Virginia's painfully long ordeal. Readers who conjectured that the novel was really Virginia's own story in some way now have witness testimony to its actual origins. What remains remarkable is the length of time between Virginia's hearing the premise of the story and her actually writing the novel. She later claimed in a newspaper interview to have written it "one night, while I was in bed. It was a 22-page handwritten draft. I typed it the next morning."

Continuing to trace the origins of *Flowers in the Attic* and its characters, and what of Virginia's own life contributed to the tale, we have to ask from what height, in what place, and at what time during this difficult and painful journey would she have garnered the view of a grandmother who would give her grandchildren the worst nightmares, even before they had gone to sleep?

The religious zealotry depicted in both Foxworth grandparents could have come from Virginia's own maternal grandfather, who insisted that they attend "hellfire and brimstone" sermons every Sunday at the Methodist church in Portsmouth. Virginia claimed her mother resented the services and didn't want to go, but she forced Virginia to attend nonetheless. Surely the author relied on these experiences when she created the Foxworths in *Flowers in the Attic*, a family dominated by a fanatical invalid father, Malcolm, and a wife, Olivia, who carried out his gruesome religious commands for reasons that went beyond religion, beyond her belief that the children were the devil's own because they were born of an incestuous relationship. Mother-daughter jealousies proliferate between Olivia and Corrine, punctuated with the revelation that Olivia is not Corrine's birth mother, despite Malcolm being her birth father. Furthermore, Corrine was named after Malcolm's mother, who deserted him and his father, Garland, after five years. Malcolm never lost his infatuation with and almost religious love for his mother, which is one of the reasons Olivia is so jealous. Malcolm transferred that love to his daughter and basically had no love relationship with Olivia. Olivia retreated into a fanatical view of her religion, terrorizing the children in the attic with biblical quotes and stories.

We know from her family's recollections that Virginia was not a fan of organized religion. She talked often about her belief in reincarnation, even claiming she had lived in Rochester at an earlier time. In *Faces of Fear*, she said, "I think I have a free-wheeling religion of my own. I have all kinds of beliefs. I happen to believe in reincarnation."

Virginia's version of reincarnation didn't have a structure in the way, say, the Buddhists describe. Simply put, she believed she was born with memories of times past.

She complained about her church experiences, especially in Portsmouth. Her family had taken her to the Methodist church in Rochester, but according to her interviews about her early life, that was not as unpleasant as church in Portsmouth. From the way the family members describe their memories of that, it seems clear she was actually frightened by the fanaticism she encountered at her grandfather's church, together with what she had experienced with organized religion, and so she chose a more independent way of thinking about God.

Again in *Faces of Fear*, Virginia reinforced this view when she said she had grown disgusted with attending church because the church-goers "were there mainly to show off their new clothes." As an adult, she no longer had to attend services and did not belong to an organized religion. She said she believed in God but not in church: "I think you can have church in your own heart or make your own little temple."

Although Corrine wants to convince her father that she has repented, there is no real reference to her own religious beliefs, only to her parents' beliefs, references that we see mirrored clearly in Virginia's own experiences.

"When I was growing up, with my two older brothers," Corrine tells Christopher Jr. and Cathy in the attic, "we were literally forced to go to church. Even if we were sick enough to stay in bed, we still had to go. Religion was rammed down our throats. . . . We were ordered to control our thoughts, to keep them off lusting, sinful subjects for they said the thought was as evil as the deed. . . . Our parents, in seeking to make their three children into living angels or saints, only succeeded in making us worse than we would have been otherwise. . . . I should have warned you that your grandparents are fanatically religious. To believe in God is a good thing, a right thing. But when you reinforce your belief with words you take from the Old Testament that you seek out, and interpret in the ways that suit your needs best, that is hypocrisy, and that is exactly what my parents do."

Did Corrine ever go to church after she and Christopher Sr. ran off to start their new life? Note the absence of any references to God or commandments until Corrine and her children are in Foxworth Hall. What did Corrine believe in? What did she worship? More and more, Virginia developed this character as someone who believed in her own beauty and pleasure, worshipping that even at the expense of her children. We see it so clearly when she parades her new clothes—her new exciting life—before them while they are suffering confinement and a lack of socialization with children their age. She seems not to care about all they are missing. It's as if she worships what she sees in the mirror above all else.

Olivia is clever enough to see through this and keeps Corrine chained to sin in her view. Religion is used as a weapon. Just as she employs it to control Corrine, she uses it to dominate Cathy and Christopher Jr. She wants them to believe they are products of sin.

There are no references to church or church attendance in Virginia's letters to her family, but her own testimonies in interviews underscore how much of this "products of sin" message she garnered from the religious zealotry around her among her family and family friends. And her unflattering view of religion certainly continued to play a strong role in her novels. Later, in *Heaven* and *Dark Angel*, she would even portray the town minister, Wayland Wise, as someone sexually preying on Heaven's sister Fanny and impregnating her.

Was this the way Virginia came to view religion, as a weapon against human frailty, human desires, and sex itself? Her mother, Lillian, certainly didn't believe what Virginia did, especially the parts about reincarnation. Yet in none of Virginia's letters, in none of her descriptions of her life with her mother after her surgeries and even after her publishing success, does she refer to any religious arguments between them. Lillian might have influenced Virginia's view of the hellfire-and-brimstone years before when Lillian refused to attend her father's—Virginia's grandfather's—church in Portsmouth.

Despite what many fans believe, Virginia wasn't using her mother as the sole model for her depiction of Olivia Foxworth. Her mother was conservative and religious but not as fanatical as Olivia becomes in the novels. Many have made an argument for this comparison by pointing out that Virginia's mother, like Olivia, did hold the key to her daughter's freedom and was the one who approved and disapproved of any outings after her surgeries. Was there any truth to that comparison between the control over Virginia's confinement and the confinement of the Dollanganger children? Is there proof of Virginia's resentment? Can we find it in her letters and the vivid testimony of her close cousin Pat?

We keep returning to the question of how much of herself Virginia incorporated into the character of Cathy in *Flowers in the Attic* as our only way to find an answer. The question has fascinated and continues to fascinate readers. We know from family discussions that the name Dollanganger was most likely inspired by Virginia's next-door neighbors' name, Garminginger. The theory that it came from combining *doll* and *doppelgänger* into Dollanganger was never verified by Virginia, and the neighbors' name makes that, at best, a poetic coincidence.

In another element of *Flowers*, Virginia drew from her actual experiences. We know that the famous hair-hacking incident was most likely inspired by Virginia's memory of playing on a street in Rochester when they were putting down fresh tar. She was running and fell, rolling around and getting it in her hair. Her mother was unable to get it all out, so she had to chop it out the way Olivia chopped off Cathy's hair. We know how such an event would affect a little girl who drew so many compliments for her hair. It's a memory Virginia would not forget. It's not too far-fetched to believe Virginia gritted her teeth as she described the scene in the attic, the feelings in herself still vivid, making it that much easier to depict what happened to Cathy.

In an article titled "A Writer's Way to Profit from Memories," quoted often on fan sites, Virginia wrote: "Since my first novel was published [*Flowers in the Attic*], not long afterward many letters came to fill my mailbox: clearly indicating that most of my readers think I am writing about my own life. Only [in] some ways is this true. Cathy Dollanganger is not me personally, but me only in her way of responding to the traumatic events in her life. Her emotions are my emotions, her dilemmas are somewhat similar to mine, but not in any way precisely. It is difficult to say where a writer leaves off and the character takes over."

In terms of drawing from real life for the character of Cathy's brother Christopher, let's consider the facts. Neither of Virginia's brothers had anything to do with the profession of medicine. Her younger brother, Gene, was in sales, married, and traveling often, and Bill Jr. had left home at sixteen to try his luck at becoming a trumpet player. Neither served as a good model for the character. By contrast, the young doctor at the University of Virginia apparently singled her out, spent private time with her, and is therefore a credible model for the character of Christopher Jr. Unfortunately for Virginia, her terrible days in the hospital and all the medical problems she sustained afterward gave her more than a simple layman's understanding of medical issues, knowledge Christopher Jr. would exhibit in *Flowers*.

The most extreme elements of *Flowers* are not things that Virginia could have drawn from her own life. There was no family fortune to inherit, no large family mansion to use as a setting, and no credible incidents of poisoning or murder. *Flowers in the Attic* is a wonderful example, however, of how personal events and memories can be married to an otherwise quite fictional plot.

The medical aspects, beginning with the doctor-patient relationship in the hospital, are carefully woven into the story and reflect knowledge Virginia earned the difficult way, by enduring. Unfortunately, the horrible results of all this medical attention came to light for Virginia on the day her full-body cast was removed. Rather than heal her, the cast failed to correct her injury and diminish the bone spurs so that her body was free of the arthritic fusions; it had done just the opposite and frozen the debilitating melds and unions precisely where they shouldn't have been, through arthrodesis. She was thus faced with a life on crutches and in wheelchairs from her late teens, just when the world for a beautiful and very talented young woman was meant to open and provide her with social encounters, dances and dates, further education, travel, and the interesting experiences that could have expanded her artistic and writerly worlds. This tragic event sharply and firmly closed off those opportunities that she might have had. She was only seventeen.

Her parents' lives were radically changed as well. Did the new responsibilities that fell to her mother create unending guilt for Virginia? Was this the major reason Virginia put up with and accepted her mother's "rules"; rules that became so confining that her cousin Pat envisioned Virginia back in her body cast? As suggested earlier, more than one relative recalls that Virginia's infirmity caused her mother, Lillian, to become angry and embarrassed.

Virginia's cousin Pat specifically recalls one occasion when she was young, visiting Virginia and finding her on the front porch. "There were two conifers on both sides offering total privacy." She remembers Lillian actually saying, "Let's not allow anyone to see my 'afflicted daughter.'" Pat felt the implication was that imperfect people were ugly. This strengthens the theory that Lillian suffered some guilt over the situation. Although there is nothing deliberate about it, a parent's indication that their child has inherited problems from them lingers like a persistent irritation on the conscience.

Pat did witness much to make us wonder about Virginia's relationship with her mother, especially after her body cast had left the young artist so immobilized. Pat lived with Virginia and her mother after Virginia's father died in 1957, from 1959 to 1960, and saw firsthand the restrictive life Virginia endured. Years later, before they found a new home close to Gene and Mary, Lillian and Virginia would live with Pat and her family at Pat's invitation. Pat believes her house was perfect for caring for Virginia. But it wasn't a smooth transition, even as a temporary situation. Pat quickly began to find herself in conflict with Lillian and Lillian's relationship with Virginia.

A memory that stands out for her resulted from Lillian's insistence every night that Virginia—then an adult woman—eat everything on her plate. If Virginia did not, her mother would taunt her about not getting dessert. One night, Virginia didn't eat everything, and her mother refused to give her a cookie and sent her to bed with her bedroom door shut.

Pat says she went in and asked Virginia how she could stand everything her mother "dished out to her."

Virginia replied, "I take myself away from it all. I imagine I am a princess in a castle enjoying life."

Eventually, years later, Pat discussed Virginia's medical problems with her brother, who was a heart surgeon and knew a great deal about osteopathy. He believed, as do many, that her medical problem began rather early in Virginia's life and that the violent twist she incurred on the high school steps may have simply escalated a condition that was already there. His diagnosis was ankylosing spondylitis, a type of arthritis in which there is a long-term inflammation of the joints in the spine, even though this is something that affects more males than females. It typically occurs where the joints in the pelvis are especially affected.

Whatever the cause and however badly the family believes the two hospitals and doctors may have handled her case, the fact remains: Virginia's life and her future were totally changed by the time the body cast was removed. As we will see, her body wasn't all that had been frozen. She was truly frozen in her adolescence for years. As a result, she had a uniquely childlike vision of adults and grew into an adulthood filled with childish longing. The only places she found any relief from the frustration were in her art and in her writing. Her characters certainly reflect the same passion.

Ironically, it was precisely because her personal life was so restricted as a result of serious illness and injury that Virginia better understood a young girl's yearning to taste adult experiences that continuously loomed and yet remained seemingly forever out of reach. It was surely painful to stare at the gold ring so close but so unattainable.

In "A Writer's Way to Profit from Memories," her article about writing in 1980, she admitted, "I realize I do pour a great deal of my-self into my stories. I suffer when my characters suffer." As she said in a *People* magazine interview, "I really feel sorry for my characters because I put them through hell."

Virginia was indeed a prisoner inside herself, locked in her own attic and yet refusing to curl up and be forgotten.

Creating any art requires a large degree of self-isolation and privacy, which is clearly more difficult for strong and vigorous younger people. Teenagers are by nature social creatures, eager to have friends and go to parties and dances. Healthy young people who avoid this are the subjects of ridicule, considered weird or different, and rarely sought after. Peer pressure is a bigger challenge for younger artists and writers. They are drawn to the artistic impulse but too often keep it closeted for fear of being the object of peer ridicule. In an ironic sense, Virginia didn't have that problem after her medical treatments left her with a life sentence of convalescence. Her peers were gone. No one her own age was there to view her as "different."

After she was withdrawn from school, Virginia went through a number of medical treatments and surgeries and was confined to her bed and a wheelchair. For a short period, she had art instruction at home, but once she was in her body cast, her life became even more restricted. Her ability to join any friends she had made in school was seriously reduced. There wasn't anything close to what we know as homeschooling back then, but she continued to be an avid reader and to work on her art and her fashion designs.

Perhaps nothing terrorizes a young person as much as seeing someone their age seriously ill and bedridden. Youth carries with it a sense of immortality, infallibility. Virginia had seemed so perfect to her peers, envied by her girlfriends and cherished by her teach-ers. If this could happen to someone like her . . . it was easier to ig-nore and forget her. Especially at that age, who wants to think of similar things happening to them? They left her alone with her mother. Her condition had locked her up. She was in a true sense deserted, left to staring out the window, looking back at her good childhood memories.

There was no other way out for Virginia than to do as she had done in her fantasies most of her young life: become someone else.

Eventually, that was just what she did.

She became V.C. Andrews.

chapter four
To the Attic

To TRAP A THING of beauty in itself is surely a tragic irony of nature. Virginia Andrews was beautiful, intelligent, and sociable, all the attributes anyone her age would need to make her Miss Popularity. But she was diverted from that life.

Her health issues made it difficult, if not in some cases impossible, to participate in events with her contemporaries. Schools, buses, and so on did not provide special access for disabled people. Besides, she was involved in many medical visits and tests and had to spend a lot of her time recuperating from them. As we all know, medical experiences can be exhausting both mentally and physically. Virginia reached beyond her one simple escape from all this through reading books to express her imaginative ideas in sketches and paintings that were beautiful and interesting enough to attract buyers and give her something of a career.

However, despite all these distractions, it remains a fact that because of her spine abnormality, she was unable to participate in high school dances or plays or to continue her formal education. No one would have blamed Virginia for falling into the darkest of holes, contemplating pulling the blanket over herself and, in a sense, disappearing. Her whole world surely seemed to have frozen along with her spine and her legs, and to add insult to injury, as a result of her condition, there were more medical issues lying in wait.

In a letter to her younger brother, Eugene, she complained that her "dear doctor, who thinks he takes such excellent care of me, prescribed a cough medicine for me three years ago . . . then all sorts of terrible things began to happen, like blood clots in my eyes, swollen out like red beads, then I developed a numbness in my derriere. . . . When I called him and told him what was going on, he put me on an antihistamine. Only then did I learn from the pharmacist that I'd been taking one of the most dangerous drugs on the market and for three years!"

During this long period of adjustment, being in a wheelchair, although blessedly in a house with no stairways to travel, she found her world had become restricted to her bedroom, the living room, and the front porch. Virginia was dependent on her mother to prepare and bring her food, shop for her needs, and keep her hygienic. They couldn't afford private nursing care. Facing the reality of her permanent condition, a young Virginia sought an escape from her deep depression and turned to the outlet her art talent provided. When she could no longer attend school, she enrolled in a four-year art program at home. Her mother's complex reaction to all this was highlighted by her pride in Virginia's work despite what the arthritic condition had caused.

Early on, Lillian got the Norfolk/Portsmouth Schwartz Department Store to show and sell Virginia's paintings—oil paintings on velvet made with a palette knife, depicting beautiful flowers and leaves, among other things. Virginia had a theory about her mother's pride in her artwork. Lillian was not as supportive of her daughter's writing as she had been of her art. The art, however, was something she could see, approve of. According to Virginia, later, when she spent time alone in her room, the door closed, writing, her mother was suspicious. Lillian never saw the proposal or the manuscript for *Flowers in the Attic*, and as Virginia said herself, her mother never read it.

Virginia's foray into commercial art brought her at least some income. Interestingly, she was able to parlay her paintings of beautiful objects and dress designs into portrait painting as well. Of course, we all remember the famous portrait in *Flowers in the Attic* of Malcolm Foxworth's mother, Corrine, the first Corrine. And as we have seen in earlier excerpts from the novel, she referred to her knowledge of the crafts and the mechanics of art when creating Cathy's character.

Beside the added income, the commercial artwork helped stem the frustration Virginia felt at not being able to go anywhere by herself and finish her schooling. The family remained a tight-knit Southern family finding joy in one another during an obviously difficult period. Eugene Andrews's wife, Mary, recalls first being introduced to Virginia and Eugene's parents in 1955. Virginia had been living with her disability for well over a decade. The family was still on Atlanta Avenue in Portsmouth.

"Virginia, of course, was in a wheelchair," Mary Andrews recalls. "She was beautiful and charming, and I liked her. I also especially liked her dad, a sweet dear man. Lillian had prepared a Southern fried chicken for lunch with all the trimmings. After lunch, we all went out on their front porch, and Grandma Lucy Parker and Iris Guille, Lillian's sister, who lived just down the street, joined us. Grandmother Lucy was a hoot, lots of fun.

"Virginia did not appear spoiled, and it was only normal that both parents were attentive because of her disability. From what I learned over the years, Virginia was a happy girl, with friends and a fellow she liked a lot until her 'accident' at school."

Other surviving family members recall Virginia's buoyant personality during this difficult period of her life. With a smile so bright she could light up hearts and cheer others, Virginia had emerged from this prognosis for her future. One can reasonably argue that she had accepted her situation long before her mother would. Her comment to Gene and Mary about that was, "I've never had a life of my own, in which I could rule my own destiny. My health has always been the captain of my ship, and I fear it will always direct my course."

Eventually, she found ways to ride along with it.

"I really first met Virginia, or 'Ginny,' as some relatives called her, when I was ten years old and in the fifth grade," Virginia's cousin Pat Mock tells us. "My dad, her mother's brother, was the Navy chaplain at the Portsmouth naval shipyard, where Virginia's father once worked. Before his Sunday sermon, he would drop me off at Virginia's house on Atlanta Avenue. She really looked forward to a ten-year-old spending the day with her. Aunt Lillian went out of her way to make me feel welcome. She always fixed tuna-looney, Lillian's name for tuna melt sandwiches and homemade cookies. She was known to be a fabulous cook.

"Virginia was always dressed and very well groomed for any guest who might arrive. She wore beautiful ensembles, complemented by nice rings, bracelets, and any other jewelry to help her escape to her 'castle.' Her makeup was always jaw-dropping, exquisite. Her personality matched her personal beauty. She never whined or griped. Even though she struggled to walk with the aid of her crutches, there never was a whimper. She was the first warrior I met, and she has influenced me more than I will ever explain, and probably more than I really knew. She was an idol to me."

Evidence of male admirers during this period is nonexistent. Some in the family blame her mother's domineering and protective manner. They recall that years before she would play a more active role as "guardian of the gate," Lillian was almost constantly hovering over her daughter. Customers for Virginia's art were one thing; courters were another. When a customer for her art arrived, Virginia was always dressed in a very beautiful and elegant peignoir.

Cousin Pat recalls that Lillian did buy Virginia pretty things so she could keep up this glamorous appearance and be pleased with herself. Perhaps with some suggestions from Virginia, who had clearly demonstrated an understanding of color, material, and style, Lillian chose what her daughter would wear. From the start of her extreme medical issues, Virginia did not go to a store to shop for herself. Her mother shopped for all her needs and more, often choosing expensive things to compensate for her daughter's incapacitation. To illustrate how Lillian always wanted to downplay how dire Virginia's condition was, Pat says, "Lillian always told the salespeople that 'my daughter is sick, so if this is the wrong size or color, can I return it?'" Of course, Virginia was more than simply sick. At this point, there was no hope for a full recuperation. Lillian found ways to blot out her own depression. Keeping Virginia out of the public eye helped keep Lillian from facing reality.

However, whatever extravagance Lillian employed to please Virginia was about to end. Virginia's ESP about her father was about to come true. She had predicted this moment; the smile so many loved was being wiped away. The air of Southern charm and pleasure to compensate for the family's struggling would fall into a darkness making its way back into the comfortable house on Atlanta Avenue in Portsmouth.

Virginia Andrews's lovable father, the man who led her to books and helped create her imagination, suffered a fatal heart attack on February 22, 1957. She had lost not only a father but a friend and the one person who saw her art and her imagination as extraordinary. Her grief was deep. And the family's grief was compounded by financial hardship. William's pension was much less than his salary. Lillian didn't drive, didn't have any sort of career, but she had a daughter with great needs and an obligation to provide for her family.

Lillian sold their Portsmouth home in 1957 with the intention of finding a place closer to Virginia's brother Eugene in Manchester, Missouri, and Virginia continued with her artwork to subsidize the family's income. But her creative writing wasn't put in storage even though it took second place to her art. The shift of her creative energies totally from art to literary endeavors wasn't going to occur overnight. The family recalls that she was writing her short stories and planning on doing more writing even as she was working on her art commercially.

Years later, her niece Suzanne asked Virginia what made her turn away from her art and start writing. As a little girl, Suzanne had watched her aunt create pictures and do needlework. She was quite taken with the talent she had for it. Why put it aside? She remembers Virginia advising her that if you wanted to do something right, be successful at it, you had to devote "all your energy" to it. She told her she couldn't stop the stories from unraveling in her head, even while she was doing a painting.

She said a similar thing in Winter's *Faces of Fear*: "If I turn all of my interest and concentration on one thing, I am usually successful. Problems begin only when you do a little bit of this and a little bit of that."

Surely she was recalling the advice her elementary school principal had given her when the family had to leave Rochester: he had told her she had many talents, but it would be wise to settle on one, develop it, and stay with it. That advice had impressed her enough to remain sharply in her memory nearly fifty years later.

Virginia repeats this thought in *Flowers in the Attic*, when Chris tells Cathy, "Your trouble is, Cathy, you have too many talents; you want to be everything, and that's not possible." What better example do we have of a writer employing something of her personal experience, her impressionistic memories, than this?

Of course, Virginia basically lost all her art customers with the move from Portsmouth. She wasn't really making any money from it anymore anyway. "She told me, however, that she invested some of art proceeds in the stock market," Suzanne recalls. "I remember how proud she was of being successful at that. She said she could make more money in the market than she could painting, so she started to lose interest. From what I knew, that was about the time she seriously started writing."

In the 1986 interview in the *Virginian-Pilot* and the *Ledger-Star*, Virginia referred to this same period of her life and said, "Painting was messy. I was allergic to the turpentine so one day I said why put up with all these smells when writing is so neat? So I picked up a copy of *The Writer's Handbook* [by Writer's Digest Books] and started out."

She wouldn't really concentrate on writing until she and her mother had moved back to Portsmouth in 1973. Nearly six more years of effort and constant rejection were to follow. However, to our benefit, Virginia and Lillian's first move put them just across the street from Eugene and his family, giving Suzanne and Brad Andrews opportunities to visit with Virginia.

Suzanne says Virginia had the living room in her house in Missouri looking like a winter wonderland, a scene from *The Nutcracker* or the movie *Camelot*. "She loved romance, sparkles, clowns, fairies, ballet dancers. . . . Christmas at their house was a feast for sure! She had sewn all the 'horseman's clothes' on the Cinderella carriage, gave the princesses fur-trimmed collars with pink ribbon, and even put a red bow on the lead reindeer."

All this was decades after her body cast had been removed and the inevitability of a lifetime of disability and restriction had colored her usually bright and sparkling world with gray realities.

Suzanne recalls sitting on Virginia's lapboard, which rested on the arms of her wheelchair. "Mama said Virginia was the only one who could brush out the tangles in my hair and not hurt me when I was four. I never felt a strand pulled. She would try different pretty clips to make me feel like a princess, too.

"She would let me watch her sew a bit until Lillian would come and get me. I would sit on her lapboard when she would call over her bird from its cage. It had a full playground, I might add, where it would sit and play with us. She would chase it, walking her two fingers, and the little bird would come back at her, chirping. Then she would play 'kiss a pretty baby,' which the parakeet would say back to the toy."

Virginia's nephew Brad recalls visiting his aunt's house when he was only eight, and Virginia would show him her books and urge him to be more of a reader. She hadn't yet become the well-known author she would be, but her enthusiasm for novels, or indeed, anything to read, was quite evident to him. "She moved about on crutches, robot-like because of her stiff legs. I was afraid she'd fall, but she never did. She was always pleasant and eager to talk to me, especially about books."

His younger brother, Glenn, always wanted to visit Lillian and Virginia, because Lillian would have freshly baked cookies for him. Welcoming her grandchildren after being forced to move to a strange new place was clearly reassuring to Lillian, and Virginia's influence and the memories of her that her nephews and niece gathered were especially cherished following her death.

Suzanne remembers, "At Halloween time, Virginia was working on my gypsy costume, collecting 'only the best costume jewelry' for trick-or-treating, and Daddy's haunted house October BBQ shindig had a lot of neighbors. Virginia and Lillian came. I think it was a pajama party thing.

"I watched *The Wizard of Oz* before bedtime and did not want to sleep. It was late, but I wanted to watch scary movies. I remember Aunt Virginia dressed in sea-foam chiffon night attire—she always seemed like a romantic princess trapped in a castle to me—but she was getting ready for bed. I pleaded with my mother to watch *Hush . . . Hush, Sweet Charlotte*, starring Bette Davis, on the old Zenith TV with foiled rabbit-ear antennas. Virginia distinctly gave Mamma permission for me to watch it." Mary was afraid it wasn't suitable, but Virginia won out on behalf of Suzanne.

These are precious family memories of Virginia for her niece, but there are some darker revelations as well from these later years in Manchester.

"You are aware that Virginia kept the books, called the shots? [Referring to the accounting and expenses.] Unlike most, I remember Grandma submissive to Virginia. I cannot imagine the guilt Grandma Lillian carried around with her . . . did not speak to anyone unless it required a yes or no. Small talk made Grandma feel like people were prying [which left room for judgment], and Lillian stayed away from church for that reason. I remember at Easter, we showed up at church, invited Lillian, and she responded in such a way that I sensed a feeling of shame coming from her. She had the sweetest eyes, held a lot of pain behind those eyes."

Suzanne's impressions of her grandmother give more reason to believe that Lillian, as Virginia herself indicates in her letters, was ashamed of and embarrassed by her daughter's physical condition.

Those memories of her niece also underscore Virginia's dependence on books and movies when we look deeper into her struggles. Like the children in the attic she created, Virginia found a way to escape through books and thus permit herself to experience vicariously what every person should enjoy to make his or her life feel complete and worthwhile. To the world and, more important, to herself, she confessed the determination to do so.

So many exasperations plagued Virginia during these years of travel from one state to another, one house to another, seeking to re-create the home and family she and her mother had left in the happier days back in Portsmouth. Suzanne could sense the frustration that slept beside her aunt. "She was unable to follow through on her art career because of the loss of clients and known retail purchasers and so dependent now on others for any life outside of her home. Yet she managed to surround herself with beautiful 'girlie' things.

"I remember these glass kaleidoscopes. They were heavy and jeweled, embellished on the outside. She kept them high on the shelf but would let me look through them sometimes."

Virginia's art sales were inconsistent at this point; she would sell a dress she had designed and sewed, sell a recent painting she had done. But she maintained a craft room in the Manchester home, a room filled with buttons, ribbons, sparkles, beads, doll body parts, needlepoint, paints, brushes, and, of course, a sewing machine.

"Everything was highly organized in clear boxes," Suzanne continues. "I remember her letting me watch her cut out patterns, thread bobbins, and sew a little."

Yet, even though her workroom was separate from her bedroom, the reality of her malady was not far away despite the distractions and games. Her hospital bed had a bar hanging above her head that she could grab to shift her body weight. "She used it sometimes to get herself up and out of bed when she had to. She told me Grandmother Lillian would sometimes make her wait, and she had to lie there for hours, until she finally had gotten this handle thing."

Why would her mother make it necessary for her to wait for her, speak to her harshly, and then suddenly treat her lovingly? The complexity and intensity of Virginia's relationship with her mother grew subtly after her arthritic pain had sent her to hospitals and doctors years earlier with only a dire projection of meager recuperation ahead of her. Their relationship continued to intrigue both strangers and family. Even as a child, her niece was confused by Virginia's and her mother's hot-and-cold reactions to each other.

"I do remember four or five happy outings with them," Suzanne tells us. Suzanne's mother, Mary, would drive them to Stix Baer and Fuller, a department store. "I just remember Virginia looking at art supplies, frames. Grandma would purse her lips, trying to readjust her dentures all the time. I would hide in the clothes displays. Virginia would always ask for extra samples at the makeup counters. She would giggle because the ladies would give her handfuls of stuff. I remember her saying she would never have to buy anything again. She could live on the free samples."

Years later, Virginia would write to Eugene, Mary, and the children, describing a California tour sponsored by Universal Pictures, which was going to distribute the *Flowers in the Attic* movie, and again amusingly mentioned free samples, clearly enjoying the fame her novel had brought. On that California trip, she and her mother visited the elegant Giorgio Beverly Hills. "The manager came running out and asked if I was V.C. Andrews—and then he was wanting to know why I hadn't bought anything in his shop. He offered to give me a little sample of the perfume—to which I replied, 'Why not a big sample?' He came out with two tiny samples apiece for all of us, promising me if I bought a 'little' sample dress he'd fill the window with a display of my books."

Suzanne's memories of her aunt and grandmother were enhanced by the fact that whenever her family moved, Lillian and Virginia eventually followed. She recalls visiting them with her father in Sun City, Arizona.

"Dad got them settled in. We took a golf cart down to the grocery store. Daddy had hoped Lillian would use a cart. She never had learned how to drive a car. I have to say, at thirteen I knew nothing of depression, but that place made me feel strangely alone . . . like a hollow in my heart and the pit of my stomach."

Suzanne recollects that Virginia was depressed about her isolation and the control her mother had over her. Suzanne says she didn't truly appreciate the depth of the darkness Virginia was experiencing until many years later, when she was old enough to fully appreciate the tension in her aunt and grandmother's home.

Surely a great part of the sadness and depression Suzanne saw came from Virginia being frustrated now not only with her condition but also with her mother not establishing a permanent home for them. The pair seemed to be in continual transition. When Gene transferred again, this time to Gainesville, Georgia, Lillian put her home in Arizona up for sale so they could follow, and eventually Lillian and Virginia moved back to Portsmouth in late 1977. They lived in their second Portsmouth home until Virginia's success gave them the funds to buy a beautiful house in Virginia Beach, where they finally found a sense of permanence and belonging and where they lived until Virginia's passing in December 1986.

When they were forced to leave Cousin Pat's home in Gainesville, Georgia, because of Pat's terrible fight with Lillian, which Pat will describe later, Lillian and Virginia moved in with Gene and Mary in Missouri. Mary describes the arrangements this way: "The lower level in our home was the family room, wood-paneled with a big stone fireplace. It was where the family gathered at night to watch TV, play games, or whatever. The guest room was a big room that Virginia and Lillian shared. Gene had a hospital bed brought in for Virginia. She had her own shower, and she could go out on the patio. Virginia always had a sketch pad on her wheelchair desk. She did a lot of colored pencil drawings and we had quite a number framed after she died. I also have a black-and-white pencil drawing of my daughter, Suzanne, in my bedroom that we found among her sketches. She signed it for my daughter after the publication of *Flowers in the Attic*, and she recalled the day and year she had drawn it: *Suzanne, September 22, 1973. V.C. Andrews.*

"When they lived with us, Lillian still took care of her daily needs, and we all took turns bringing trays down to her, often eating on TV trays to be with her. Lillian helped me in the kitchen and would fix a couple of her dishes we liked. All the children were there, Glenn, Brad, and Suzanne. Gene traveled, so he wasn't home all the time."

Mary recalls that the strain wore on everyone after a while, especially on Virginia, who was dependent and isolated because of the stairways. It was during this time that Lillian decided their next home should be back in Portsmouth. "She thought they should return to what they knew best and hoped to settle within walking distance of all their needs." Because of the time it would take to find the home and secure it, Gene had been the one to suggest to Cousin Pat that she take Lillian and Virginia in for a while in Decatur.

Pat believes the true motivation was Virginia's descent into deeper and deeper depression. Actually, Pat's home was more conducive to meeting Virginia's needs, and Pat had once spent months living with them. Despite the age difference (Virginia was nineteen years older), she and Virginia were close friends as well as cousins.

Virginia's nickname for Pat was "Pittypat," from *Gone with the Wind*. In the novel, Pittypat Hamilton is the biological aunt of Melanie Wilkes and Charles Hamilton and aunt by marriage to Ashley Wilkes and Scarlett O'Hara. She is most often referred to in the novel as Aunt Pitty or Miss Pitty.

Pat and Virginia's relationship began when Pat's father would drop her off at the Andrewses' Atlanta Avenue house when Pat was only ten. Years later, when Pat was a junior in high school, she had a boyfriend in New Jersey and had saved up money to buy a bus ticket so she could attend the junior-senior prom with him. Virginia was in her thirties and designing and making clothes more frequently. She heard about Pat's date and sketched her younger cousin's prom gown. Pat says, "She ordered the most beautiful aqua blue shimmering silk organza and created my tea-length strapless gown with an arrangement of silk roses in the back. I remember her standing at her table/desk to do all of her tasks: sewing, painting, typing."

The two had always remained close, explaining why Eugene thought of Pat first when they needed to move.

"I had three young children when Virginia's brother Eugene called and told me about their situation and asked if Lillian and Virginia could live with me until a new home was found and acquired. I was thrilled. I had a large house with perfect accommodations for Virginia. Virginia was light, and I was young and strong. I took her up a flight of steps every day on my hip so she could shower by herself. She loved it.

"She always did show me her artwork, and she would frequently use her sketchbooks while having the TV on in the evenings. She read a lot, drew a lot, and sewed, often making beautiful clothes. She went through a period of making some jewelry . . . nothing very special, but she sold some bracelets. She always appeared to be happy and cheer-ful, but that facade appeared to be a cover for her depression. I knew her too well to misread it.

"When she was living with me, Virginia asked me to teach her to play chess. I bought a chess set at the local drugstore where I would go to get her milkshakes. I taught her to play and never won another game. Miss Smarty-Pants. She caught on fast to everything. Often, but not nearly enough, I would tell her to get extra dressed up as I had my housekeeper coming to babysit.

"Amid Lillian's screaming and carrying on one time, we left for the Marriott hotel in Atlanta. We headed right for the bar and lounge, ordered dinner and a drink, watched the dancing, and loved the music. Dinner was not over until the bananas Fosters were ordered and set afire at our table. . . . The poor girl hungered for fun and excitement. No one appeared to notice her affliction or her wheel-chair. I took her, chair and all, to an epic religious film in Atlanta, too. Movies were not off-limits for us. Popcorn and all!"

Pat describes Lillian's continual screaming, her complaints and warnings about taking Virginia out of the house, but the cousins ignored her as best they could.

"One day, I told her to dress for shopping at the mall. We went to Atlanta to Phipps Plaza, Saks on one end and Lord & Taylor at the other. Carpeted! We went despite Lillian's objections. We got into the car and started laughing. Virginia told me she had never been in a shoe store since she was sixteen. She must have tried on a million pairs. We did go into a wig store, and she bought a wig. Before be-coming wheelchair-bound, she'd had a voluptuous head of hair, but it was thinning.

"She loved the mall and getting out of the house as much as her mother hated us doing it. I think she was ashamed of my beautiful and perfect Virginia. I was always proud to be pushing her wheel-chair. I was proud of her before she was famous. I never saw her after she became so."

Pat's memory of this time contributes a great deal of complexity to any understanding of Lillian and Virginia Andrews's relationship. While there was always love, perhaps too much motherly love, we can see that it was in her home that Cousin Pat says she witnessed Virginia's struggle to capture some independence and feel less like a burden. While Lillian complained about the drain on her and the responsibility of caring for her daughter, she was reluctant to surrender any aspect of it and, from what Pat tells us, constantly opposed Pat's efforts to give Virginia a social life.

Regardless of what the motives for Lillian's thoughts and actions were, her command of practically her daughter's every breath hastened their departure from Pat's house and prevented the cousins' friendship from continuing. It wouldn't resume until years later in letters, when Virginia's talent and success brought her some of the independence she had cherished and sought during her younger years.

Early on, Pat was sensitive to Virginia's longing for some independence, and in trying to service it, she found herself more and more in conflict with Lillian. It finally culminated one night.

"One evening prior to Virginia's being 'put to bed,' she told me to come to her bedroom to talk. We had adjoining bedrooms downstairs on the same floor with the family room. She had intimated that she was writing a book . . . or about to do so . . . and she was planning on telling me about it. When she invited me into her room that fateful night, the only thing I can think of is that she wanted to discuss her book. She may have also wanted to tell me that we needed to stop going out on the town too much, as her mother was agitated by it.

"As we started to talk, Lillian came busting into the room, telling me to leave Virginia alone and to let her get some rest. Virginia was in her forties! Her mother was still telling her when to go to sleep!

"I told her Virginia had asked me to come in to talk with her. Lillian didn't care and ordered me out. Virginia told her it was okay.

At that moment, Lillian lunged at me, pushing me against the wall. I told her this was my house and I would not be pushed around in it. Therefore, she needed to pack her bags and leave. She was no longer welcome. Virginia could stay, and I would take care of her.

"Lillian called Eugene, who drove from Gainesville to get them. He picked them up to take them back to his house."

Soon after, Gene took his mother back to Portsmouth to find a new home. They found the perfect house, close to the train and bus stations and within walking distance of many stores. Lillian no longer faced the dependence she had felt while living in Missouri, Arizona, and Georgia. There was no longer need for anyone to drive her anywhere.

"I cried when Virginia left us," Pat recalls. "I felt I would never see her again. I spoke to her only when Virginia called. Whenever I did call, Lillian always told me Virginia could not come to the phone.

"One year, I think at Gene's home in Gainesville, she had a birthday party to which I was invited. When Lil mailed the invitations, she must have tossed mine into the trash bin. Virginia called me and asked why I did not come. When I told her, she did not want to believe her mother would do something like that.

"My father had often preached a sermon about Virginia, leaving her nameless. He spoke of her having an affliction—likened to a grain of sand in an oyster and its making a pearl from its irritation. Choked me up every time I heard it.

"Virginia made many pearls in her lifetime."

chapter five

Opening the Attic Door

VIRGINIA ANDREWS NEVER FORGOT the premise of *Flowers in the Attic*: children locked away in a mansion for years.

It resembles what's called a pitch in Hollywood and publishing. It's the start of a serious discussion about the rest of the story and whether the concept is strong enough to be the basis of a movie or a published novel. There are key words to further the development of interest and discussion: *children, locked, mansion, years.*

A story has to be unique in some creative way and yet stir feelings common to us all. What sound in all your nightmares has the same frightening resonance as the sound of a door, the only way out, closing and the lock snapping into place? It's supposed to be a sound reserved for the worst in our world, the criminals, those who have hurt others seriously and need to be kept isolated from the rest of us.

Suffering the loss of choice and free movement is meant to be the punishment for bad deeds. Because reasonable society abhors the idea of being sadistic and unjust, the underlying justification for punishment is that it will theoretically lead to repentance, and that repentance will lead to social reacceptance, a return to self-respect and meaning. Unless they live under tyranny, those being punished will know exactly why this is happening to them.

In a real sense, Virginia Andrews saw herself as a victim of tyranny, the tyranny of arthritis and its effects, which, of course, had no logic or reasoning in its punishment of her. If not a casualty of medical blunders, she was at the least a victim of medical failures, well-thought-out procedures in highly respected institutions that weren't as beneficial as the doctors believed they would be. Her parents and she gave these institutions their trust. Most of the family members aware of Virginia's medical details agree that the body cast was perhaps the biggest mistake of all.

The obvious question anyone, especially at that age, would have is "Why me?" "Arthritis" and "arthritic" are words usually attached to aging. In most of her letters to family, Virginia avoids talking about her infirmity and rarely expresses self-pity. In a July 1978 letter, she wrote, "There are ten million things for me to do, and I meet frustrations all the way!!! Damnation, why couldn't someone else have had arthritis and not me? I wish I could pass it around the family, and let each person be me for an hour a day . . . and then, maybe they'd understand."

In another letter after Gene and Mary had invited her to Marco Island, she expressed her frustration again. "We will visit when we can," she wrote. "But to be honest, by the time summer is over here, I'm sick to death of heat, and I don't fish, and I can't swim, and I can't stroll the beach and pick up shells, nor do I give two cents about acquiring a suntan—so what would I do in a place like that? . . . except stay two weeks, and then go home to do what I like most—Write."

She highlighted her frustration and came the closest to self-pity in the quote we saw earlier in the letter to her brother and her sister-in-law: "When Mother is gone, if I should live that long, I will have to pay for every service performed. I have to save for that day. I've never had a life of my own, in which I could rule my own destiny."

How easily and clearly could these same words be uttered by Chris and Cathy in *Flowers*? Or even Heaven or Audrina, although we should add emphasis on Chris and Cathy because it is they who have the physical experience of that lock being turned in the door, an incarceration surrounded by swirling promises, the kinds of promises children are most inclined to believe: the promises a mother or father makes.

Flowers in the Attic truly explores the parent-child relationship most of all. No one wants their parental love to be challenged. No one wants to face the reality that their mother's love for them might be less important than that mother's love and ambition for herself, as we see depicted so dramatically in *Flowers*. Indeed, being a mother requires you to be less self-centered when it comes to the needs of your children. A mother and, for most of the novel, a grandmother who are just the opposite of what is required can be gruesome and threatening to their own children and grandchildren.

In the 1986 *Virginian-Pilot* newspaper interview, Virginia addressed it this way: "Don't we all have a primal fear that Mommy and Daddy are going to betray us? Hasn't each of us been left alone in a department store at some time, wondering, *When is Momma coming to get me?*"

However, as she worked, Virginia did not see herself as a horror writer in the traditional sense. The fears she imagined for the children in the attic were fears suffered by most children. They were ubiquitous—*natural*, not supernatural. Virginia explained in *Faces of Fear*: "The face of fear I display in my novels is not the pale specter from the sunken grave, nor is it the thing that goes bump in the night. Mine are the deep-seated fears established when we are children, and they never go away: the fear of being helpless, the fear of being trapped, and the fear of being out of control."

Maybe she had Cathy say it best right after she and her siblings were brought into the large mansion through a rear door and then rushed to the restricted world they would inhabit for more than three years: "And we were alone. Locked in. All the lights were turned off. Around us, below us, this huge house seemed a monster, holding us in its sharp-toothed mouth. If we moved, whispered, breathed heavily, we'd be swallowed and digested."

Did Virginia's doctor at the University of Virginia describe it this way when he told her his story? Were he and his siblings compliant until they, too, realized that they had suffered one of the worst betrayals a child could suffer, parental betrayal?

Virginia knew the themes she wanted to stress as she developed the novel. Almost at the very start of *Flowers in the Attic*, when the children's father has been killed and all their worldly possessions are threatened, Cathy struggles with being a child and being forced to think more like an adult. Necessity, after all, is not the mother of invention—it is the mother of maturity. Observe both the maturity and the childishness in Cathy when her brother Christopher Jr. confronts her with their new reality after their father has been killed and they've become financially destitute. He treats her like a child. She certainly is one, as is he, but she doesn't want to be as helpless as that. Was Virginia talking about herself while she was writing, even in her fifties? Was Cathy speaking for her?

"Was I a windowpane, so easy to read, that even he, my arch-tormentor, would seek to comfort me? I tried to smile, to prove to him how adult I was, and in this way gloss over that trembling and weak thing I was cringing into because 'they' were going to take everything. I didn't want any other little girl living in my pretty peppermint pink room, sleeping in my bed, playing with the things I cherished—my miniature dolls in their shadowbox frames, and my sterling-silver music box with the pink ballerina—would they take those too?"

Suzanne recalls her aunt Virginia's "girlie" bedroom during another visit in Missouri. "Her bedroom was very feminine, with cream and gold dressers. A mirror tray on her dresser had real crystal perfume bottles on it that she had filled with colored waters. She had a sterling silver brush set, pink porcelain birds, and glass clowns.

"Aunt Virginia would not let me touch her first-edition Shirley Temple doll. It was real porcelain, with real hair, and had eyes that moved. She kept a hair net on it, wrapped in a blanket in her bottom drawer."

This occurred before *Flowers in the Attic* was completed, but from her niece's memories, we can wonder if the adult Virginia was clinging to childhood innocence the way Cathy was. Like all young girls in V.C. Andrews's novels, Cathy is caught in a crisis of identity. She realizes that events are stealing her childhood, and because of that, she is forced to be more adult. And thus, any challenge to childhood results in adultlike behaviors and the destruction of childhood if one is to survive. But as Virginia was to so aptly capture in *Flowers*, Cathy wanted to resist, to remain a child, and to keep her innocence.

In another letter to Gene and Mary, Virginia delved deeper into her view of herself as a writer and explained, "I never think of *Flowers* as a scary thriller, but a sad, heart-breaking story of betrayal. Writing *Flowers in the Attic*, I lost twelve pounds it upset me so much, for I lived through everything those children suffered."

She was constantly aware of the possibility that most of her readers would think she was writing literally about her own life. She told this to her family and explained the same thought in a number of interviews. In one of her letters, in fact, she sounded annoyed that her readers believed that *Flowers in the Attic* was autobiographical. "It's filled with too much emotion streaming from Cathy"—that emotion she said the fans described as only someone talking about herself could express. This was clearly a result of Virginia's descriptive powers. She confessed in her description of writing in the "A Writer's Way to Profit from Memories" article from

1980 that her and Cathy's situations were similar in that both were trapped.

One can truly sense the longing she felt for a "normal" life when she told her sister-in-law Mary how much joy she found in talking to Suzanne, who had grown into a beautiful, intelligent young woman. It reminded her of what she had missed during her adolescence, but it gave her an insight that would find its way into the novel. In one of her letters, she said she would never forget the differences between how adults rationalized everything in contrast to the literal way a child looked at the world and life.

"It was the first time I ever heard her even suggest that she envisioned her own children and becoming a mother," Mary recalls. "I think recalling that conversation helped me understand what she was attempting to do and did do in *Flowers in the Attic* with those children and that mother."

All these thoughts, the haunting story premise, the visions of the mansion—they were brewing and brewing until she finally put words to paper. But it took most of the five years between her and her mother's return to Portsmouth and the letter she would write to literary agent Anita Diamant on January 13, 1978, for Virginia to wrestle with the premise of *Flowers in the Attic*.

It is in this letter that Virginia admits to the book's being based on a real event. Although she would avoid the description of herself as a horror writer in later interviews, in describing her novel, she wrote, "Real children who struggled to survive under almost unendurable circumstances. Basically, a horror story."

As we have seen, many book reviewers grappled with this characterization of her works, as did Virginia herself. She would retreat from what she had said in her pitch letter. To her, it wasn't horror, because she saw horror more in something beyond reality, and what she was desperate to capture was essential truths and real events.

To be sure, the Dollanganger children lived in terror and eventually experienced a most horrifying event when they realized what their mother was doing. It wasn't like scary things jumping out of the forest, the creatures Virginia had fantasized about and frightened her young brother Gene with when they walked along those Portsmouth streets. Those were fairy-tale monsters.

And yet she was often quoted saying that *Flowers in the Attic* had something of a fairy-tale aspect to it. Perhaps that's true if we think about Cathy's continuous reliance on her imagination, her fantasies, which she played out with her uncooperative brother until the scholarly, coolly objective boy followed her into what he came to realize was their only true escape: make-believe that became the bridge to sexual maturity.

The fantasies were most likely easier for Virginia to capture. She had been living with and in them herself for most of her life, and it was easy for her to depict a young Cathy driven with the same full imagination. However, as the story in the attic came to encompass years of confinement, this titillating transition to sexual awareness that she wanted Cathy to experience, this confined but vibrant entrance into adolescence, was still a reach for Virginia to capture, even at the age of fifty-five, when a woman would normally be capable of looking back and advising her teenage daughter, niece, or granddaughter. However, that tableau of personal knowledge of male-female intimate relationships was practically blank.

She was not fond of romance novels. She said they lacked "thrills and chills," which were obviously code words for more graphic sex.

In the *Virginian-Pilot* interview in 1986, Virginia responded to the reporter asking if she was in the dark about sex: "I couldn't talk about it. I wanted honesty, and no one gave it to me. Instead I was handed fairy tales. So I went to the library and got out a book."

What she read, which was analytical and scientific, was clearly not enough now that she was trying to capture realism in an adolescent. She wanted to know the feelings, the passion. Seeing that her niece was a very attractive young lady and knowing she had romantic relationships, it was understandable that Virginia would seek, just as she did with anyone she met, to learn something real from someone else who could and did have the experiences she was denied.

Suzanne recalls her next-to-last visit with her aunt Virginia and the conversation between them, which is very telling in this regard. Her memory sheds light on Virginia's thirst for "real" sexual knowledge, as opposed to what she could imagine and feel from her endless reading.

"I was seventeen, and my aunt was in her late fifties then. I had just broken up a relationship with a boy," Suzanne says. "We were living on Marco Island, Florida. I visited and stayed with Grandmother Lillian and Aunt Virginia for a month. I knew she was constantly writing and did not want to disturb her. However, we did have private talks. I specifically recall one night when she asked me personal questions about sex and the sensations a girl felt leading up to intercourse. She wanted to know about seduction, what I recall her calling the Game. It was uncomfortable for me to discuss such things, but in a way, I welcomed the self-examination. I was visiting them to discover myself in the first place.

"I wondered about my own attractiveness. Breaking up with someone leaves you questioning your own sensuality. You wonder if the fault was mainly yours. So it was of some benefit to me then to share my experiences with her. I naturally wondered if she was looking for some sort of comparison to her own experiences, although I couldn't imagine Aunt Virginia having an intimate relationship with a man, especially in her house with Grandma hovering over everything.

"Aunt Virginia surprised me, however, when she started talking about a stockbroker who had jet-black hair, soft curls, and gorgeous green eyes. She said she had many dreams of him. It was easy to read between the lines and realize these were sexual dreams.

"I knew she was writing about young girls and hoped I had in some way helped her. I did feel better about myself after our talks."

Cousin Pat recalls Virginia talking about the same man she had described to Suzanne. Pat says Virginia claimed he had asked Virginia out on a date, but "Lil saw to that, it would not happen. Of course, people probably did not really understand that Virginia was like a large board. She was stiff like a plank. Lots of pillows to lay her on in a car, wheelchair in the trunk . . . lift her in and lift her out. Lots of touching Virginia, and maybe Lil was concerned about a man's hands all over her virgin daughter. Upshot: a date never happened. He may have visited often, but I'd put money on it that Lil was right there for every minute."

One of Virginia's most revealing comments about sex and romance came in a letter to her aunt Baby Sis. "My life has changed so much," she wrote in September 1980, almost a year after *Flowers in the Attic* was published. "I feel like pinching myself to see if it's really me. There is also romance in my life, two men who may, or may not, be after my money . . . but even so, it is fun to play the game, and even more fun to know I can play it expertly. (Cathy taught me that.)"

In a letter to Mary and Gene in June 1981, Virginia identified her "two men": "I'll have to inquire around to see if I can get someone to drive us to the airport to meet you. Perhaps my attorney or my stock-broker, who are both friendly. My attorney is very handsome and has been the first man to take me out on a date since I was seventeen. My stockbroker is good-looking, too, but sometimes I think of him as a little boy who just couldn't handle me like Doug, the attorney."

While nobody has been able to confirm that a date with Doug actually occurred, it appears to be the general belief of her sister-in-law Mary that one did.

Her reference to Cathy in *Flowers in the Attic* when she was talking about her own flirtations further confirms her own belief that she was putting much of herself into the character. Earlier, in March 1980, Virginia had told her cousin Pat about another man whom she found attractive and attentive. In reference to attending a publishing convention in Chicago, she said, "Of course, I need a man to help, but can you picture my mother letting me fly off with a man? After years of 'manless' living, suddenly I have several to choose from. And

I choose the handsomest and the largest, six feet two of strong muscles, and sensitivity. He's very nice and has so much in common with me. He's an artist, a professional photographer and architect. I met him in a studio where I had my publicity shots taken, and he's been to my home to take a hundred others. . . . He has just recently divorced his wife and seems rather desperate to find another woman."

As she had told her niece Suzanne and her aunt Baby Sis, she was still charmed by her stockbroker, too, but now, more than ever, she wondered if men were after her "fortune." The royalties from *Flowers in the Attic* and the contract for book three had put her income at seven figures. In another letter to Pat, she wrote, "Oh, the price we pay to be rich. Once I used to think it was my charm and beauty—now I have greenbacks in my eyes."

There is something very innocent and childlike in these romantic descriptions, because she had so little experience with male relationships, never really going out on a serious date. In another letter to Pat, dated June 15, 1980, she considered what it would be like to ever become truly serious about a man. "As for getting married, I'm having too much fun with five men on the line, and each day I add another. Or so it seems. I still like my photographer the best. He gave me a beautiful prize-winning photo, matted and framed. Of seagulls against a deep blue sky. It's unbelievably beautiful, and so sensitively done."

Since Virginia was so successful and in the public eye, her interviewers would ask if there was anyone in her life. She was coy about it, suggesting in some interviews that she had been or was in love, but always keeping the real details buried in vague references to a cadre of male admirers. Except for what she wrote in letters to her family, she told interviewers very little besides that she was in love or was pursued.

What role her mother played in keeping any romance from becoming something more serious is a matter of conjecture. However, from the testimony of her family and the fact that Lillian accompanied Virginia anywhere she went, we can be assured that any moments of real privacy with a man were severely limited.

Perhaps Virginia felt more unfulfilled than we imagine or than she ever revealed in her letters. She claimed in conversations with her niece that she had nothing to offer a marriage and then, when pressured about it at times, declared she had much more to do before thinking about settling down with someone. The innocent tone in her letters, especially in those to her cousin Pat, underscored how as a grown woman she was still experiencing adolescence.

One thing is clear: Virginia was far more determined to become a professional writer than to become someone's lover. She was constantly pursuing anything that would help her craft her descriptions and characters so that they would feel as real as possible on the page. Her own awareness of what a character would feel was therefore important and explains why she was always questioning her niece, her nephews, and her cousin. In her writing and talks, notably in "A Writer's Way to Profit from Memories," she made clear that whether you experienced it vicariously or really did tiptoe into something of a real romance, it was essential to the process of fiction to explore passion so your characters were no cardboard cutouts: "A writer can and a writer must embroider and embellish what might be a simple tale without all the imaginative trappings. To take one's own life story and tell it exactly as it happened (unless you've led one very exciting life) usually makes for less than suspenseful story. A novel has to be paced so it has peaks of excitement that grow higher as it approaches the climax. Life just doesn't move along speedily enough as a novel must. Dialogue in reality can be so mundane as to be absolutely boring."

For Virginia, the art of literary creation—the rules, so to speak—had replaced the Bible. It had become her credo, what she most worshipped and preached.

Professional writers know that writing is rewriting. Although Virginia in a *Family Circle* article claimed that she seldom rewrote until she had a book finished, few professional writers will deny the importance of it. Every published writer will have an editor with opinions and will go through a copyeditor's suggestions. A literary agent often will make suggestions. After all, they have the responsibility of trying to sell the book. There are agents who are driven by the winds of change in the market as well as the achievement of the story and the writing, maybe more so today than ever. Writers have changed their protagonists from male to female or vice versa because agents and/or editors have suggested that one or the other would sell better. Many other things might be considered and changed because of the input of cover art editors and promotional executives.

But the plot for *Flowers in the Attic* that Virginia described in her letter to Anita Diamant remained basically the plot of the final rewrite and the published manuscript.

"Plot: A young wife is suddenly widowed. Left with four children. She is totally unskilled for the labor market, and deeply in debt. Her home and all she has are repossessed. However . . . she has one choice. She is the sole heir to a tremendous fortune. If she can deceive her dying father, and never let him know she is the mother of four children whom he would despise.

"Four children are imprisoned in an upstairs room of a huge mansion. Their playground is the attic. The two older children are twelve and ten, named Christopher and Cathy. The younger two are twins, age three when they go to live upstairs. Without sunlight, Cory and Carrie cannot grow. Their lives become a virtual endurance test to outlive the dying grandfather, who stays always on the first floor, taken care of by a private duty nurse, and a staff of servants.

"The years pass. The grandfather doesn't die. The mother marries again and gradually drifts away from her children."

In her letter, Virginia emphasizes that the children's grandmother considers them "the devil's issue. Born out of unholy wedlock between half-niece and half-uncle."

She emphasizes the truth of her story by ending the letter, "I call my novel, which is not truly fiction . . . *FLOWERS IN THE ATTIC*."

And then, in an article in the *Norcom Gazette* in 1980, Virginia claimed *Flowers in the Attic* was based on a grain of truth. Elaborating, she added, "My favorite character is Cathy because she is me; my personality in her." In the same article, she stated that she knew the character Chris in reality and that, furthering our intrigue with Olivia, there were "twelve people combined to create the grandmother."

Her family recollects that Virginia's mother was completely unaware of what her daughter was doing and did not know at first that she had written to a literary agent or that the agent had agreed to read the manuscript. Mary Andrews recalls her mother-in-law's surprise, as do her sons. "She had yet to realize what this book was about," Mary recalls, "but she was nervous about it."

We have taken our time to reveal and illustrate the complex relationship between Virginia and her mother, Lillian. According to Mary, Virginia knew she had become a burden to her mother. Many close relatives and friends saw how torn Lillian was between being proud of her daughter and ashamed of Virginia's infirmity. It is not surprising for Lillian to have had these feelings. Even now, with all our transparency, people sometimes hide their illness as if they were ashamed of it, as if they adhered to the puritanical idea that we are punished on earth for the evil we do on earth. Virginia's cousin Pat especially believed that Lillian suffered from some religious guilt because of what had happened to Virginia, which had in a medical sense been inherited: the bone spurs and arthritis.

Whatever embarrassment or guilt Lillian felt was about to get many degrees more intense when her daughter published *Flowers in the Attic*. If there had been complexity and confusion for Lillian before, it was about to return in hurricane-like waves washing first over their small Portsmouth home and life. Mary relates that when Lillian found out more about this book, "She realized it wasn't about flowers, something Virginia had often drawn and painted. She knew that people would read it, but she could not, none of us could, imagine that 'other people' would be in the millions."

The evolution or maturing of Virginia as a writer accelerated greatly once a successful literary agent agreed to take on her story about children locked in a small bedroom and an attic. That locked door was pried open with every new page, corresponding with a more expanded view of the relationships within families and between men and women. Virginia's understanding and development of the creative writing process was going at high speed. She realized quickly that for any writer, it's a constantly ongoing effort to improve.

Virginia was now a committed writer, and for committed writers, the whole process becomes as important as the air they breathe. Likely this was especially true for a writer who had spent most of her adult life up to this point looking out of windows. Virginia had managed a turn to find a new window, the fully opened window of her imagination, and now nothing could stand in her way. She was in it for the ride all the way, and nothing she had cherished would replace it.

"Loneliness has its reward when you employ it to advantage as I do," she wrote to her nephew Brad. "I'd rather write than eat, than stare at the boob tube, or read, or paint, or sew, or anything." This was a serious point for her, the belief in how much a creative person must isolate. "You have to move into the story and live it. You have to forgo friends, and other activities, and keep the story always on your mind, first and foremost—and in that way it comes alive."

She was proud and defensive about how she worked. In a letter to her aunt Baby Sis, one sees anger when others don't understand: "You asked on the back of your Christmas card if Virginia was painting or 'just writing.' JUST WRITING? Forthwith, let it be known here and forever, writing is not JUST doing anything. Writing happens to be the MOST difficult of all crafts, including painting, sculpturing, poetry, or musical composing!!! Writing not only makes the reader see, but feel, live vicariously, suffer, laugh and cry . . . and when a writer can do that . . . all of that, he or she is an artist. Was the skill hard to learn? You bet it was! The list of books I've read and studied would be three feet long.

"And I have been told by those in the know . . . professional editors and publishers, that I happen to be not just a good writer, but equal to any being published."

She firmly believed she had arrived along with that contract for *Flowers in the Attic*. What a journey it had been—from the disabled young woman who moved frequently, survived a controlling mother, and fought to support her family in any way she could. Is there any doubt that her story, her actual life events, would easily serve a writer's need to create an impressive character with all the drama and passion to capture compassion and inspire any reader?

Virginia was always reaching out to her family to explain and to share her journey; in a letter to her nephew Brad, she admitted that writing had been very difficult for her in the beginning, but "Words that used to float always out of reach, now are within my easy grasp, and that is due to practice. Like physical exercise, the more you write, the more your mental muscles grow."

In that same letter, she said her writing had gotten to such a point that she didn't need to depend on complicated plots. Her characters were so strong, so believable and likable, that they carried the story along on their own. She said the characters she created, and the torments they suffered, were a million times more fascinating than any ten people she knew blended into one. She was intent on getting beyond what she would call mediocre and ordinary in life and in people. She feared that for herself.

Ironically, even though at first she resisted having her full name reduced to V.C. Andrews, partly to hide the fact that she was a woman, she did reveal in letters and talks that she herself favored books supposedly designed more for males than females: fantasy and science fiction. On this theme in her writing and because of the books she had read, she concluded that women were basically concerned with romance, but she believed that romance, in and of itself, wasn't enough. Those thrills and chills had to be added to the "game."

Because Virginia led such a cloistered life, she constantly referred to the power of her imagination taking her to places and to conflicts she couldn't literally experience. But there were times when she thought she might have gone a little overboard with that active imagination of hers. She even expressed sympathy for her characters and what she had created for their obstacles and crises.

In a letter to Eugene and Mary, she described her agent visiting for lunch, laughing and remarking on how cruel Virginia could be to her characters. "But you base your stories on normal people who get themselves into bizarre situations, and I like that," Anita had apparently told her.

Anita was confirming that Virginia's purpose, if a writer has to state one, clearly was to seek out the unusual, even the horrid, in families and the way adults treated their children.

When Virginia's uncle asked her if she wrote about the things she missed out on, she replied, "No, because a lot of the things that happen in my books I wouldn't want to happen to me. But I enjoy the awful things because they are kind of fun."

She was clearly referring to the excitement that came from exposing some of the intended or even unintended cruelty, jealousy, and even sadism in the guise of religious teaching she had seen in other families and read in books. In her letters, she noted feeling uneasy reading horror books with mutilation, blood, torture, and so on. She liked the horror books without graphics. She preferred buildup and suspense without bloody details.

And yet, not without some longing, she bitterly suggested in her letters that even after acquiring a *real* agent, all this was not really enough. She repeated her belief that the perfect life is one in which you are the captain of your ship, master of your fate. But life gets out of hand, and wrong decisions are made. That was what she said she wrote about: life and the unexpected curves it throws. She was not fond of books with what she thought were "tacked-on happy endings." She was never going to write like that.

In a letter to Gene and Mary, she wrote, "A novel is a problem that has to be solved before the end. And it doesn't have to be a happy ending. In fact, happy endings are out of fashion."

She was clearly preparing them for the ending of *Flowers in the Attic*.

Even though there were surely things she wanted to expose, like the underlying and destructive jealousy between a mother and a daughter in *Flowers in the Attic* and the underlying failure to fulfill parental responsibilities later in *Heaven*, she made it clear in *Faces of Fear* that she didn't want to be thought of as someone imposing morals or in any way being pedantic: "I write mainly to entertain. I don't think people want moral lessons; in fact, they come up to me and say, 'You never make a moral judgment.' That is one of my assets. Readers like the fact that I don't say whether I am for it or against it. But if you read between the lines, you can tell."

Her stories were first and foremost meant as entertainment. She wasn't writing what she was writing with the intent that it be used as some sort of a textbook. She liked the fact that readers were left to draw their own conclusions. This concept surely related to how much she hated being lectured about morality and behavior, especially in a "hellfire-and-brimstone" church.

With such clarity of purpose, such love of "a good story," and such a dedication to what was real and true in people, she had the usual challenges any good writer would have—but tacked on to those was the imposing weight of her severe physical impairment. For me personally, writing while having a common cold is difficult. What powers of concentration Virginia must have had to call from inside herself to accomplish what she did under the circumstances that "caged" her. One can only be in awe. There are so many smaller, perhaps technical, challenges she had to meet, such as not being able to sit long to type but having instead to stand for hours.

Virginia claimed she did not adhere to a writing schedule; neither the clock nor a fixed number of pages dictated her daily output. Rather, she simply stopped writing when she felt so inclined. Of course, her mother was often knocking on her door and telling her to go to sleep, but she admitted to her brother and sister-in-law that she occasionally worked right through the night nevertheless.

These were now the days after she had given up on her artwork, but although she had stopped selling art and was totally devoted to publishing her writing, she continued to envision color in everything. She went further than mere descriptions and interpreted color, finding meaning and feelings in different tones. It helped her crystallize her thoughts and the emotions she wanted to see moving through her novels. She said that each chapter was "allotted its own color page" as she wrote a book. Mary Andrews says they are that way in their storage cartons. More important, perhaps, Virginia admitted that color had always affected her, affected her moods.

There are many examples of such use of color in *Flowers in the Attic*. It certainly crystallized her descriptions. The visual artist in her sat beside her as she typed. Maybe the customers for her velvet pieces and her portraits were gone, but she was painting now with words, something she had always envisioned she would do:

"Evil was dark, crooked, crouched and small—it didn't stand straight and smile at you with clear sky-blue eyes that never lied."

"Patience. I colored patience gray, hung over with black clouds."

"Summer's old dark green turned overnight into the brilliant scarlets, gold, oranges, and browns of autumn."

One of the best uses of color perhaps is this line: "Black shadows don't have shiny sharp teeth unless your skin is emerald green, and your eyes are purple, and your hair is red, and you have three ears instead of two. Only then is black a threat."

She even had color as a chapter title: "Color All Days Blue, But Save One for Black."

As technology improved, so did the pace of Virginia's writing. Like most writers of the period, she transitioned from handwritten notes to typewriters to a computer. She was amazed at her own productivity, and when it came to writing letters to family, it wasn't unusual for them to be ten to twenty pages in length.

She quickly had discovered, even before she had that first publishing contract, that writing gave her a new and exciting sense of herself. It built a new confidence and a new vision of her future.

In fact, in one of her letters to her nephew Brad, years after *Flowers in the Attic*, she wrote, "A writer must have a great deal of self-confidence or else the writer will not feel liberated enough to make himself or herself vulnerable to ridicule or praise. Some may even consider any writer an egomaniac or an egocentric—and why not? To believe in yourself is to believe in the one person in this whole wide world you can fully control."

So dependent on others for most, if not all, of her needs, she found that when she closed her door and began her creative work, she was truly once again the master of her own fate, something she hadn't felt since that day she twisted herself so badly on the high school stairway.

This expanded freedom came amazingly quickly for a first-time writer. In less than five months, she would acquire a major New York literary agency, Anita Diamant's Writer's Workshop, and a contract with one of the biggest publishers in the industry, the Pocket Books imprint of Simon & Schuster.

Soon after, she would write to family and say it all in her own words. "As you can see from my own experience, it [writing] is very gratifying. The financial rewards are great, but even more important is the wonderful sense of accomplishment it gives. To reach for a goal, a very difficult goal (and writing is the most difficult of all the crafts), and achieve that goal, not in a mediocre way, but in a rather sensational manner, makes me feel not only happy, but fulfilled."

In describing her efforts in another speech she gave to fans and would-be writers after her first three books had skyrocketed on bestseller lists, she borrowed a story from Henri J. M. Nouwen's *Clowning in Rome: Reflections on Solitude, Celibacy, Prayer, and Contemplation*: "There is a beautiful story of a child who watched a sculptor chisel on a huge block of marble for months and months. The child never spoke until the sculptor had almost finished, and then the child asked, 'How did you know there was a lion in there all the time?' That is success for a writer to know there is a lion in one's mind, and finally, at long last, we have produced it. *Flowers* is my lion, *Petals* is my tiger, *Thorns* my elephant—but just wait until you read my dinosaur!"

Of course, that dinosaur was probably to be *Seeds of Yesterday*, fourth in the Dollanganger family series, though she would publish *My Sweet Audrina* before that.

The time bomb of her cancer was ticking away, but Virginia would go on with the first two books of the Casteel family series, *Heaven* and *Dark Angel*, and then her fantasy, so different from everything else she had published, *Gods of Green Mountain*, her only published sci-fi novel, about a planet with two blazing suns.

Not long after, that window of achievement would close for her—but thankfully not before the sculptor had revealed her major accomplishment.

The process of publication and the accolades that followed would fill her life with the excitement and attention she craved. The exponentially growing cadre of domestic and international fans, the awards, the effects on her family and on herself and her mother, and her new wealth and fame escorted her out of the small house in Portsmouth, from the city with all its wonderful and tragic memories, from the echoes of her lost family, and from the place where she had seen her father's smile for the final time.

In her heart, she had to believe that he was smiling for her now, that strong, handsome man who had taken her hand and led her into the library for the first time. They were beyond her wildest expectations, those shelves and shelves of books. Every cover opened to reveal another diamond. Surely he had seen the ambition blossoming on his daughter's face.

A dream, perhaps, but whatever it was, it gave her the courage and the stamina to slip into that place reserved only for the most famous and cherished of people and crowned her with the byline *V.C. Andrews*.

These, then, however short they were, would be the most exciting years she would have.

chapter six
Into the Attic

MARY ANDREWS RECALLS THAT Virginia was happily overwhelmed with the speed at which *Flowers in the Attic* had taken her to new heights. She was fifty-six in 1979 and had been writing for some time, but it still felt like quite the overnight success. She was now and would for the rest of her life be known as V.C. Andrews. The adulation, the excitement, and the encouragement were followed rapidly by more book contracts, editing, and promotion for her works. There was talk of a Broadway adaptation of *Flowers in the Attic*, and a number of movie producers were making serious inquiries. The first option to create a feature film came on February 2, 1980, only three months after the book's publication.

Mary remembers, "There was so much excitement and happiness for her in the family, and she did tell us, 'On the way to becoming a celebrity, plus fame and fortune and all that goes with it, has me a bit overwhelmed, to put it mildly.'"

Virginia's first published work was going to be launched as what was known as a total release, the lead title of Pocket Books' published works for that season. She would receive the personal attention typically reserved for major bestselling authors. She told her family the initial print run was 750,000 copies and would have a cover price of $2.50. Given the modest $7,500 advance she received, the title represents one of the best investments a publisher ever made in an unproven author.

"Now let me tell you of the latest news," she wrote to Mary and Gene in July 1979. "Pocket Books sent out 15,000 of those promotion books to the leading newspapers and literary magazines around the country, plus many bookstores I can't reach [. . .] the orders are coming in by the thousands! They are thrilled to death up there [in New York], for I am a new author, and customarily they don't risk so much money in promoting a new author's first book. They think of me as an especially good writer, and well worth gambling on. Book publishing is a gamble, after all, for you never can tell what the public will go for. Also, because I can't travel and appear on TV like other authors, they have given me special radio and magazine coverage. . . . Thursday, the Eastern Sales Manager for Pocket Books called me on the phone, telling me he was in this area, selling my book, as thousands of other salesmen are in other sections of the country too. He said the book is going over fantastically well."

She was very proud of the publicity pamphlet for the novel and wanted to be sure that Mary and Gene had seen it, especially quoting: "*Flowers in the Attic* has a salability far beyond any 'category' suspense novel. A rich and expensive cover treatment, and very provocative preview booklets—along with four separate radio spots—will alert consumers to this novel. *Flowers in the Attic* will work for you in a big way."

Her excitement continued in a November 14, 1979, letter to her cousin Pat: "Dear Pit-Pat, Life has become so exciting. I wake up each morning and pinch myself to see if I am still me. I am second on the Walden's bestseller list, and third on the B. Dalton's list—so this means I should place near the top of *Publisher's Weekly* (the Bible of the publishing world), and thusly, I will be included in the

New York Times bestseller list. That means I've made it BIG! B. Dalton and Walden's represent the largest book sales in the country."

In fact, *Flowers in the Attic* would be on the *New York Times* bestseller list for fourteen straight weeks. The first sequel, *Petals on the Wind*, was an immediate bestseller and rose to the number one position. It remained on the list for nineteen weeks, bringing *Flowers* back to bestseller lists as well. The same sort of overwhelming sales would be seen for the sequels *If There Be Thorns* and *Seeds of Yesterday*.

There are many surprises to come for a newly published author, but one that surely seized Virginia's attention was that almost immediately upon publication, *Flowers in the Attic* was banned from almost every high school library as well as adult ones, some bookstores, and especially by many parents who forbade their children—daughters in particular—to read the novel.

What had Virginia revealed in the young female characters she captured that so unnerved or challenged these people who wouldn't open the cover of one of her novels? What were they afraid to read? A young girl like Cathy Dollanganger coming alive, feeling things she had never felt—what woke her at night, "pulsating, throbbing, excited," knowing a man was there with her, doing something she wanted him to do?

Were Virginia's revelations about a young girl's sexual curiosity too much like their own, too much like their own fears and desires, perhaps even ones that flashed incestuous thoughts? Were these surreptitious readers afraid that someone watching them read *Flowers in the Attic* would see them blushing and ask them why? The protagonist was so young, the intimacy so adultlike.

Many blame the negative reactions simply on Virginia's weaving incest into the story. Some were also turned off by what's been called the Southern-fried religious fanaticism Olivia and Malcolm Foxworth practiced. Others point to the vivid depictions of child abuse. Likely, the combination of all these things was what offended many readers and especially parents who wanted to keep it from their teenagers and young daughters. Eleven- and twelve-year-olds who equated reading with taking castor oil were flocking to it.

Yes, the book is critical of fanatical religious beliefs, and it does vividly portray the torture and vicious punishment of innocent children, but I suspect discerning readers will tell us that there is more, much more, that is personal, making Virginia's work alluring and forbidden simultaneously. Simply put, it was what reading *Flowers in the Attic* awakened in the reader and not just what it vividly displayed to the reader that made it so *forbidden*.

These are heavy themes for a novel that was supposed to be something of a fantasy, an escape read, that truly became one of the most successful literary experiences for an audience of adolescent girls as well as grown women. In mass-market paperback format, *Flowers in the Attic* at first looked like just another example of a diversion, entertainment, perhaps just another story to read on the beach. But with remarkable speed, the first readers spread the impact of their reading experience so quickly and enthusiastically that Virginia's debut zoomed to the top of the bestseller list in two weeks. By September 1981, there were over 3 million copies in print. It probably didn't need the heavy promotion Pocket Books and Simon & Schuster were giving it. Word of mouth, the most cherished sales goal for any publisher, was turning the novel into one of the fastest-selling books in publishing history.

Timing is everything. A novel that includes incest would certainly not be banned as widely today, but Virginia was clearly not driven by considerations of what was or wasn't offensive. From all she wrote and said about it, we can see that she was determined to be true to her story and characters. In author-speak, she was not writing for any market. But she was not oblivious to what went on in the world around her. She was a voracious reader herself but less of contemporary fiction and more of the classics.

Around the time *Flowers in the Attic* and its first sequels were published, there was a great deal being written about child abuse. There were headlines in newspapers that rivaled any shocking premise

Virginia could come up with. According to John Philip Jenkins, writing in *Britannica* (February 27, 2020), child abuse had become a serious social issue in the United States and other Western countries. There were claims of incest, abduction of children, and even the murder of children, as well as the operation of organized child-abuse rings. The information was gathered through social workers and psychotherapists who interviewed suspected child victims. Jenkins came to a fascinating conclusion that the increase in child-abuse reporting also resulted from "the controversial practice of some psychotherapists of attributing the problems reported by adult patients to repressed memories of sexual abuse suffered during childhood."

In Winter's *Faces of Fear*, Virginia admitted, "It was an odd sort of coincidence that I would start writing about child abuse right when it became very popular to write about it.

"There are so many cries out there in the night, so much protective secrecy in families; and so many skeletons in the closets that no one wants to think about, much less discuss. I tap that great unknown. I think my books have helped open a few doors that were not only locked, but concealed behind cobwebs."

Tackling sensitive topics is always a difficult decision for a writer. Will the controversy cause the publisher to reject the work? For years, Hollywood avoided stories that put incest on the screen, but Simon & Schuster did not hesitate to publish Virginia's work. It is true that incest has always been easier to digest in print than on the big screen, but despite its shocking incidents, the general public and most reviewers did not consider *Flowers in the Attic* gratuitous.

More important, Virginia did not shy away from her premise even though she was well aware of how such a story point would resonate with her family, her mother in particular. She expressed the opinion often that Cathy and Christopher Jr. weren't to be blamed as much as their mother, who had cooperated in and later reinforced the situation that nourished the incestuous event.

In Rubin's 1981 "Blooms of Darkness" interview in the *Washington*

Post, Virginia accented this opinion, saying, "I don't see why people find the incest so shocking. I felt it would have happened naturally. It's the mother who is shocking. It's her fault they're in the attic in the first place."

Whatever conclusion you reach, there is the adage, "If you want to sell something, ban it." The forbidden is often the most desirable, not that this was the complete reason for the success of *Flowers in the Attic*. Nevertheless, it was undeniably part of the appeal for many.

And yet, from what the surviving members of the Andrews family recall, it's extremely doubtful the word "incest" was ever even uttered in the Andrews home before the publication of *Flowers in the Attic*, save perhaps in allusion to a biblical passage in which the act was referenced (e.g., Leviticus 18:10). Readers might be surprised to know that Virginia's mother was the only other immediate family member in her household during the book's writing and publication. According to Virginia herself, when her mother heard what topics her daughter had written about, she avoided reading anything by her in the future.

Virginia wrote to her brother Eugene and his wife, Mary, about this during the early stages of the publication of *Flowers*: "Mother has not yet read my book. I doubt she ever will. Her attention span is very, very short—and she gets sleepy. I feel, however, if she can manage to read it, she will be shocked—and shocked more when she reads my other two books."

And yet, when success came and the public demand to see—and even touch—her daughter was wrong, Lillian Andrews would be at her daughter's side willingly. Family members witnessing it would describe those protective eyes scouring the adoring fans for anything she thought inappropriate. Lillian would reveal to her daughter-in-law Mary that she was wondering what the readers' mothers were like.

Did they know their children were carrying *Flowers in the Attic* in the manner in which they should be carrying the Bible? What were they so in love with? Why were they so fascinated? What had the world come to? And how did her daughter do this? These were questions in family discussions, even occasionally voiced in Virginia's presence.

As they say, the rest is history—although it is a continuing history, with the Dollanganger series still selling domestically and worldwide. Even now, new countries acquire publishing rights to the books, and those territories that had done so keep renewing their agreements to continue publishing the titles, perhaps energized by the Lifetime channel's adaptations of *Flowers in the Attic* and three of its sequels. When the movies aired internationally, the market for Virginia's work again expanded across all formats.

Although Virginia had vowed never to talk about her personal life after what she felt was devastating coverage in *People* magazine, the compounding success of the sequels and all the advertising and subsequent publicity—the demand to know V.C. Andrews—made it difficult for her to ignore those who now wanted to speak with her. There were questions coming at her from every media source, domestic and international.

Nevertheless, she remained as tight-lipped about her personal life as she could be and began deliberately giving out contradictory information about her illness, any romances, and especially her age. In Rubin's *Washington Post* article in 1981, he says, "No one has been able to pin Andrews down on her age. 'Say I'm 37,' she finally blurts out after hemming and hawing about it. She is no more 37 than she is in her late 50s, as one magazine reported. The best guess is that she is in her late 40s."

Like some coquette, she tantalized reporters with comments here and there, and so it's a testament to Winter that he was able to get Virginia to be so revealing when they spoke on the porch of her Virginia Beach home.

After what we have already learned about the close-knit Andrews family, its battle to survive the Great Depression together, its tragedies and losses, and its reactions to the horrendous struggle of one of its cherished members, we can only hope to catch a sense of the impact that Virginia's international fame had on this Southern family of modest means.

Remember how restricted she was, how few social relationships she was enjoying, her acquaintances disappearing after she dropped out of formal schooling and before the publication of *Flowers in the Attic*. At this point in her life, her world was mainly populated by doctors, nurses, and family. For years after her father's death, she lived quite isolated with her mother, meeting strangers who wanted to buy her art but only after her mother had put the customers through a filter. Most of her school friends had deserted her. The isolation was compounded by her and her mother's moving from house to house, from Portsmouth to Arizona to Georgia and back to Portsmouth, because her mother wanted to be close to her son Eugene and also when possible to have her older son, Bill Jr., assist them. As we know, Lillian couldn't drive and provide for herself and Virginia.

Virginia was not a traveler following the onset of her medical problems. Consequently, she didn't go on vacations with her mother to see other cities until after she had written her bestsellers and her publishers were keen on getting her more exposure. Up until then, her research about people and places was still limited to what she could draw out of libraries or other books she was given or managed to buy and information she could garner from those family members she felt comfortable questioning and in whom she was just as comfortable confiding about her personal struggles.

It all emphasizes again how important books were to her, even after her success, and how important it was what she attributed to her dreams. From the tenor of her letters, one can feel confident that she was constantly starving for interactions to learn, to fill in her visions of people, especially families. She did say when she was discussing her work in "A Writer's Way to Profit from Memories" that although there was "the magic of memories . . . A writer can, and a writer must, embroider and embellish what might be a simple tale without all the imaginative trappings." Following this theory, she did take time to

Six-year-old Virginia with her father, William H. Sr., at his home in Portsmouth, Virginia.

Courtesy of the V.C. Andrews estate

William Sr. on leave from the Navy and vacationing with Virginia's mother, Lillian, and her older brother, Bill Jr. (Baby Virginia is at home with her grandparents.)

Courtesy of the V.C. Andrews estate

Virginia at age four, after the family moved to her father's hometown, Rochester, New York.

Courtesy of the V.C. Andrews estate

Virginia with her father, William, her older brother, Bill Jr., and her grandmother at her grandmother's home after her grandfather's death, in 1927.

Courtesy of the V.C. Andrews estate

Virginia and her older brother, Bill Jr., at their grandmother's home. (Bill Jr. would eventually run off to pursue a career as a trumpet player, at age sixteen.)

Courtesy of the V.C. Andrews estate

Virginia in a family photo. Present are her grandfather's brothers; her mother, Lillian; Bill Jr.; and other relatives.

Courtesy of the V.C. Andrews estate

Lillian, Bill Jr., and Virginia on the front steps of their Rochester home, in 1930. You can see the "For Sale" sign to the right of the door.

Courtesy of the V.C. Andrews estate

Eugene Andrews, Eleanor Parker, Eric Guille, Iris Guille, Virginia, Bill Jr., and Grandmother Lucy Parker in Portsmouth, Virginia, 1938.

Courtesy of the V.C. Andrews estate

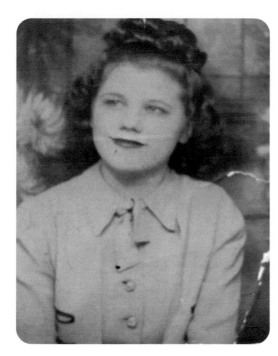

Virginia at age fifteen. (She was in school plays around this time.)

Courtesy of the V.C. Andrews estate

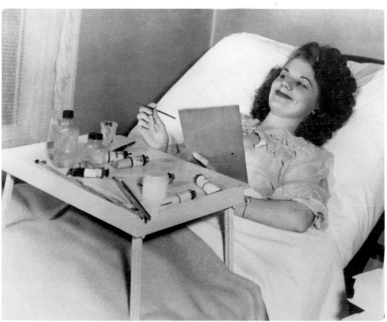

Virginia in the hospital after her first serious surgery, and the setting for a fascinating start to *Flowers in the Attic*, coming years later.

Courtesy of the V.C. Andrews estate

Virginia at age thirty-four in her home on Atlanta Avenue in Portsmouth, Virginia, with her cousin Lucy. Note her floral paintings on the wall.

Courtesy of the V.C. Andrews estate

Virginia typed *Flowers in the Attic* on this red IBM typewriter.

Courtesy of the V.C. Andrews estate

V.C. Andrews's first
published novel.

*Courtesy of the
V.C. Andrews estate*

Virginia with
the Dollanganger
family series.

*Courtesy of the
V.C. Andrews estate*

Lillian took pride in her
successful daughter.

*Courtesy of the
V.C. Andrews estate*

Lillian enjoyed her
daughter being on the
bestseller list.

*Courtesy of the
V.C. Andrews estate*

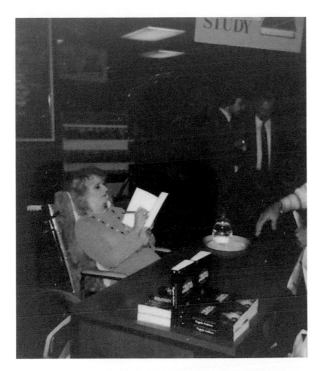

Virginia at one of
her earliest book-
signing events.

*Courtesy of the
V.C. Andrews estate*

Virginia with her mother, Lillian, at a Virginia Beach book-signing event.
Lillian had come aboard to help promote the book.

Courtesy of the V.C. Andrews estate

Virginia Andrews
███ *Michael Lane*
Portsmouth, Virginia 23703

June 15, 1980

Dear Pitty Pat,

Last Saturday, June 7, Mother and I flew off toward the "Windy" city, and Chicago fully lived up to its reputation. First we had to circle O'Hare for one hour waiting for electrical storms to travel eastward, and then we had to wait our turn to land, and all the while the fuel was running low. Off to a great dramatic start!

But...we made it--one hour late! Already the assembly of guests were waiting at the banquet table in a fabulous resturant where I was to be guest of honor. Four girls from POCKET met us, and one man, and from all the comments on how pretty we looked, I took it they didn't want us to take the time to change into formal clothes. Damn! I had four cocktail dresses and had the chance to wear only two. I sat at the right of the president, Ronald Busch, and by the time dinner was over, he'd not only promised me a trip to New York City, but London, Paris and Rome! Beware the man who sits next to me!

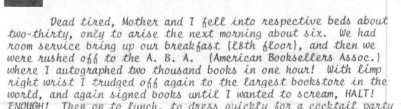

Dead tired, Mother and I fell into respective beds about two-thirty, only to arise the next morning about six. We had room service bring up our breakfast (18th floor), and then we were rushed off to the A. B. A. (American Booksellers Assoc.) where I autographed two thousand books in one hour! With limp right wrist I trudged off again to the largest bookstore in the world, and again signed books until I wanted to scream, HALT! ENOUGH! Then on to lunch, to dress quickly for a cocktail party before we sail onward toward another formal dinner--and this time we had the chance to really dress for the occasion.

Seated at the right this time of the Director of Publicity, Advertising and Promotion, I soon found myself snowed under by a very handsome man who seemed to have his eyes bedazzled enough to want to spend his two weeks vacation at Virginia Beach so he can take me to dinners and the theaters. My dear darling mommy piped up she'd have to go along too--and that's when I said, "No you aren't!" Causing everyone to laugh, and Mother to blush.

(Some information redacted.)

Monday morning we were up again at six, only this time room service was so busy we had to go downstairs for breakfast, and couldn't find a table in three tries. With growling stomachs, my agent's assistant, named Humprey (he looks a bit more attractive than Tiny Tim), rushed everywhere to hunt up coffee and Danish pastries. We gobbled those down and took off for Marshall Field where I sat in a back room with six other authors and pre-autographed about fifty books to get a head start on the outside traffic. I met Stephen King, the author of THE SHINING, SALEM'S LOT, THE STAND, DEAD ZONE, etc. A full faced arrogant man whom I didn't care much for.

Then, outside to pleasantly be greeted by many fans, some of whom had fan letters they didn't mail when they saw I was appearing in person--"A real live author" is the way most of them put it.

It's a mad wacky and wild but wonderful world, and very exausting when you're accustomed to living in an ivory tower. Somehow Mother and I survived and managed to reach home before we fell into bed. The Big Apple can wait. I'm tired! And it wasn't over even then...the next day I did a live radio show over the telephone, originating in Boston. I have two more of those coming up due to public demand. Have you heard the radio advertisements of PETALS? Listen carefully to the woman's voice-- she's imitating MY voice! I've been asked to read both FLOWERS and PETALS on cassette tape. It seems my publicity director thinks I have a very unusual voice on tape and he thinks an author reading her own novels will have national sales appeal. (Talking books for at home but most of all for cars.)

So far, the British rights, French, Spanish, Norweigian, Swedish, Danish, Greecian, Turkish, Hebrew and Finland have all been sold. I can't wait to see all those translated versions-- especially Japanese.

My third book is finished, in New York, and will be out next March or April. This week my literary agent is in Hollywood with my theathrical agents, holding conference with movie producers interested in the film rights. I'm asking for script and cast control, and 10 percent of the gross. I'll probably settle for less, but one has to ask more then bargain.

As for getting married, I'm having too much fun with five men on the line, and each day I add another, or so it seems. I still like my photographer the best. He gave me a beautiful prize winning photo, matted and framed, of seagulls against a deep blue sky. It's unbelievably beautiful, and so sensitively done.

I'm sorry about Paul--but what else can I say? Good luck to you and your aspirations. And next time come to visit--or I'll made a Voodoo doll and stick in pins!

Love,

P.S. In two weeks I'll be in the number ONE spot on The New York Times bestseller list! That's the best you can do!

Virginia Andrews
█████ *Michael Lane*
Portsmouth, Virginia 23703

February 7, 1981

Dear Mary and Gene,

        Sometimes life becomes so hectic there is
hardly time to think, much less time to write letters.
Since we've moved from Portsmouth, to Virginia Beach,
the days seem so short--perhaps because it takes us
longer to get from one room to another. We have about
5,000 sq. feet, and that's a lot of house.

        I'd like to say Mother adores it here, but she
doesn't, as usual. She misses Portsmouth where life
was so convenient. We were depending on Bill and Joan
to stay and drive her around, but they came shortly
after New Year's Day and stayed four days and then left.
They have put their things in our maid's quarters, and
this keeps us from hiring a maid to make work easier
on Mother. There was an English butler I could have
hired, if we'd have had that room and bath at his
disposal, but everyone kept warning me to BEWARE. He
refused to give me adequate references, and who knows,
he could have been another Jack the Ripper, although
he sounded very nice. He would have been our chef,
housekeeper, done the laundry, gardening, driving.
and catered our parties. Sigh, sigh, how wonderful
a butler would be.

        IF THERE BE THORNS is finished, and will be
for sale the middle of May, total distribution June first.
In September THE OBSESSED will be on sale in hardcover
only. THORNS will be published in hardcover and paperback
simultaneously.

        I've started on another book, but some of my
bubbling enthusiasm for writing has worn off. I feel
tired. I have had some trouble with my right foot that
has grown a bone spur that has to be removed in March.
It's just office surgery, nothing major, and I'll go
home to recooperate. Then there will be no bone under
my little toe to grow more calluses.

        My living expenses have taken a tremendous jump
since buying this house. We still own the other one too.
The real estate business is just about dead. If we don't
sell soon we will have to rent as our electricity, gas
and etc, is still going on.

(Some information redacted.)

Two weeks ago, Saturday, I went to Willis
Wayside and bought a fortune in furniture, only the
best. I think this house is going to cost 100,000 just
to furnish it properly. We're ripping up soiled carpet
and putting down new. Our family room furniture and
decor is Pan-Asiasn. Our dining room wall units and
dining table are waiting for chairs to be upholstered
in the fabric of our choice.

Mother is scared to death, naturally. But I
do have the means to pay for what I buy. However, I
am not a millionaire. Simon & Schuster may owe me
more than a million, but they have sticky fingers and
ten dozen reasons why they have to hold back 20 and 25%.
(Expecting a few book returns) Most authors have 40 to
50 percent held back from their royalties. If I
weren't a bestselling author they would treat me the
same way.

I'm sorry I can't affort to support both my
brothers and their families, but who will look out
for me in the way I want to live but myself? I don't
want a brother telling me what I can and cannot do in
my own home. In this house I am the boss, and what I
want comes first. When Mother is gone, if I should
live that long, I will have to pay for every service
performed. I have to save for that day. I've never
had a life of my own, in which I could rule my own
destiny. My health has always been the captain of
my ship, and I fear it will always direct my course.
But I do have more control now, due to that money you
make so light of, Eugene. I cannot "give half" to
anybody. When love has to be bought it doesn't mean
a damn thing.

We haven't taken any pictures of this house
since the yard is a mess. In the spring we'll hire
men to come and clean up the building materials that
the former owner (a building contractor) left for seven
years. Sand, wood, bricks, are all over the place.
However, he did have the grounds professionally landscaped,
then let them grow wild. Bill has promised to clean up
the yard and trim the shrubs and trees when he comes back.
We have Lynnhaven Oysters in our part of the bay--our own
oyster bed. And do they taste wonderful when fresh!
The house is of natural white brick, French Provincial,
and really beautiful. It will be even more beautiful
when I've finished everything I plan to do.

The best of everything,

Love,

June 21, 1981

Dear Mary and Gene,

I'm thinking you'll get a kick out of seeing my new corperation letterhead stationery. Once a month I have to hold an executive meeting with my president, treasurer and secretary-- which means I meet with myself in the dining room and put down minutes in my book. Which also means my attorney will do that for me. (The dining room will be business deductible too.)

But...I do use it for business when my literary agent, editor, and journalists come to lunch or dinner. Next week I have four interviews set up with various newspaper and magazine reporters. Being the hottest author in THE WORLD keeps me irritatingly, yet sometimes pleasantly, busy, busy.

Bill and Joan left for Canada last Thursday and will be returning in September or October, hopefully with enough money to see Bill through the winter. Golnick is such rotten pay I fear he's wasting his time, but he was determined to do it nevertheless. Bill has done a great deal of work in our yard which is almost three acres, and overgrown with underbrush. He's cleared most of that out near the long driveway. I'd like, later on, to have a circular driveway for this one has to be backed out of.

Yesterday Mother and I were driven over to Portsmouth in my Van (the driver paid by Pocket Books) to attend an autograph party. I was overwhelmed by the huge crowd standing and waiting, we were only a few minutes late. Five hundred at least! I signed so many books a blister raised on my index finger, right hand. Then, at four we left and were driven to Lynnhaven Mall, not so far from home, and there I signed only 65 times. That mall is so new all the stores haven't opened as yet. But I had the chance to watch a "Bird show"--lots of noise as Macaws pulled little toys and shot off toy canons.

Anne Maitland, my publicity director, called and told me about the Marco Island newspaper story concerning Captain Gene's broad smile, and Captain Gene's wife's smile because of my success. It was amusing to hear, and they are sending me a copy even if you don't. You don't know this, but the govenor of Virginia declared June 6, 1981 officially V. C. Andrews day in Virginia. Joan and Bill went with us to Richmond to a huge celebration, autograph parties, luncheons and formal dinners, and an official speech that I made in their largest library auditorium. This part might come as a surprise, for we connived to call Bill and Joan --Gene and Mary,

(Some information redacted.)

Vanda

just in case a certain greedy ex-wife should read about this
in her newspaper. The UP and AP both covered the story, plus
many other newspapers. I used to get a wee bit nervous at
flashlights going off in my face, but now I ignore it like a pro.

My reading fans are a delight. You'd think they really
knew me from their affectionate greetings. I think I may start
a trend of incest from the remarks I hear--heaven forbid!

Thanks for the Papaya seeds. They arrived the day
we were leaving, and since we've come back we haven't had time
to put them in the ground. But Mother is doing that today.

As for the Mango--well, I guess that sort of thing
requires a certain taste. I didn't like it. Maybe I would after
some practice. I used to think Mexican food was atrocious too.
I don't even like Smithfield ham as much as I once did.

I'll have to inquire around and see if I can get someone
to drive us to the airport to meet you. Perhaps my attorney or
my stock broker, who are both friendly. My attorney is very
handsome and has been the first man to take me out on a date
since I was seventeen. My stock broker is good looking too, but
sometimes I think of him as a little boy who just couldn't handle
me like Doug, the attorney.

Brad wrote a wonderful long letter, and please don't
scold him for not writing more often. ████████████████████
████████████████ He enclosed an essay he'd written. His
writing is very good, and I hope he won't give up and turn to something else when he shows so much talent. I wanted to type up his
script, but when I tried I found myself changing his phrasing to
the way I'd say it, and that wouldn't be fair to him. Everyone has
to develop his own style. Mine is so ingrained, I can't even copy
my own work without constantly changing and improving--or so I think.

By for now. I'm back to the novel I have to finish by
Octor--or the latest, January. And I'm only on page 55.

Love to Glenn & Susan too,

Virginia at around age thirty, in Portsmouth, Virginia.

point out that "dialogue in reality can be so mundane as to be absolutely boring." She was not a reporter; she was a fiction author. She was not a photographer capturing what everyone could see; she was an artist capturing what only she could see and then help others see.

The power of the descriptions in her novels, whether of people or of places and things, emanated from her artistic talent. She knew how to use color and shade, find meaning in the tint of eyes, and especially draw on the color of hair to reveal softness or fear in a character. Her settings are detailed, with her descriptions of rooms with carefully drawn curtains, chandeliers, and statuary. She could describe the portraits of characters' ancestors, ascribing meaning to their smirks and smiles and glares. Frank Lloyd Wright, who had commented on her drawing when she was a child, would surely have appreciated the way she described the intricate stairs in Foxworth Hall and the interiors of Whitefern in *My Sweet Audrina*. One could easily assume she had lived or traveled extensively in the "willies" of West Virginia when reading her descriptions of them in *Heaven*.

Obviously, Virginia had drawn from a deep well of her own reading to feed her imagination and create her new worlds. The same was true for her characters, their traits and gestures, all that revealed who they really were. She observed as much as she could about human behavior from watching her family and those she had known in her aborted school life.

In a letter to her brother Gene, she wrote, "I put myself into Cathy's body and in that way, I could make her real." Referring to her own nephews, she wrote, "I put a lot of Brad and Glenn in the twins (Cory and Carrie) concerning what they liked to eat . . . the finicky picky ones who didn't want anything grainy, lumpy, or funny looking." Elaborating on the character of Christopher Jr., she added, "The boy, Chris, I patterned after someone I used to be in love with . . . someone you don't even know about, Eugene."

The point is clear: although nothing for any writer or artist is solely drawn from the well of imagination, a writer's way of interpreting reality almost provides a third eye. This is the ability to see what everyone else sees but in a unique way. It's not so much imagination as it is an interpretation. It's why a good writer is both a reporter and a psychiatrist. Much of that special vision for Virginia was drawn from within her own feelings and fears. It's the sculpting a writer does to create a character that is real both to them and, most important, to the reader.

In *Flowers*, it enabled Virginia to turn an ordinary little girl into a Cathy Dollanganger. It's almost impossible to discover from where imagination comes, anyway. It's doubtful that it's something taught or learned. As we have clearly seen, Virginia was employing the magic as soon as she developed speech and could manipulate a pencil or a paintbrush.

Virginia herself believed in the mystery. She often noted that she merely had to close her eyes and drift into sleep, where she felt another world would open. After the success of *Flowers in the Attic*, she noted the power of her dreams and struggled to turn them into stories, claiming she had a sheet of forty more plots she had garnered from her dreams. She made the same claim again in Rubin's "Blooms of Darkness" article that she had sixty-three brief synopses of future novels tucked away, although none of these has been found in her collection of papers. Constricted, restrained, and isolated, she dug into the craft of writing with a refusal to fail. It was the only way to throw off the chains.

We know from Virginia's own testimony that she wrote nine unsuccessful novels and about twenty unpublished short stories before she came up with *Flowers in the Attic*. Do her isolation and restriction explain what took her so long? Why did she first write nine different novels, claiming that if one failed to be accepted, even on its first try, she'd start another? Not until after the first nine did she turn to the famous attic. She had first heard the premise forty years earlier in the University of Virginia medical facility—why had she kept it on the back burner?

Was she afraid of something, a little terrified of the revelations? Worried about how her mother or other members of her family would react? It would seem not.

However, it should come as no surprise that Virginia wanted to share her experiences and success with her family. Besides family offering a real sense of comfort and protection when she suffered her illness and became so dependent, it was the place where she would begin her exploration of character and plot, find her themes, and develop her driving philosophy.

In this small but precious circle of brothers, aunts, niece and nephews, and cousins, she would find an audience willing to hear details about her interchanges with her publisher, her agent, reviewers, fans, and other writers, many of those writers surely envious but all eager to learn the answer to the big question: *How did you do it? How did you capture the magic? We know you worked hard and you were determined, but how did you get millions of readers to confess, at least to themselves, that you were revealing what they had hidden and deliberately forgotten about themselves as children and young adults?*

Some would try to define *Flowers in the Attic* as if it were any other phenomenon: "Sensational," "An event!" Because of the way readers were reacting and the sales were going, it was clearly a literary wonder. Some commentators and reviewers found they were using contradictions to describe it: "This is so simple; it's a young adult's book, and yet it's not."

It wasn't? Then what was it?

In an interview in *USA Today* in 1986, Virginia was asked, "Do you write for adults or adolescents?"

"I write for adults," she replied, "but teens seem to identify with my books. . . . My themes have to do with a struggle for independence, daydreaming, fantasy, learning and struggle for control with parents. I get letters from teenagers saying they feel like my characters. One girl said she wished she could be locked away to learn about life. Remember, I'm in the same bind. I live at home with my mother. My disability limits my breaking away."

In the same interview, she repeated her lifelong theme: "I'm intrigued why people do such terrible things to the people they love."

Or, as Cathy summarizes the novel for us: "I think of us more as *flowers in the attic*. Paper flowers. Born so brightly colored, and fading duller through all those long, grim, dreary, nightmarish days when we were held prisoners of hope, and kept captives by greed."

Kept captive by their own mother and grandmother. How horrid! How fascinating—Virginia's theme, "people do such terrible things to the people they love." Or are supposed to love. This contradiction is at the heart of what draws us to the story. At the start, it doesn't seem that horrible; it seems painless. *Stay in your room until you apologize, change your tone, do your homework* . . . but it doesn't really stop there.

What is it about knowing you can't get out that makes you wish you had had a spanking instead, especially when you are young and thrive on the sense of freedom? Was sadistic Grandma watching them through a peephole, waiting for them to commit a sin, perhaps even enjoying their discomfort and fear?

Perhaps the most interesting part of the production of the novel *Flowers in the Attic* lies in the creation of the keyhole cover. The keyhole in the center of the book cover opened to a splash of characters and setting. Some reviewers and commentators saw it as another symbolic way to show how Virginia gave the reader a sort of peephole view into the secret world of Foxworth Hall and the attic and, especially, Cathy's growing adolescence. Such a cover concept would quickly become identified as a V.C. Andrews signature.

Because there was so much excitement and interest in V.C. Andrews book covers—and because they were expensive and innovative—Pocket Books released a detailed description of their creation. They began with the statement: "The story behind the covers of the V.C. Andrews novels is a chronicle of a whole new trend in paperback design."

How fitting that a novel with such an original style would inspire innovative and creative cover art. According to the release, "Pocket Books art director Milton Charles was given the task of creating the cover for *Flowers*. He hired artist Gillian Hills to execute the cover painting and together they developed a 'look' for the novel and subsequent series that has succeeded beyond anyone's dreams.

"On their third try, Charles and Hills hit on their bestselling look. Charles decided to make the cover a die-cut with a step-back painting. The front cover is a stark black and red house with silver embossing. This was the first time that foil had ever been used as art. A child's face showed through the die-cut."

Most lifelong V.C. Andrews fans recall their instant recognition of the sequels, as well as of *Heaven*, *Dark Angel*, and *My Sweet Audrina*, via the same step-back covers on the bookracks in drugstores, airplane terminals, and bookstores. They stood out like flashing neon signs on the bookshelves, announcing the arrival of a new V.C. Andrews tale.

Virginia wrote that she was particularly excited by the *Flowers in the Attic* cover "because of the way Grandmother Olivia loomed over the huddled children in the step-back . . . to show four children inside, haunted by fear. When you see it," she told Mary and Gene, "it is quite striking."

Virginia told them that the novel had a $100,000 promotional, advertising, and publicity campaign, with thirty-six-copy floor displays, known as "dumps" at the time. The launch was truly a muscular avalanche to introduce the title, but word of mouth was more like the lightning that every publisher dreams will strike a title they've developed.

What really happened at the start of all this was that reviewers and commentators were caught unaware. By the time they looked at a copy of *Flowers in the Attic*, it had sold tens of thousands of copies. After ten weeks on the *New York Times* bestseller list, the "Paperback Talk" column reported over 1.6 million copies had been sold. The words of detractors fell so quickly by the wayside that they were practically trampled out of existence.

The *New York Times* wouldn't officially review it, but it *would* review Stephen King? So what?

A *Washington Post* reviewer called it "deranged swill." Who cared?

The detractors were all like mythical Dutch boys putting their fingers in the holes in the dike to prevent the flood of the city. While they stood there quaking, the water rose and rose and went over the wall of naysayers; *Flowers in the Attic* became a worldwide phenomenon. The multitude of fans who wanted signed copies would figuratively push the detractors aside with a *Get out of the way!*

To be sure, there were some very complimentary reviews of *Flowers in the Attic*. In *Panorama*, Nikki Janas wrote: "Andrews travels subtly into a sinister world and develops a tale that is cinematographically polished and meticulously crafted." Kay Jarvis wrote in the *San Diego Tribune* that Andrews "displays great narrative power and marvelous imagination," and Deanie Johnson in the *Norcom Gazette* said, "If you're looking for a book jam-packed with suspense, terror, and intense emotion, then search no further—*Flowers in the Attic* is the novel for you."

Fortunately for us, Virginia detailed her publishing achievements in her letters to her family from 1978 until her passing. As we shall see, despite her success and rapidly developing fame, Virginia was still the naive young woman who had twisted her body on that high school stairway and then struggled with becoming a mature woman, free to be who she wanted and do what any other young woman could do. Her early complaints about her publishing experience and later about her promotional participation had a certain innocence.

She went from outright indignation at times to explosive joy and amazement. Her family would see that she was out to share with them her success and fame, sometimes sounding like a seasoned bestselling author before a single copy of her book had been sold. Her ride was amusing, edifying, and wondrous.

She wanted her family to participate with her in as much of the publishing experience as she could share. She enjoyed providing them with the details, as we can see in this excerpt from one letter:

"Dear Mary and Gene . . .

"First, I did receive the contract to sign . . . and try to understand. I had books to guide me along the way—thank God—for it is one complicated jumble of legal mumbo-jumbo jargon. And whether or not I cheated myself, I signed, hoping for the best, and trusting my agent, who said it was a very fair contract. *I gave the publishers permission to use my real name as the author, and not the pseudonym I had on the manuscript.*"

The pseudonym she was referring to was not V.C. Andrews.

That is another story to unravel.

chapter seven
Living Life in the Attic

V.C. ANDREWS WAS A different pseudonym from the one she claimed to have used for more salacious material, such as the famed undiscovered story "I Slept with My Uncle on My Wedding Night." (See the excerpt at the back of this book on page 243.)

Virginia had not been as secretive earlier. At the start of her success, she was willing to share the details of her financial gain and her possibilities with her family. She was clearly unsure of that pending wealth when she received the early income from *Flowers in the Attic*, the $7,500 advance.

She wrote: "I am allowed to make 3,300 dollars above my annuity—but my royalty advance is more than double that amount . . . and therefore, this year, I will have to pay income taxes, too. It means I will have to live stringently, unless my agent manages to sell the right I have 100% of" (that is, unpublished and unencumbered works in her file).

Despite the celebrity treatment Virginia was already enjoying from her publisher and agent, she was cautious about predicting her success. She told Mary and Eugene in July 1979, "Here's hoping you like the story well enough to give me rave reviews. Being a perfectionist, I think I could write it better today than when I did. That's the way I was when I painted too."

Because she was a first-time published writer, she was frustrated by the process and the length of time it took to get her contract signed, sealed, and delivered. "Yesterday, after the mail came I could stand the suspense no longer, so I put in another call to Anita, my agent—(collect too) to find out why two weeks had passed and still no contracts . . . she explained she had to take the contracts back and make them change a few phrases—and that took the legal department at S and S ten days."

In the meantime, still aware of her finances, she faced the reality most first-time published authors face when they experience the income improvement. "I don't have enough deductions! I can't claim Mother, since I am now contributing more than one half to her support—as she used to claim me for the same reason . . . it's all so darn complicated."

In time, when looking back, these concerns would seem almost comical. Nonetheless, they were short-lived, as the impact of *Flowers in the Attic* and its sequels was soon to be felt and seen in both her bank account and her brokerage statements and make her one of the most financially successful authors of her time.

She ended another letter by showing her pride and new self-confidence as time went by. In a tongue-in-cheek way, before she had received her royalties, she chastised her brother Eugene's boss for doubting her impending success after Eugene had bragged about her. "And if Golnick still doesn't believe you have a sister soon to be famous—give him his shoe to eat when the fact hits the newspapers, the TV, Variety Magazine . . . and whatever else may pop up any day, any second . . . and tonight you can bet I'll be taking at least two tranquilizers!"

In a letter, she described her older brother, Bill Jr., hinting in a phone call that he wasn't quite believing in her great success by stating (incorrectly), "You sure must have had some fantastic agent to sell it the first time it's shown." She reacted immediately with, "There's an old adage in the writing business, that the BEST agent alive cannot sell an unsalable manuscript . . . in fact, even the worst agent in the business will refuse to handle a manuscript that is unsalable. And to hear that an editor at a giant publishing firm like Simon & Schuster tell me mine is the most unique and exciting script to come into their offices, if you think that didn't inflate my ego, which is often depressed, then God didn't make Virginia Andrews . . . or anybody else named Andrews."

With her pride and confidence exploding, in a July 7, 1979, letter to her brother Gene and sister-in-law Mary, it is easy to see and understand Virginia's initial reaction to first seeing the book cover for *Flowers in the Attic*. However, the birth of her famed name came as a complete surprise. And not without some indignation:

"Dear Mary and Gene,

"When I received the copy of the book cover, a sample book, and the publicity pamphlet I went into shock! They used V.C. Andrews and not Virginia Andrews as was in the contract! Once you have your name established—that's it, and I don't like V.C. Andrews!"

"She was so upset about it," Mary Andrews recalls, "that we called her to ask if there was anything she could do. Gene thought she should see an attorney. She told us she did call and they told her it was a printing error that would be far too expensive to correct."

Later, she said she had found out it was a deliberate decision. The publisher was after a male audience and thought keeping the sex of the writer secret for a while might work.

"After the book was published, none of us could complain," Virginia wrote to Brad.

In the same September 1980 letter, she told him, "You'd be surprised at how many of my fans address me: 'Dear Mr. Mrs. Miss—or whatever, Andrews.' Whatever? You know they meant possible Mr."

Even though she didn't want to be in the category of horror and terror on bookshelves and in reviews, Virginia could see it was not easy to escape this fate. Unfortunately, this was a genre most readers thought only men could do well. Reluctantly, even though the situation didn't make her happy or comfortable, Virginia ultimately came to the conclusion that turning her into V.C. Andrews was probably wise.

Nevertheless, she complained to her family and others about the discrimination against women even reaching into what they could create in their imaginations. Everyone, she said, expected her work would simply be more romance stories, as if that was all women could do. She wondered what would be the result of a man writing a romance novel. Would everyone think he couldn't possibly do well in that genre just because he was a man?

She relaxed her indignation in her final conclusion that what she had essentially done was create her own field, so in the sense that it was now hers forever, her pseudonym was sacrosanct. In a number of interviews, she expressed the belief that she was so unique in her approach, style, and plots as to have her own genre. Her style, her voice, was simply too unique to put into a category or relegate to any common category. It was an immediate challenge for reviewers, booksellers, and retail outlets. Stores love to pigeonhole the book and the author to make the display coordinate with what they have designed already.

When *Flowers in the Attic* was launched in November 1979, it was immediately placed on a variety of bookstore shelves, ranging from horror to thriller to general fiction to young adult fiction, but the novel would persevere regardless of how it was shelved—or mis-shelved. In time, it would find its own place, just as Virginia had predicted. It was still on the bestseller list four months after its publication.

Nevertheless, her fortune was still to come. Except for 50 percent of their advance on signing a contract and the remaining 50 percent on publication, authors have to wait for their royalties, assuming their sales have produced enough income for them to cover the advance that had been paid. Considering how small her advance was in relation to what the sales of *Flowers in the Attic* would be, and with the accumulation of foreign sales, Virginia still should have had good reason to anticipate her impending wealth.

In July 1979, about four months before the release of *Flowers*, Virginia wrote to Eugene to tell him the sequel was finished, "and they chose my second title: *Petals on the Wind*. I always send a list of alternative titles when I'm not confident about a title. *Flowers* was so perfect I knew they wouldn't change that."

Readers were clamoring for *Petals*. What happened to these three remaining children? In her first fan letter—written by a man, it should be noted—the reader asked, "Did they ever get revenge on their mother and grandmother?"

Flowers in the Attic almost immediately suggested the possibilities for the sequel. Virginia indicated that sometimes her characters just took over and ran with the baton. In letters to the publishers and in her fan mail, she could see that her fans were insisting on *Petals on the Wind* to finish their story. There were too many questions left unanswered, and more important, perhaps, they were too invested in the characters to just let them go by closing the cover of the novel. And the success of *Flowers* demanded it.

The plot for *Petals on the Wind* wasn't going to be any less dark just because the children had managed to escape from the attic. All teenagers dream of running off and having their independence and chance for adventure, but for Christopher Jr., Cathy, and Carrie, there would be dark and trying complications in *Petals*, even if they had found a welcoming home where everything they needed was provided. Strange romantic relationships occur, and the haunting effects of being locked in the attic are explored. Virginia never let us forget: these were still damaged children. Their dark memories were haunting, and the way they thought, trusted, and explored love was very much influenced by their incarceration in the attic. If this was going to be a fairy-tale life, there were still many monsters lurking in the shadows.

"It's a good thing I love to write, for it is hard work," she wrote to Eugene. "You wouldn't believe how fast I can type without one error made—how fast I can dream up plots from just one good opening line—and I have a sheet of forty more in my bedroom desk— dreamed up in one sleepless night before I began to take tranquilizers. Now I sleep too well to dream up anything but DREAMS."

What a rebirth she was having in her mid-fifties! Successful publication had opened so many doors, doors to her own mind. She was ecstatic about her own abilities to create and to form characters and develop plots. With her growing wealth and fame, Virginia had to adapt to a more active life than what she was previously accustomed to. In a short discussion with her brother Eugene about someone she had grown to like and someone she depended on, an employee, she reveals a nagging fear about how her needs impacted those around her. It is perhaps one of the most telling and revealing quotes from her letters.

"Hank found me a nice man, John, to act as my 'chauffeur.' Of course I paid him each time according to how far he had to drive and whether or not we had to take the chair. . . . [W]e were going to Willis Wayside to look for a chair, another, larger desk for my study and a service wagon. He seemed happy to do what he could, saying he got in his wife's way since he retired and he was dying of boredom. I think he stayed an hour after we came back telling me of his war wounds. He'd stepped on a landmine and it tore off his face and his ear. However, the doctors managed to sew it back, all but for an ear which was half-missing. They could do nothing though to remove the pieces of shrapnel lodged in his brain so he had constant headaches for thirty years. Then, on the very day we thought John was driving us to Willis Wayside—Hank called up and said he'd died! Fifty-four, and healthy enough appearing—and dead that quickly. *You don't know how guilty his death makes me feel—like somehow I brought on whatever killed him. (The lifting, you know . . .)*"

Although she had become royalty in publishing, she was always cognizant of the ways in which her disability impacted her relationships, particularly regarding people she employed.

Fortunately for her, if not appreciated half as much by her mother, Virginia's skyrocketing celebrity would bring smiles and excitement enough to drown out any dwelling on her unfortunate physical condition and the restrictions it imposed on her. She was determined to be a full-time, successful author, someone with important things to say about the craft and someone who would engage with her fans. And that included travel and public events.

Virginia participated in autograph-signing events almost immediately after the launching of *Flowers in the Attic*, and those would increase after *Petals on the Wind*. In the November 14, 1979, letter to Cousin Pat, she said, "Yesterday, I completed my first three autographing parties, driven there by a chauffeur in a limousine. This limo is at my disposal anytime I need to go anywhere—even shopping."

Remember those days described earlier with Pat taking her to a mall for the first time? It was like going to the moon, and keep in mind how upset that had made her mother at the time. Fame and success made denying Virginia these simple pleasures impossible.

She could barely catch her breath before the second novel's success proved equally overwhelming. In her March 10, 1980, letter to Pat, she was obviously quite ecstatic: "*Petals on the Wind* will make its debut this June both in hardcover and paperback. *Flowers in the Attic* will also be in hardcover to make a boxed set. They've set the first printing for the hardcover at 35,000, and the first paperback printing for *Petals* at 1,500,000! That's a lot of books! And this time my percentage will be much greater. The book has not even gone into galleys and still they have sold thousands of *Petals* from the cover alone—and all the people who keep demanding the sequel. *Get ready for some more suffering—bring out your Kleenex—your towels and tranquilizers.*

"It was amusing when your brother, Joe, asked if anyone would die in the sequel, for he didn't want to cry again. I answered: 'Death is a natural part of living.' He answered, 'Oh, God! Now I have my answer!'"

During all this, Virginia kept in touch with her nephew Brad, who she knew would be excited for her and fascinated with what was happening so quickly. In September 1980, the same year *Petals on the Wind* was released, Virginia proudly told him, "Last Sunday I gave my second public speech before an audience of three hundred or so, and believe it or not, at the end I received a standing ovation. This was a real achievement for me, for as you know I am not accustomed to public speaking, but with the belief in my abilities, I tackle anything and somehow it works out."

Rather than shy away from and be frightened by all this public exposure, she now embraced it with her nervous mother at her side. She went on to tell Brad, "In March of next year, I've been invited to speak in Chatham, Virginia, at several of the colleges and universities up that way. I'll stay overnight in a guest cottage (and Mother too) so it should be a nice small vacation, as well as being profitable.

"Saturday, I finished the third in the series concerning the 'Dollanganger' kids, titled, *If There Be Thorns*. It should come out next spring."

She makes her feelings regarding women's representation in the trade clear in the next comment to Brad: "I thank you for that flattering title of 'Authoress extraordinaire.' However, remember this is the age of women's lib—and that stilted title 'Authoress' has gone out of style. An author is either a woman or a man now, as it should have been all along. The sex of a writer, or doctor, or whatever should not be mentioned at all."

Early in November 1980, she revealed how she had embraced her fame and the fans who came to her book signings. She told Cousin Pat, "I also have my own fan clubs of high school and college students who follow me around and just revel in being near a 'celebrity.'"

In a *New York Times* article on June 14, 1981, about the third book in the Dollanganger series, *If There Be Thorns*, the legendary reviewer Nan Robertson described the cover in vivid detail and predicted it would be the biggest-selling novel of the summer of 1981. She credited Pocket Books' art director Milton Charles and his illustrator Gillian Hills for creating the bestseller-making packaging.

Flowers in the Attic and *Petals on the Wind* together sold nearly 7 million copies in original paperback editions. *If There Be Thorns* had a first printing of 2.5 million in paperback and took the number two spot in its first appearance on the mass-market paperback bestseller list.

Robertson wrote, "So many readers of the Dollanganger saga expressed a wish for copies in a more enduring form that Simon & Schuster took the unusual step of publishing hardcover editions subsequent to the Pocket Books ones.

"Terror tales are not a new fictional genre by any means: They have been part of the English literary tradition since the early 19th century, when Mary Wollstonecraft Shelley wrote 'Frankenstein.'"

Despite this comparison with Shelley, as noted earlier, Virginia would not have appreciated being categorized as another terror writer. On the heels of this comment in the *Times*, she continually emphasized, and most commentators and reviewers eventually agreed, that she was in a class by herself— and a very popular one, at that.

In another letter to Mary and Gene, dated June 21, 1981, a week after the *Times* article appeared, Virginia wrote, "Yesterday Mother and I were driven over to Portsmouth in my Van to attend an autograph party. I was overwhelmed by the huge crowd standing and waiting, we were only a few minutes late. Five hundred at least! I signed so many books a blister raised on my index finger, right hand. Then, at four we left and were driven to Lynnhaven Mall, not so far from home, and there, I signed only 65 times. . . .

"You don't know this, but the governor of Virginia declared June 6, 1981, officially V.C. Andrews day in Virginia. [June 6 was her birthday.]

"Joan [her sister-in-law] and Bill [her older brother] went with us to Richmond to a huge celebration, autograph parties, luncheons and formal dinners, and official speech that I made in their largest library auditorium . . . the UP and AP both covered the story, plus many other newspapers. I used to get a wee bit nervous at flashlights going off in my face, but now I ignore it like a pro. Everything was happening so quickly.

"My reading fans are a delight. You'd think they really knew me from their affectionate greetings. I think I may start a trend of incest from the remarks I hear—heaven forbid!"

With the money that was now coming in, Lillian and Virginia had begun to look for a bigger, more luxurious home. They had settled on one in Virginia Beach and closed on it on November 20, 1980, underscoring the whirlwind that had come raging from the New York publishing world. When one compares the modest homes described earlier with this one, success is easy to detect. In her usual detailed way, Virginia moves us in with her and her mother when she describes the house to Cousin Pat:

"The house has ten rooms. A huge kitchen with Lazy Susan corner cabinets, a walk-in pantry, breakfast nook, utility room, Florida room, a family room 21 x 30 ft. with a wet bar at one end as large as the kitchen we have now, living and dining room, three baths, five bedrooms. I'll use the office it has now for a storage room as I need more space, and convert one of the extra bedrooms into a big office. There is also a kitchen in the garage for cooking smelly things like fish, or roasting in the summer, and in the garage is a complete workshop with cabinets overhead. We even have two dishwashers, two stoves, for parties given.

"My bedroom is so huge I could move in there and never come out—especially the bathroom with its sunken tub, a huge shower with a steam room, dressing room with the Hollywood mirrors, lights all around, and even a bidet—which will probably never be used unless my next operations are very successful. I'll have two giant walk-in closets for my own use, plus in the dressing room, a long row of narrow cabinets for makeup, shoes, handbags, linens, etc."

She told Brad in a letter that "the house is French Provincial style, white bricks (not painted but made of white clay—or whatever) and has its own private road so the house cannot be seen from the street, and one acre of land."

She summed up her own amazement at her success by telling Pat: "And who would ever believe a small paperback book like 'Flowers' could buy such a home?"

Virginia had finally found her fairy-tale castle. The expense was easily justified once *Petals on the Wind* was released. Virginia had written it under intense pressure to produce the story for a demanding new global audience. Still in a writing frenzy, she had completed *If There Be Thorns* for a March 1981 publication. When she had first conceived of *Flowers in the Attic*, she had no concrete plans set down for sequels and certainly not three of them, with a fourth on the drawing board. Her work habits and productivity made it all possible. (And she managed to publish another fan favorite, *My Sweet Audrina*, in the middle of it all, too.)

The public events, the demand for more interviews, the accolades, the new financial responsibilities, all accumulated within a little more than two years and highlighted by another move to a bigger and newer home, were navigated well, with Virginia assuming more and more control of her life. She chose her interviews carefully and directly participated in the choices for their new home. But she did admit to the strain of all this, always with a touch of hope.

In a very revealing passage in a February 1981 letter to Mary and Gene, she wrote: "I've started another book, but some of the bubbling enthusiasm for writing has worn off. I feel tired. I have had some trouble with my right foot that has grown a bone spur that has to be removed in March. It's just office surgery, nothing major, and I'll go home to recuperate. Then there will be no bone under my little toe to grow more calluses."

It's always in hindsight that we find symbolic or prophetic utterances or events. At the time, only someone truly prescient could read anything into "bubbling enthusiasm for writing has worn off. I feel tired." Despite her ailments and physical disabilities, Virginia's enthusiasm for her work and achievements clearly seemed to overwhelm her disadvantages. She took on any and every challenge she could.

As she herself described it, merely going to a department store was like a safari. Lifted, carefully placed on pillows, shifted to a wheelchair, wheeled about, lifted, and carefully placed again for the ride home, her mother hovering with a hawk's eyes, slamming down on the slightest carefree act or dangerous shift, Virginia clearly understood what every journey meant, no matter how short or long. If she was in pain, she knew she couldn't voice it, or her mother would cut the trip short and send her back to bed. We already know that Lillian was fiery and firm enough to take command, even of a daughter who had become world-famous.

Virginia, however, wanted to see and feel her international fame despite any fatigue and any recurring pain. In September 1982, a trip no one would have predicted Virginia would ever undertake was arranged. She and her mother and her agent were going to London, where Virginia would do publicity events and tour historic places, and then go to Paris.

"Dear Eugene and Mary,

"Here we are again, about to set forth into the huge world for the third time in a few short months. It seems we are making up for all those years when we did nothing but stay home. . . .

"I've mailed Brad my British itinerary, so you can see from that, we will be busy, especially when you realize they won't tell me everything in advance, or else I might back out. . . . I've heard they are giving me the most expensive publicity tour they have ever given ANY author.

"Not to be depressing, but if anything should happen, everything you will need will be left in my filing system, inside the Scandinavian desk in my office. Remember I have two desks in there. The Queen Anne desk has my CPT on top, which would have to be returned since I only lease it, with the option to buy when I have paid in the full amount. The printer also goes with the CPT. To program the word processor, you use the Word Processing disk in the black case. To process the computer, you use the math disk in the green file folder. That program disk is labeled, CASH ON HAND. (My code to keep my affairs private.) The Xerox is mine, paid for."

Her detail about her possessions, her organizational specificity, and the clarity of her directions to her brother and sister-in-law before she left tell us much about her character and her sense of responsibility. Her mother had little or nothing to do with her work, her business affairs, or the organization of her materials; Virginia held her own life together at this point.

This would be the first of the two big trips she would take, London and Paris—and then Hollywood.

chapter eight
Leaving the Attic

IN ILLUSTRATION OF HOW Virginia Andrews's fame had crossed the
ocean ahead of her, we have the letter from the secretary to the
deputy master of the household at Buckingham Palace replying to a
request made by Mark Gray, Esq., the promotions manager of her UK
publisher, Fontana. The request was for Virginia to be permitted to
stand in the forecourt to watch the Changing of the Guard ceremony,
something reserved for celebrities and highly respected members of
the realm.

Permission was granted.

On September 6, 1982, a reporter from the *Times* of London
called Virginia to interview her so that the article about her would
appear when she arrived on September 17. Her publisher in the UK
had to make a number of intricate arrangements for her, including pro-
curing a special van. The *Times* described her in a cruel and inaccurate
manner, a reminder of why Virginia disliked interviews: ". . . paralyzed

from the neck down. [Untrue.] She must travel in an outsize wheel-chair in which she is tipped back at an angle, necessitating her wearing a bib when she eats. [Not any more than anyone would, handicapped or not.] She needs a custom-built van with a hydraulic lift before she can glide through the carefully-measured doors."

The trip was a full nineteen-day tour. Although there was no doubt Virginia needed special assistance, the reporter's depiction of her made her sound like an incapacitated woman, which suggested a publisher was dragging around a fragile person just to make a buck.

On the contrary, Virginia was filled with excitement and energy. When Anita Diamant asked before the trip if Virginia would mind a cocktail party and a formal dinner every night with the press and other media, Virginia's answer was, "Of course I don't mind."

This was not the response of someone as helpless as a baby, uncomfortable in social settings, and constantly in pain.

The *Times* reporter highlighted some of the more negative comments about *Flowers in the Attic* as well. Perhaps it was a bow to sensationalism, or perhaps this reporter was reminded of her own mixed feelings during adolescence and was haunted by the novel. Whatever the case, it certainly underscores why Virginia had showed such reluctance about the so-called in-depth interview since the *People* magazine experience, which she considered nasty and devastating and which featured photos that, in her opinion, portrayed her in the worst light, almost as distorted.

The press notwithstanding, in her letter to her nephew Brad, we can clearly see Virginia's vitality and excitement in her description of preparations in the days leading up to the big trip:

"This Thursday and Friday, Mother and I are off to autographing parties in local shopping malls. We've been doing that ever since we came back from New York. This coming Saturday is our day off, during which 'free' time we will have to finish packing to leave on Sunday for JFK airport. We will be staying there overnight at the International Hotel, and catching British Airways at ten on Monday."

Though Lillian was far more introverted than her daughter and never one to encourage her to travel and socialize, Virginia's success and fame obviously had an effect on her. She was proud to escort Virginia and become part of the festivities, standing alongside her daughter amid the endless waves of admiration flowing their way.

Virginia wrote to her nephew Brad, "Think of me as going drunk and stuffed all through Britain, and into Scotland. They are leaving out Ireland where we could be bombed.

"At the end of our promotion tour, we'll have three days in which to explore London, and the British countryside, and do some shopping, before we fly over to Paris and spend another three days there, and then back to New York where my American publishers have more promotion stunts on schedule."

This demanding agenda could easily exhaust anyone, but Virginia was not only energized but constantly enthralled with the attention and the festivities the whole time.

Her niece Suzanne recalls Virginia telling her how impressed she was when publishers were "sitting at a large round table, and she had a parade of servers in white coats come toward them with plates covered with silver domes. They were all set down at the same time and the lids lifted in unison.

"My aunt just loved this part! And in France she loved the French portions because she 'could eat a lot of different things without getting so full.' When she told me the story of her foodie adventures, her wheelchair would wiggle, she'd writhe with excitement! It was so cute!

"One other thing I do recall was simply a purchase she made at the department store. It was a $700 all-inclusive, decked-out-to-the-max makeup kit/collection. I just recall her saying that she'd never in her life have thought about making such an extravagant purchase. The brand name was Pupa . . . it was a red box that folded out in half, then kept folding out, pull-out drawer, folding mirrors, and everything 'makeup' a woman could need . . . even four mini nail polishes. Glosses, shadows, mascara, liner, creams . . . it was the most amazing kit I have ever seen! She loved shopping but needed reminding that she could afford it, and much more! It was the boost she needed . . . stories came pouring out after that life-affirming social adventure."

Anita Diamant remarked that Lillian was constantly critical of the spending, talking her daughter out of purchasing much more expensive things. It was surely difficult for Lillian to get her arms around this kind of wealth; Lillian had come through the Great Depression, and she and Virginia didn't have any money of note until 1979. Lillian wasn't working, and until Virginia began selling her artwork, their income had come from subsidies and pensions and what profit they could manage from sales of their houses when they moved. Perhaps Lillian didn't trust her daughter's understanding of finances, even though Virginia was keen on her investments in the stock market. The push and pull between mother and daughter didn't come to an end with Virginia's success and fame.

In fact, after Virginia bought the new home and began thinking about furnishing it, she told her brother Gene: "Two weeks ago, Saturday, I went to Willis Wayside and bought a fortune in furniture, only the best."

In one visit, she had spent $25,000.

"I think this house is going to cost $100,000 just to furnish it properly. We're ripping up soiled carpet and putting down new. Our family room furniture and decor is Pan-Asian. Our dining room wall units and dining table are waiting for chairs to be upholstered in the fabric of our choice. Mother is scared to death, naturally. But I do have the means to pay for what I buy."

It was true. In 1982, with the trips, the autograph events and parties, and the publication of *My Sweet Audrina*, Virginia was having one of the best years of her life, financially and socially. She and her mother were enjoying their large new Virginia Beach home. Adding to her buoyancy, Virginia still harbored the hope that—someday—

some medical procedure would restore her legs and enable her to live a fuller life. That year, the decision was made to write the next sequel to *Flowers in the Attic*, and sales of the Dollanganger series continued to skyrocket around the world.

Meanwhile, *My Sweet Audrina* seemed like a one-off, a story from out of the blue. Why she wrote it right in the middle of all the excitement around the *Flowers in the Attic* sequels was a bit of a puzzle. It was published in August 1982, whereas *Seeds of Yesterday*, the final Dollanganger sequel, wouldn't be published until 1984. *Audrina* was obviously a story line that had seized her imagination.

In "A Writer's Way to Profit from Memories," Virginia revealed some of her thinking about the book: "One of my greatest methods of finding story ideas is to take one situation from my life and ask, 'What if I hadn't run as fast as I had? What if I had been caught? What then? Would I have suffered? Been kidnapped, raped? Then killed?'

"In my newest novel, *My Sweet Audrina*, due out in mid-August of '82, the first and best Audrina meets her fate in the woods, while I could have met mine in the valley between a ring of low hills that swallowed my screams for help. I was lucky enough to have escaped. Pity my poor character that didn't.

"For a certainty in a novel I write the worst is bound to happen. But fortunately I was a fast runner, and clever enough to avoid most pitfalls. My characters are clever enough and fast enough, but by playing God, I always trip them up in some way, so as to allow what I escaped to happen to them, and then the fun begins. (Or terror.) It chills my blood to think maybe God up there is just another aspiring novelist hoping to entertain himself too by letting the worst happen, heaven forbid."

The story takes place in basically the same time frame as the Dollanganger sequel novels, the 1960s and '70s. One particular review in the blog Renee's Bookcase, years later on April 24, 2019, seems to sum up most of what the dedicated V.C. Andrews readers thought at the time of its publication and shortly thereafter: "Throughout the book, I found myself changing my opinion about each and every character several times, i.e., liking, hating and finally feeling sorry for Audrina's father and Cousin Vera."

The story line is truly dark and probably one of the things V.C. Andrews published that comes closest to a true gothic novel. The basis of the conflict for the character is purely psychological. As the novel unfolds, the reader is drawn to the truth but in a sense abhors finding it out at the same time. What has Audrina's father done to her? Despite its darkness—or perhaps because of it—*My Sweet Audrina* was another big worldwide success for Virginia.

Interestingly, at least a couple of bands used the book to develop songs: the Norwegian band Ancient recorded a song called "Audrina, My Sweet" on its album *Proxima Centauri* in tribute to the novel, and a post-punk rock band in Sydney, Australia, Toys Went Berserk, recorded a song based on the book called "Audrina" for its 1987 album *Pieces*.

Furthermore, in a bizarre incident in 1989, an American woman, Tara Leigh Calico, had disappeared from Belen, New Mexico. A photo of a bound woman was discovered and publicized, and in it a copy of *My Sweet Audrina* was at the woman's side. Calico's mother claimed it was one of her daughter's favorite books. While it remains an open case, one wonders how Virginia might have reacted to knowing one of her books might have helped identify a missing girl and show that she had been kidnapped.

Between the publication of *My Sweet Audrina* in 1982 and the third *Flowers* sequel in 1984, Virginia Andrews and her mother would make another long trip, this one to Hollywood. In February 1981, Virginia had entered into a feature film option with producers Jeff Begun and Sy Levin. The option was renewed in August 1982 by Chuck Fries, a highly successful television and movie producer. There were other moves to get the book into production. Fries would extend the option periodically until at last the movie began production in 1986 and hit theaters in November 1987.

Every movie needs a distributor. In 1983, at the time of Virginia's Hollywood trip, that was Universal, although when the movie was released in theaters, distribution would be taken over by New World Pictures with Chuck Fries Productions, Inc. Because of the overwhelming success of the novel and the sequels, everyone was eager for the book to be adapted, but it took nearly seven years. Nevertheless, because of her continual success, by the time she and her mother set out for Hollywood, Hollywood knew who Virginia Andrews was.

Virginia kept a detailed diary of this trip, celebrities and all. By all accounts, Universal was a host determined to make the most of her presence, and I don't think anyone could have described the adventure better than she did in a June 28, 1983, letter to her brother Gene, which almost reads as if she is writing an episode in one of her novels:

"We were met at the airport not only by Anita, my New York literary agent who went with us to London, but also by a girl named Suzanne Hobbs, Sy Levin's secretary. . . . It wasn't until we drove to the hotel that I met Sy—and here he comes, the man I'd pictured from his slow measured way of talking to be somewhere in his sixties—and Suzanne told me was only thirty-six. (He's since had a birthday since we left.) Suzanne was the one who read FLOWERS IN THE ATTIC and brought it to Sy's attention. She started the ball rolling. Then Chuck Fries's daughter, Allison, began to prompt her father to make a movie of FLOWERS . . . as I've heard every son and daughter of all the movie producers have urged their fathers to do the movie versions of my books. My young reading fans are behind me all the way, and when they have influential parents, that helps. It was a difficult movie to sell because they feared so many interior scenes, to say nothing of the incestuous relationship."

Virginia was experiencing what most novelists go through once their books have been optioned. Someone once said there are probably two hundred and fifty thousand options for every movie actually made. It would take an additional four years after the book was optioned before someone on a set for *Flowers in the Attic* would say "Action!" and many of those interior scenes Virginia made reference to were cut, including the incestuous affair. Virginia continued with her detailed report to her family:

"Suzanne is a lovely tall girl in her late-twenties, more than half her height being in her legs. Never saw such long pretty legs. Her hair is waist length, straight, dark brown to match her eyes . . . and right away we became good friends. It was very funny to watch Sy's reaction to me, for he'd seen only the photographs that PEOPLE magazine had published, and as you recall, they weren't flattering— to say the least. I should sue. Time and again he remarked on how young I was . . . how pretty—and thin. When I later on toured the headquarters of Universal, everyone kept saying I wasn't at all what they expected, which you can bet I asked what were they expecting? Somebody like a witch, I presume, and somebody with a grim out- look. As it was, they found out I can be a great deal of fun.

"We were driven to the Sheraton-Universal Hotel, located in the studio lot itself, and there we had a suite of rooms, with Anita's room adjacent to ours. Mountains all around, lovely gardens directly below, with the obligatory swimming pool, and outside tables for breakfast- ing, etc. Immediately we had to unpack, bathe and dress for a formal dinner in THE MAGIC CASTLE. The very favorite restaurant and theater of Harry Houdini who used to perform there often.

"We drove a long way to reach this castle high on a mountainside, swerving around mountainous curves that had Mother gasping and ex- claiming. It did really look like an old European castle until you go in- side. The walls are stone, and plastered all over with old posters advertising Houdini and a few other famous magicians. Each year they have contests to find the 'best magician of the year.' We ate dinner in near night darkness (you know how Mother enjoys that), with Jeff Begun, and his girlfriend, Roberta Collins, an actress I've seen in a few TV shows. She looks a bit like Bo Derek. We discovered we were both chocolate and cheese freaks. Joel, my Hollywood agent, was there to be my escort, another man in his mid-thirties, and already going bald on top like Sy . . . although Sy has enough thick beard to cover ten heads. I wore my most expensive cocktail dress this night . . . and lived to regret it, since every night called for a change of clothes, and I had to supplement my wardrobe with another dress when we shopped on Rodeo Drive the next day.

"Roberta was the one who captured good seats for us after the dinner, for that's when the best magicians show their stunts on a small stage where I was seated so close I could see wrinkles and individual hairs. I fixed my eyes on their hands and tried to see just how they made objects appear and disappear. No such luck . . . I still don't know how they do it. The best magician was, naturally, saved for the last—the real spellbinder. A Japanese man who was TALL! and powerful looking. He stood up there with his straight slick shoulder length blue-black hair, his huge head, and his face was both handsome and sinister in an interesting way. He's been the winner for the past five years of all contests for magicians. Being so close to the stage, of course he saw my intense interest, and he kept giving me cynical smiles, with one eyebrow lifted, as if he knew I was trying to catch on to his tricks. He didn't speak, just moved those expressive eyebrows, curled his lips, and bowed when everyone whistled and shrieked at some of his more incredible performances. He made doves, rabbits, and cards come out of the air, out of a thin baton . . . and I didn't see where they came from or where they went. He threw a whole pack of cards out, and they fell to the floor randomly, then when he gestured, one by one they leaped into his hand. His facial expressions were so distracting—I'm blaming that on my lack of understanding his tricks . . . at least that's the reason I'm giving.

"Back to the hotel, full of strawberry daiquiri, champagne and wine. To bed by three, and up the next day at six to dress for an interview, and then we're off to shop on Rodeo Drive.

"The weather is hot, no smog but surprisingly, it's very cool and breezy in the shade. But to travel from shop to shop kept me out in the sun and gave me a tan despite myself. I'd look at this and that, and to be really honest, I was disappointed. The clothes are too trendy, too flashy, too fallish (summer is over in the fashion world). I picked up a pretty belt . . . I'm big on belts this year, and it was a mere $350.00. If I had liked it, I would have paid their exorbitant prices."

Virginia was being wined and dined by Hollywood. Nothing makes someone in Hollywood as important as representing and developing a star, whether he or she is a top actor or a world-renowned bestselling author. Where once a trip to the mall was akin to a major expedition, especially in her mother's eyes, Virginia was now out on the town with ease and grace. And the best was yet to come.

". . . and back to the hotel to dress for dinner at Chasen's, the crème de la crème in the Hollywood set—taking the place of the Brown Derby, which is closed down. I was told when Elizabeth Taylor was married to Richard Burton and they lived in Beverly Hills, all their meals were delivered to their home from Chasen's. That night I wore the new black and white cocktail dress, Mother wore white, whereas the night before she'd worn red. This was our first meeting with Charles (Chuck) Fries, and he'd brought along his daughter, Allison, since his wife was with her mother who was ill. Chuck is in his early fifties, having recovered from open heart surgery last winter, and a wonderfully likeable fatherly man who insisted that I try his favorite dishes. Sy had already found out he and I like the same kind of cocktails, and I believe he had three strawberry daiquiris to my one. Mother had her usual, Pink Squirrel. Sy tried this, too, and said it was good, but a bit too sweet.

"I ended up by eating 'Hobo' steak, the house specialty. They take thick New York strips and marinate them in a thick salt coating full of seasonings for 24 hours. This salt coated steak is shown to you before the salt is scraped off at the tableside, and then it is broiled. I like mine medium rare—but more rare than medium. It smells wonderful while cooking beside the table. With the steak, I had their other specialty 'hot chili'—and was it hot!—and an artichoke salad, and for dessert, chocolate mousse. Again Roberta and I were the chocolate freaks. We had champagne or wine with this meal.

"Now, here comes the part you're going to like most. Behind our table was seated Johnny Carson and his date, Morgan Fairchild, along with Ed McMann (I'm not sure about that surname spelling), and his wife who looks young enough to be his daughter. At another table Carol Burnett was eating with five people, and seated down a ways (we had the banquet table) was Charlton Heston. Sade Thompson was eating alone. Of course Chuck and Sy seem to know everybody, and aren't a bit shy about interrupting their meals. However, I know I don't like it when fans cause my food to grow cold, so I wouldn't let them introduce me until I'd finished eating, and they had too.

"As the result, Carol Burnett and Charlton Heston finished first and escaped out of a back door. But Johnny and his group were there when we went in, and there when we went out. I was introduced to Johnny, and Morgan who is very pretty, just like she is on TV. She was wearing pink knit embroidered with crystals, and Eugene, pink *does* make a lady look pretty. Johnny is a very small, very pale, thin weak looking man with absolutely no sex appeal in my opinion, although he was gracious. Ed McMann??? is the comedian. He warned me that when he shook my hand I had to be prepared for electrical chills and sexual thrills so violent that I'd rip off his clothes. Then I said I was afraid to shake his hand if this would happen . . . he laughed and said his wife had his leg manacled to hers to keep him from going wild.

"On our way out, a news photographer ran up to snap photographs of me . . . just in case you don't think I'm a real celebrity. The next day we started off to tour Universal City, seeing the special effects that made E.T. fly on a bicycle through the sky, and how they make earthquakes, burn down buildings, etc. I was introduced as the celebrity in the audience, and somehow they made me flash on the screen. It was fascinating to see what they do with models. There was a one acre lot under a black tarp which they told me covered a miniature model of the entire city of New York. They were filming this movie all at night (therefore the tarp to keep out the sun).

"We ate lunch in Universal commissary where only the movie stars and movie bigwigs are allowed (tourists in the cafeteria), and again I saw Morgan Fairchild, only this time she was wearing a cotton pink skirt with white stripes, and a blouse with the opposite coloring. She didn't look as glamorous this time. We also saw a number of lesser movie actors and actresses, the kind on TV. They say the big ones don't dine out often, but keep to their mountain lairs—and many don't live in California at all, but are scattered all over the world.

"After lunch, more touring of Universal, including a trip up into the Black Tower where Charles Fries has his posh office, along with dozens of other producers. I saw Sy's office, met everybody there, including the man who handles the budget—and here was where I heard all their gasps because I wasn't the grim old woman they'd seen in People. (Detest that magazine.) But nobody is my booster as much as Sy. His office displayed my books everywhere. Chuck Fries in his office surroundings is not quite the benign friendly fatherly man I met at the dinner. More businesslike as he discussed budget, and costs, and when, how and where. The filming will begin this March, April or May—as soon as I approve of the final script. I'm expected to fly there again for that. He did assure me that he never optioned a book that he didn't make into a film, so that was good to hear, although if they keep renewing their options, I'll get richer just from them.

"While in his office I couldn't keep my eyes off of a stunning oriental cocktail table with a matching breakfront. Silver and gold leaf formed trees with birds and flowers. Of course I was thinking they were just perfect for our family room, but I couldn't figure out just what kind of wood would be that shiny. Then, when we left his office, both Sy and Suzanne whispered to me, they had tried to "steal" the cocktail table . . . both prepared to lift up something tremendously heavy. I'm sure they were only joking about stealing it. Suzanne, being quicker than Sy, hefted first with such might she almost threw the table through the ceiling. It was made of *plastic*!

"That's Hollywood . . . all facade."

Had it taken Virginia that short a time to realize the dazzle was not to be taken seriously? Of course, she was enjoying herself. Few in the Hollywood circles she was moving in knew the details of her journey or were going to bother finding out. The emphasis is always on the "property" and what can be gotten from an association with it. Note, however, that Virginia had done something few successful novelists do or get the opportunity to do: she maintained approval of the movie script deriving from her book. She would reject five attempts, and when the final one was in process, the changes and cuts were truly Hollywood dazzle.

Before they would leave the Hollywood scene, Virginia and her mother were taken to a nightclub where Virginia said transvestites "mimed Julie Andrews, Judy Garland who turned into Liza Minnelli before our eyes.

"There was Marilyn Monroe, Marlene Dietrich, Barbra Streisand, Diana Ross, and a huge fat man/woman with a billowing white wig, inch long lashes, and a very pretty face and legs, played the role of Little Orphan Annie, a madam, and several other funny parts. When she was Annie, she held a big doll dressed like her, with a smaller doll dressed the same, holding a tinier doll, and on and on ad infinitum. During her song and dance the doll was kicked, slapped, brutalized until she fell apart. It was all hilarious. Even Mother, whom I thought might be shocked by some of the jokes, laughed and seemed to enjoy herself. We had tried to finish our superb dinner before the show began, but we were finishing up when the host called 'Gypsy' came to our table, directly in front of the stage, and had to meet me. He'd read 'Flowers' and commented the title conjured up in his mind the notion the flowers were those who couldn't make it to the closet.

"There were three front tables, and we had the best one. Marty Allen had another, and Dennis Cole, a TV actor once married to Jaclyn Smith, was at the third. The host, Gypsy, between acts would come out in the craziest costumes, tell jokes, poke a few at me, after I was introduced to the guests, and without pity ribbed Dennis Cole during the entire evening, as if being straight was being wrong. Naturally, Sy had to bring them over, and we had our pictures taken with Gypsy, Dennis Cole and Marty Allen, and the big fat lady-man. This was my favorite evening."

Virginia didn't leave Hollywood without being taken to a private screening of *Psycho II*, which she pronounced "absolutely inane. Alfred Hitchcock should spin in his grave."

In so many ways, June 1983 was the pinnacle of Virginia's career. The power of *Flowers in the Attic* had brought her to the attention of the most important producers, agents, and publishers. Her international status continued to grow. Through her constant sharing with her relatives in letters and phone calls, holidays and visits, she held on to family. Her fan mail was overwhelming her. Yet through it all, she somehow maintained her work ethic and productiveness.

On March 15, 1984, *Seeds of Yesterday*, the third sequel to *Flowers in the Attic*, was published. It was number one on the *New York Times* bestseller list by April 8. Virginia was now concentrating on her next series, the first book of which was *Heaven*. In an early edition, she would write this letter to her readers, explaining why it was a challenge:

"Dear Reader,

"Writing HEAVEN was a new and different kind of challenge for me. In my other novels my characters have been affluent, and most of their concerns revolved around achieving those things which can't be bought. In HEAVEN the characters lack even the basic comforts which most of us consider necessities—basics such as inside plumbing, heat and light, adequate food, clothing and shelter. None of these are available to the five children growing up in mountain country known as 'The Willies.'

"As I wrote, I went back to a different time, a simpler time when life was more primitive. However, conditions such as I write about in this novel still exist today.

"I have drawn upon real events in part of our country where life is cruel, and youth is fleeting, where children come too easily . . . and are sometimes sacrificed to adult desires.

"So come with me to The Willies, where the wolves howl at the moon, where obstacles higher than mountains don't prevent even the lowest from reaching for their dreams, no matter what the cost."

Later editions didn't include this letter. *Heaven* would be number one on the *New York Times* bestseller list by November 3, 1985. Virginia wrote the sequel, *Dark Angel*, and it would hit number three on the *New York Times* list by December 28, 1986, nine days after her passing.

There was a great deal left to do before this dire date. Nothing suggested its coming more than the letter she had written to her mother as far back as 1983. Despite its tone and meaning, the work she did until 1986 makes it all quite remarkable.

What was it she had foreseen?

August 23, 1983

Dear Mother:

I may still be around ten years from now, but just in case
I'm not, I want to leave you a few instructions. First of all,
DON'T PANIC! Don't you DARE give away my house without receiving
fair market value. Use professionals for advice, not neighbors
or family.

As you can see from the papers I'm going to order printed out
in a few seconds, I have a very good bond portfolio and there is
no reason why you should liquidate it when it will see you
through for the rest of your life in grand style, even without
touching the original principal. Please consult with Dick before
you do anything, and if necessary, have Errol Lifland and Eugene
there with you--but don't listen to your sons nearly as much as
you listen to pórfessionals. As you can see $126,429.42 is not
such a small sum to be sniffed at--and tax free, and there will
also be royalty monies coming in twice a year. Don't panic.
Hang in there and enjoy yourself. Take trips to all the places I
wanted to go, like Hawaii and take your family with you. Dick's
office number ▓▓▓▓▓▓.

Everything listed in our joint names of Virginia C. Andrews
and Lillian L. Andrews and V. C. Andrews, and L.L. Andrews is
left to you. YOU are rich, Mother, and don't you dare even think
it doesn't mean anything because I'm gone. Life is for the
living, not for the dead. Also, there is a list of "OTHER"
investments, so have Dick explain all the sheets to you, and keep
Eugene, Mary, and Bill around so they can help you understand.
But never, never give up the major portion of your inheritance to
ANYONE--provide for yourself first, for that is the way I want it
to be.

Also realize I'm not sorry about dying, only sorry I never
really had the chance to live. I look back on my life and know,
I haven't lived in the true sense. The best part of my life has
been in my imagination, so let's both hope and pray there is such
a thing as reincarnation and the next time around I'll receive
the physical rewards as well as the fame, riches, and beauty I
like to think I deserve. You see, I want the whole bag of beans-
-and nothing lesser will do.

I hope all of you enjoy living, and you in particular, won't
go around saying eternally, and borincly, "Poor Virginia."
Virginia is not poor, nor has she ever felt poor--even when she
was. Inside I knew all along that I was someone special and
chosen...for what I don't know...but in Heaven's Inexplicable Way
I've had to live out my life, harassed and badgered by a fragile
skeletal frame. That's why I once wrote my autobiography and
called it, ONE UNDER A PARASOL, for always my poor health has
kept me in the shade, and out of the sunshine of happy
fulfillment.

All the jewelry I didn't list on my will, I leave to you, to
do with as you will, and all other possessions not mentioned, are
yours. If you want the gold and pearl ring I left to Joan, then
you keep it, and any other article I've given to Mary or Suzanne.
You come first.

Goodbye, and good luck, and thank you for being a very good
mother, and doing the very best you could for someone who wasn't
always easy to please.

Your loving daughter,

Courtesy of the V.C. Andrews estate

chapter nine
Leaving Foxworth Hall

IN 1983, THREE YEARS before she died, Virginia drafted a frank letter to her mother. Virginia's sister-in-law Mary doubts very much that Virginia ever gave the letter to her mother, who "would have been devastated, hysterical. I can't see her doing it, and none of us ever heard of her writing the letter, much less giving it to her mother."

There is definitely a logic to that conclusion, especially in 1983, almost three full years before Virginia would pass away. Remember how hard Virginia worked at keeping her disability from public view in the beginning, wearing clothing that basically hid her wheelchair when possible customers for her art arrived. Remember how insistent she was about not being depicted as an invalid and how angry she would get at being called "paralyzed."

In Dorothy Landon's article "The Pages," Virginia says, "I'd rather be like Jacqueline Susann. She had cancer and kept it to herself. It might have stigmatized her books."

Consider how devastating it surely was to have battled a condition that had stolen her legs, her ability to be independent, her chances to have a significant romantic relationship—and to have succeeded in getting people not to look at her as a disabled person so much as an international bestselling author, someone who, as we've seen, enjoyed her celebrity, gathered the strength to visit with her fans at autograph parties, and fully participated in conventions and events alongside other bestselling authors—and then have a second medical battle take it all away just when she'd reached her height.

Virginia had found her voice. She had proven herself, but she knew it wasn't going to be enough. Nevertheless, she put her health issues aside and continued to write and publish, with plans to do much more in the future. However, between her completing *Dark Angel* and finally seeing the actual shooting of the film adaptation of *Flowers in the Attic*, there were no other completed manuscripts in the pipeline. She had ideas, and despite the publication of *Heaven* and *Dark Angel*, there was a great hunger for the prequel to *Flowers in the Attic*, which later became *Garden of Shadows*. *Dark Angel*'s success was calling for another sequel as well.

There was finally real excitement developing for the film version of *Flowers*. It would turn out to be a difficult shoot. Virginia had been very concerned with how Hollywood would turn her book into a movie, and so was one of her first fans.

In fact, the one and only fan letter Virginia had in her scrapbook was sent to her on September 8, 1979, seven long years before the actual production of the film adaptation of *Flowers in the Attic*. She received the letter two months prior to the official date of the book's publication. Sample copies of the book had been distributed as part of the big promotional package Pocket Books and Simon & Schuster had planned. And complimentary copies were given to customers when they bought other books.

The fan began his letter by saying, "I have just finished the book *Flowers in the Attic*."

It was also this fan letter that was the start of a wave of fans demanding a sequel.

"Now I have a few questions that were left unanswered," he wrote. "Did the three survivors ever find Cory's grave? Did they ever have their revenge on their mother? Their grandmother? Were there any long-term effects of their imprisonment? In other words, what is the title of the sequel? When will it be available?

"Is a movie being considered? I feel it would be a success if it followed the story as written."

In a 1986 *Publishers Weekly* interview by William Goldstein, conducted on the set, Virginia would say, "No other book gives you the thrill that the first one does. I did picture the movie in the back of my mind when I was writing it."

As any novelist would, she cherished that last line in her fan letter: "the story as written." Having approval of the script as part of her contract, Virginia rejected five previous scripts that either didn't follow the story or, in her opinion, distorted some of her scenes and characters. Originally, the script was to be written by one of horror movies' most famous writer-directors, Wes Craven. He had actually completed a full draft, but according to what Virginia told her family, this was the version the producers thought too graphic, and she had expressed reservations about it herself. By the time the decision to green-light the production was arrived at, the producers themselves had rejected another version.

This should surprise no one. By now, Virginia realized that a script, especially an adaptation, goes through multiple rewrites before a shooting script is finally approved. Many times, even A-list actors have script approval or create rewrites of their own scenes and dialogue.

Virginia also had to deal with perhaps the biggest fact pertaining to an adaptation: a movie is at most a little over two hours. As with all adaptations, much of a novel has to be cut because of this time factor or the production costs of a particular sequence or scene. There are really no very expensive settings in *Flowers in the Attic*, but there are scenes and sequences that were highly debated. This was, after all, one of the first modern novels to include incest.

When there was finally a script that she could approve—written by Jeffrey Bloom—Virginia went to the set of the film to do her cameo playing a maid washing a window.

Almost all the interior shots had been completed in California, but for the exterior, the location director had found a house that was more representative of the now-iconic Foxworth Hall, crystallized in her readers' minds through Virginia's descriptions of it as well as the innovative V.C. Andrews cover. In the novel, the house is practically a character in and of itself. Virginia took great care to describe the attic, the stairways, and the looming exterior.

The movie team settled on the Crane House in Ipswich, Massachusetts, a fifty-nine-room, Stuart-style mansion erected by Richard T. Crane Jr., a wealthy businessman. The house sits on 165 acres and is a national historic landmark available for a variety of activities, including outdoor concerts. It was also the house used in *The Witches of Eastwick*, featuring Jack Nicholson as the devil, Daryl Van Horne, with Michelle Pfeiffer, Susan Sarandon, and Cher. That film would be released June 12, 1987, with *Flowers in the Attic* following it on November 20, 1987.

Virginia approved of the house, telling people it was as she had envisioned it when she wrote the novel. She was on the set in October 1986. Lillian was there, too, hovering over her as usual, protecting her even though they had a nurse, Margaret Sullivan, to look after her. Few knew how desperately she needed a nurse at this point. Neither Virginia nor her mother was revealing anything.

Lillian had come a long way from the woman who would not read *Flowers in the Attic* or anything else her daughter had written. Thanks to her daughter, she had seen London and Paris, been wined and dined at the best restaurants, and stood beside bestselling authors and movie stars, and she now lived in a beautiful new home with none of the financial woes that had followed her from the day she had married a man who was in the Navy and lived in her parents' home during the Great Depression.

Louise Fletcher, who had won the Academy Award in 1976 for her role as the dominating Nurse Ratched in *One Flew Over the Cuckoo's Nest*, seemed perfectly cast as Olivia Foxworth, who was characterized by her power and control over her four grandchildren and her daughter, Corrine. She'd be nominated for a Saturn Award, presented by the Academy of Science Fiction, Fantasy and Horror Films, as best supporting actress for her performance in *Flowers in the Attic*.

Virginia had told members of the family that Fletcher, after she had received her copy of the script, had called her to ask why a grandmother hated her grandchildren so much. "She obviously hadn't read my book." Virginia gave the actress a summary of Olivia's relationship with Corrine and why she viewed her grandchildren as sinful. By 1986, *Flowers in the Attic* was one of the biggest bestsellers. Along with its sequels, the books were approaching 25 million copies sold. Grandmother Olivia had become almost a quintessential terror creature, berating and almost starving the four children to death. Nurse Ratched would be an angel in comparison.

Fletcher was later to claim that she stayed in the character of the grandmother all the time, even when she was not shooting, such was the intensity on set.

The cast was rounded out with Victoria Tennant as Corrine, Kristy Swanson as Cathy, and Jeb Stuart Adams as Christopher Jr.

Swanson, along with most of the cast, attended a dinner with Virginia and her mother and said she was proud of the fact that Virginia told her she was exactly as she had pictured Cathy.

Eventually, the movie would be criticized for its omission of incest and for an altered ending. But for the time being, Virginia was excited to be on the set and very excited about doing her cameo. She was still able to get up on her crutches for the shot, which was basically the camera panning over Virginia captured in a window. "The camera will skim over me. If you blink you'll probably miss me, but I'll have my best window washing hand out," she told Goldstein in the *Publishers Weekly* interview.

In February 1986, she told Eugene and Mary that there had been a request for her to rewrite the science-fiction novel that would eventually see publication as an ebook, *Gods of Green Mountain*, and "Anita Diamant called to say several publishers were pleading with me to write a 'clever' book for small children that can be beautifully illustrated. And even yet another editor is waiting for my ghost story to be included in an anthology next spring."

Little else would be accomplished between this February 1986 letter to Eugene and Mary and her cameo appearance on the movie set. She had spent her last Christmas with her family in Marco Island, Florida, and they wanted her not only to visit again but to move there. Her brother showed her a beautiful home in Naples, thinking she would like to live there if she chose Florida.

Of the house, Virginia wrote: "The pictures of the Naples house bring back all sorts of memories, and help me to recall just how it looked. I see things in the photos that I didn't notice at the time. I feel some trepidation about moving to Florida, for despite what you think, Eugene, my joints did feel the dampness more than they do here. And though I don't have many mobile joints left, I certainly do what I can to hang on to what I've got, and not have them start hurting. I have not felt well since I returned from Florida.

"I knew I had something like pleurisy because my chest and back hurt so much, but it wasn't until yesterday that I finally went to a doctor. I have not only pleurisy, but a slight case of pneumonia as well. Anyway, the prescription he prescribed seems to be helping already. I believed I was very fatigued by that last day when we stopped off in South Carolina to visit Middleton Plantation. It was cold and windy and very damp, and roaming around vast plantation grounds in mid-winter wasn't such a smart idea. Especially when it began to rain on the way back to the van—and that was a long, long walk."

Ever conscious of her appearance, she added, "My beautiful long fingernails proved to be disastrous! Two weeks after I arrived home, they began to pull up from the base, bending backwards, my own nails underneath and making terrible bruises right in the middle of my nails! I had to have them removed. My nails were so roughened by the manicurist down there they look pitiful now. But time heals all wounds, and I will survive pleurisy, pneumonia and pitiful nails."

How characteristic of Virginia to keep her secret about her ill health so guarded, minimizing what was happening to her. No, time was not her friend now. She surely would rather have kept her fingers on the hands of the clock, holding them back. *Keep me as I am, with all my pain and suffering, keep me here.*

From what all her surviving relatives have said and written, it is clear that Virginia's family had only a general idea of her condition. Her vigorous activity and production of her novels, her autograph sessions, her speeches, and her travels kept everyone somewhat confused about the seriousness of her cancer. Some family members recall her talking about an inoperable lump on her breast, but the idea of Virginia having had a major surgery between 1983, when she wrote the letter she wanted to give to her mother, and her actual passing seems incredible to her family. No one in the family recalls a mention of surgery or even chemotherapy or radiation.

The details of the decline in her health remain vague, probably deliberately so. It seems highly unlikely that when she wrote that letter to her brother and sister-in-law after having spent Christmas 1985 with them, she had no awareness of how serious things had become. Yet she reduces it to a touch of pneumonia and fatigue. The family was aware that she had a lump on her breast, but because of how Virginia dealt with it, they weren't fully aware of its potential to be serious.

Theories range from her own disbelief in what was happening to that familiar avoidance she shared with her mother: hiding her wheelchair confinement; dressing and traveling with careful attention to her hairstyle and cosmetics; forbidding, avoiding, then ranting against descriptions of her that made her look like any sort of invalid.

And of course, that telling comment about Jacqueline Susann and how she'd rather keep an illness to herself so as not to stigmatize her work.

Mary Andrews confirms this theory: "We realized in 1986 that the lump in her breast was cancer that had metastasized. But she and Lillian were so not wanting people to know things. She was not taken to a hospital in late 1986 . . . she wanted to be at home and had nurses around the clock.

"Bill and Joan were living in Portsmouth then. He was at the house with Virginia, and he called Gene and told him she was in and out of a coma and he should come. He did and stayed until she passed."

Virginia's niece Suzanne recalls, "The last time I saw my aunt was early fall, the year she died. I had just married a fellow named Eric and wanted her to meet him. We drove straight through from Kissimmee, Florida, where we lived at the time.

"What I can remember, the wide-open grassy backyard, with big beautiful trees, geese, squirrels . . . we were greeted by a nurse at the front door, then taken into a sitting room. Oval-shaped, big tall windows, so it made you feel like you were sitting outside. It was beautiful!

"The nurse wheeled my auntie in . . . she was very white/gray/withered. Have you ever seen makeup on someone who is severely dehydrated? She always had such a glow, such beautiful skin . . . so seeing her like this took my breath away.

"Inside I was screaming/crying, but I smiled and introduced my husband to her. We had small talk (I hate small talk), but it's like she knew this would be the last time. I knew it would be the last time . . . my heart ached so much I could not breathe. How do you say goodbye to someone, and know it's final?

"It was like I couldn't run out of there fast enough, yet I wanted to hold her and cry buckets of tears in her lap at the same time . . . oh, God! That was so hard! Her life stolen from her . . . had I known, I would have spent more time with her."

The *Virginian-Pilot*, her local newspaper, which had been so proud of her, put the notice of her death on its front page for December 20, 1986:

"Virginia Beach novelist V.C. Andrews, a Portsmouth native who rose to international fame and fortune with a series of gothic novels, died Friday [December 19, 1986] of cancer in her Virginia Beach waterfront home.

"The *New York Times* dubbed her 'the fastest-selling author in America' after her initial success, *Flowers in the Attic* . . ."

"All my life I thought I was meant to be something special," Virginia had said. "I never knew what it was. Now I have the satisfaction of having my name recognized. And it will live after me."

Once again, she proved herself a prophet.

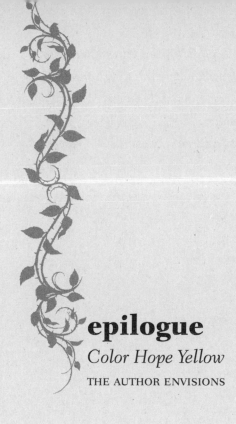

epilogue
Color Hope Yellow
THE AUTHOR ENVISIONS

WE ARE IN A *woman's bedroom with blasts of color everywhere: in paint-ings, shelves of dolls, pillows on settees, and bright curtains.*

Through the doorway to a living room, we see a small, elderly lady sitting and staring at the floor.

A music box starts to play. In the encased globe of it, the figurine of a little girl begins to pirouette.

We see Virginia Andrews turn her head toward the music box and the figurine. Virginia's hair is beautifully coiffed, and she is wearing makeup, but it's obvious she is quite sick.

As she watches, we fade out and into a much smaller, simpler bedroom.

A four-year-old Virginia Andrews, in an undershirt and panties, is pirouetting before a mirror.

The door opens, and a young Lillian Andrews peers in. "What are you doing?" she asks. "I told you your father was coming home. Get dressed!"

She closes the door, and young Virginia hurries toward her clothes.

Outside, on the Portsmouth sidewalk where the sun shines brightly, a tall, handsome Bill Andrews Sr. struts proudly in his World War I uniform, his Navy bag over his shoulder . . .

We return to elderly Virginia Andrews in her bed. Her smile widens . . .

And so it begins again . . .

note to the reader

WHAT FOLLOWS IS THE only unfinished, authentic Virginia Andrews manuscript in the possession of the Andrews family. It was their wish to include these pages unedited.

The Andrews family understood this to be next on Virginia's agenda once she had completed the prequel to *Flowers in the Attic* and the sequels to the Landry novels, *Heaven* and *Dark Angel*.

In reading this unedited material, we feel certain you will encounter the classic characteristics of Virginia's writing style. This was obviously a first draft, and we've left it in its original state so the reader can get a true feeling for Virginia's thoughts and processes in creating a novel.

It has the working title of *The Obsessed*. Her completing it was often a topic of discussion. Family members recall her talking about it, and in a letter to her brother Gene, she told him about two other novels she was writing. Referring to what follows, she wrote, "You should like the novel I've based against a background of Maine, Eugene. One of my main characters is a tuna fisherman . . . this book is going to raise a terrible fury when it comes out, for it touches upon a very sensitive area."

It is up to you, the reader, to imagine how it might have ended.

The Obsessed

By V.C. Andrews

If there's one place I'd rather be,
It's my island in the sea,
I could live there hap-pi-ly,
Throughout eter-ni-ty,
If I had you with me,
On my island in the sea.

— V.C. Andrews

prologue

ANY DAY IT MIGHT happen, she was thinking in the summer of her ninth year. She'd be on the shore, just as she was now, wearing white shorts with a sailor top. She'd look up, stare, feel overwhelmed with happiness, and just because his red sails would be headed toward her island. Perhaps her heart would panic, but she told herself no. Her heart would leap for joy for the day he came would be her day of deliverance.

Run! She had to run because she was alone. The hour was just a bit past dawn. A day so new she felt just born and happier than she'd feel at the end of the day when she had to snuggle down before the fireplace and sit meek and mild, and pretend, pretend.

Someday, Mama, she wanted to say, I'm going to find a man just as wonderful as my father. Then she'd be able to grow old feeling safe. Jamie, please be like Daddy when I get to know you. Please love me as he loves her, forevermore. Please see me as he sees her, perfect, divine, the most beautiful woman in the world—and she was, she was.

Jamie, she went on thinking, when you get to know me, really know me, you're going to be so proud when I step on stage and play with just as much skill as Charlie-Pop.

Then she was panting, her breath coming in short painful spurts. Stumbling to a walk, she willed her panicky heart to behave itself.

You're not sick, you're not! You don't have an extra heart valve, you only think you do!

Doctors, what did they know, not much. Not enough to know what to do to help her. Despite what anybody said, Mama, Daddy, Dr. Benson, she was going to live past age twenty-five—she was!

There, now that she was walking slowly, her heart regulated its wild pounding and her breath came more normally. She breathed a sigh of relief. It had been two years since she had her last serious attack, and then she'd nearly died. Without Mama and Daddy sitting by her hospital bed night and day she might have given up and gone on to a better place—if there were a better place than here.

In the frail light of the rosy dawn the old boathouse rose up stark and bleak. Its gray paint peeling, and inside was just as depressing, but it had a sink with running water and it was hers alone, that's what counted most. Somewhere to fade away in. Somewhere where she could lie on the cot and pretend she was just as healthy as any other nine-year-old girl.

What was that small noise coming from the boathouse? Startled, a bit frightened, she hesitated near one of the small square windows. Voices. How odd. No one came here but herself. Somehow she was angry, her privacy violated. Should she run back to Windown House and tell Daddy who would be writing in his study? But Daddy didn't like to be interrupted during his most creative hours, the early hours. And Mama would still be sleeping. Swen wouldn't listen; Elka didn't want anybody to bother her when she was cooking, and she was always cooking or cleaning.

If only she had just one friend, just one. Someday she would have, when Jamie made up his mind to come.

A woman's voice. She trembled—was that Mama? Then to her utter shocked amazement she heard a man's voice whispering such words as she'd never heard before! Oh, Mama!

Now what should she do? Turn around and pretend not to have heard anything? But suppose she was wrong and it wasn't Mama, but some tourists who didn't know this island was private property? No, no, she shouldn't be cowardly. She should face up to this situation herself, and rid herself of ugly suspicions. It couldn't be her mother in there with a man who'd say such coarse ugly words.

"Now look here, Therese," said the man, louder talking now. Her heart sank. It was Mama. Her bare legs began to tremble as she gingerly stood on her toes and peeked through the dirty glass of the window. "All this has been great fun, but it's also dangerous. My wife might overhear some gossip. You know damn well not one thing goes unnoticed by those village women. You know as well as I do that Jansen's store is their hangout for gossiping. I can't risk losing my children or my wife if you are only using me for your own amusement."

"Jack, Jack," crooned her mother's sweet soft voice. "You know I love you in one way, and my husband in another. We're not hurting anyone as long as no one knows, and you've been careful, so have I. Jay does nothing in the mornings but write, write, write! Sometimes I hate the sound of his typewriter!"

Oh, Mama, how can you say that? It's that typewriter that brings in the money to buy you all those beautiful clothes, furs, and jewels.

"Before we married, he swore we'd travel at least three months a year, but we never go anywhere."

"Haven't you told me before it's because of your daughter?"

"She's frail, yes, but not so frail a nurse couldn't stay with her. That's why we hired Elka Swenson, so she'd be here with Lisa. But no, Jay doesn't want to leave his precious daughter alone—and alone means without him to take care of her."

"What did you say was wrong with her?"

"Nothing is wrong with Lisa except she's selfish! She wants her father all to herself. There's no room in their relationship for me."

Oh, Mama—is that what you think? What you've been thinking all my life? She sobbed, for even as she stared at her naked mother, in the arms of a naked man whose back was toward the window, her heart was throbbing painfully.

Anger and shame made her linger on, when otherwise her sense of decency would have driven her away. She peeked again. Oh! Mama, how can you do that with that man when Daddy loves you so much? How can you deceive him with lies, while he works night and day to give you what you want!

A bestselling novel—that's all she kept telling him. "Not just another teeny-bopper thriller, Jay, but a mainstream book that will let the world know just what kind of man I married."

The light inside the boathouse was dim, spooky. She shivered as that man's bronze heavy hand fondled her mother's bare breast, and his head lowered as if to bite at her nipples.

She'd never seen her mother naked before. Never seen the backside of a naked man. Then he moved. Her mother turned on her back and pulled up her knees, spreading her thighs. Shocked again. Lisa began to gasp. Her faltering heart caught her mental panic and began its own wild drumming.

Death, always she walked on the rim between life and death, and her mother didn't even believe. Only Daddy believed. Only Daddy cared.

Wanting to leave, even if she had to crawl, Lisa watched all that panting, heaving, the upward heaves her mother made, the hard driving thrusts the man with the sandy hair made. And then it was over. They were both quiet, as if some divine peace held them both in a state of suspended animation. Time to leave now.

"Therese, you've got to decide. Is it to be me, or him? I have children, I have a wife. I have to think of them as well as you."

On her knees Lisa inched away, her heart hurting so badly she seemed caught in some horrible nightmare that would never end. Her mother's voice followed her, as if shouting. "Meet me here again when you come back. Two weeks from today. I'll make my decision by that time."

Daddy, had to get fast to Daddy. Only he knew what to do. Somehow she reached the house, her knees cut and bleeding, her body wet with the perspiration of her efforts. Still crawling, she crept closer to his closed study door. Such a big house. The library so huge, and once it had been five log cabin rooms.

"Daddy," she whispered, clawing at his door weakly, "help."

The typing stopped. Silence. She tried to speak, to call his name, to let him know she needed the oxygen mask, the hypodermic needle that would soon put her to sleep.

"Is that you out there, Lisa?" he asked. She couldn't speak as she slid to the floor and lay there gasping, hurting so much her left fingers felt numb. Daddy, don't you disappoint me too! Please, please!

one

IN HER GRAND SUITE of rooms that faced three directions, Lisa furtively hid behind the heavy blue draperies, tugging a little on the ivory sheers underneath, just enough to see outside. Faintly she could hear him moving about below. From time to time he paused, as if he stopped to listen for the noises she should be making. But she wanted him to think she was lying stupefied and scared, too afraid to do anything that would thwart his desire.

Tonight he was coming to her room to use her, violate her, shame her as she'd never been shamed before. Sobbing, she clung for support to the draperies. The weight of her unborn twins made her feel faint, too heavy—and he'd want them too, as he wanted to possess everything that was hers.

Oh, how she hated and despised him! Dead, he should be dead, as her mother had died on Hemlock Road, plunging over the preci-pice on the day she drove over to the village to tell him she could never see him again. Rain slick road. Brakes that didn't hold.

Screams torn from her mother's throat as she plunged over and fell one hundred feet, and smashed down on rocks. Then the fire. Daddy came into her room where she lay supine, staring blankly at the ceiling, knowing even before he spoke that her mother would never return.

Shame and guilt, how long she'd lived with it. Too long. Could she live with more? No! no more. Fate had slapped her down too many times, this time she was going to slap back.

There he was! On the lawn below he stood like a medieval baron surveying his domain. Handsome and tall, when he had no right to be anything but ugly. Her fingers released the sheers. Slowly she backed from the windows, and then with deathly precision, she headed for the hall, for the stairs, for the library—and the study where the gun was kept in the huge mahogany desk. The gun meant to keep her mother safe. As if anyone could be kept safe.

I won't have the nerve to do it, she thought, trembling as she descended the stairs. Oh, if only Elka and Swen hadn't been sent away on vacation. If only someone would come to save her. He'd locked the double gates to close off the bridge. Her car keys were stuffed in his wallet, the keys to the boats too. Her only avenue of escape was to swim across Frenchman's Bay to the village, and she was seven months pregnant.

Oh, God forgive me for what I'm about to do, she thought as she found the gun he'd hidden on top of the highest shelf in the library. Strange he'd thought about the gun in the study desk, when she'd almost forgotten it being there herself.

Once more she lay upon her bed and fixed her eyes on the ceiling. Not doing any of the things he'd ordered. Not bathing. Not putting on the sheer negligee with the exquisitely beaded lace and fancy feathers. How dare he give her such a thing?

She turned her head to stare at the night table with two drawers. The bottom drawer held the gun. God, forgive me for what I must do, she thought again, and then she decided she'd better fall on her knees and pray, for when the time came, she might end up loving instead of hating him, and her soul would be doomed to eternal hell.

How did it all begin? She lay thinking as the day wore on toward night.

Did it truly begin the day Daddy walked into her room and told her Mama was dead?

Nine years old, and on the bed she lay trembling, having just awakened from a horrible nightmare. "Daddy," she cried when she saw him come reluctantly into her bedroom, his handsome lean face pale, his hair windblown—and were those tears shining in his eyes? "What's wrong?"

He looked toward the windows. His hands clenched into fists before he spoke in a choked voice. "Lisa, I have just heard some very sad news."

NO! Don't tell me! Don't say the words! Don't make it real, please.

"It's your mother, Lisa."

"She's only gone to the village to fetch my medicine," she gasped out quickly. "Don't look so scared. She'll be back in a few minutes. She always drives carefully."

"It's raining very hard out there," he said in a sad stiff way, only then turning to look at her, but not meeting her eyes. "I was in my study writing when the police called. Darling, there's been an accident."

Say no more. Don't make it real.

"I couldn't believe she'd go out on a day like this.

"She knew I didn't want her to drive, especially on Hemlock Road. You know that sharp turn, just before the village is reached? The one with the sharp drop off?"

Oh, oh, there! There where she wanted to build a house someday. Where she could lie in bed and watch the tuna fleet sail out to sea. And watch the tuna fleet when it sailed into home harbors. Bringing all the men back to the women who loved them; the children who loved them. Bringing Jamie McKitrick home to me.

He sat on her bed and took her hand. His face pale beneath the bronze tan. His eyes somehow hollowed out, his cheeks gaunt, as if he'd been starving for months, when only this morning he'd looked wonderfully healthy. "There are some things you can't run away from, darling. Some things you have to face bravely. Can you be brave for Daddy?"

NO! Don't tell me what I don't want to hear!

"Daddy, I had a bad dream about Mama. I dreamed she was running away from us, and the more we ran after to call her back, the faster she ran—and then she disappeared. The fish ate her."

He shook his head. "No, sweetheart, the fish didn't eat her. She didn't fall into the sea."

Fast, she had to think fast. "Then she fell into a ditch?"

"In a way, yes, a ditch. Only this ditch is hundreds of feet deep. Lisa, hold tight to my hand; hold fast to my love and devotion, for you will always have me to take care of you. I promise to love you until the day I die, as I hope you will always love me."

"Oh, Daddy, of course I will always love you!" She sat up and threw her arms about his neck. "Hold me close, then tell me what happened to Mama."

He said it all in a calm toneless voice, though she knew he was dying inside from anguish, just as she was.

"I don't know what went wrong with her brakes, but someone saw her skid. She went right over the abutment and her car smashed down on those huge rock boulders. The doctors at the hospital said she died instantly, so she wasn't burned alive in the fire."

Stunned, gone dead feeling, she cringed closer against him, trying to merge into him, to be one with him, and let him know he still had her.

Dry-eyed. She couldn't cry. Even on the day they put Mama into the ground, she could only stand and stare. The people of the village looked at her as if at someone alien, someone who had to be strange not to cry. How could they know she'd already cried enough tears to make a primeval sea? She saw Daddy looking around at those who'd come to see her mother buried, forcing her to look around too. None of the villagers associated with the Lorraines of Birdlane Island, yet not one failed to be here. They stared at the father and daughter expectantly—hopeful they'd put on a spectacular show of grief?

Where was her mother's lover? One by one she stared at all the men with sandy colored hair. He'd have to be a big man. She saw only Jamie McKitrick standing near his sister who was two years older. Sad amber eyes that stared at her, as he always stared at her. For a moment some of her sorrow departed when she thought she saw his strong compassion. He liked her. Oh, it was in his eyes, such admiration as she'd never seen before.

"Father," she whispered, "stop looking at everyone. People are whispering."

When all the people were gone, she and Daddy still stood in the empty cemetery staring at the raw grave covered with sprays of flowers. Why was Daddy staring at that second yellow heart of roses? Two hearts of yellow roses. Mama had loved yellow roses the best of all.

Then Daddy was ripping into the flowers, tearing open small envelopes, reading cards, tossing them away, wild, wild!

"Lisa, did you ever tell anyone your mother preferred yellow roses above all other flowers?"

"No, Daddy," she whispered. Was that what was driving him wild, finding out someone else had sent her his heart of yellow roses? Jack, the lover?

"I like pink roses best," she whispered helplessly. She ran forward to pluck at his sleeve, trying to calm him. "I'll take care of you, Daddy. I'll finish teaching Elka how to cook the gourmet food you like. I'll do everything Mama did for you. You're not going to be lonely."

He stared straight ahead as they drove home. Lonely house, haunted house, no mother, no mother. "It's too bad Charles couldn't come," said Jason after hours had passed and the fire was guttering low. "Your grandfather has a way of never being available when any-thing important happens."

Straight away she rushed to Granddad's defense. So many things could keep him from coming. Concerts, appointments. Daddy wouldn't listen. He headed for the kitchen and directed Elka to leave Mama's room just as it had been. "I'll move into a guest room. Lisa, never enter her bedroom! Do you hear? Don't even peek inside."

"Why?"

"When you are a woman, perhaps you will find out for yourself."

Cryptic answer, tears in his eyes that refused to roll down his cheeks. Her heart bled for him, for his love that had been betrayed.

Cry some more in the night when he couldn't sense her shame and her guilt.

"Together you and I will hold down the fort," he said a week later, when he could manage a faint smile again. A formerly happy smile that had turned cynical. She was busy with pen and paper, trying to make up menus to please him. Trying to do all the things her mother had done for him to make him feel pampered.

"Lisa," he said, looking up from the newspaper, "run outside and play. Life is too short to spend so many hours waiting on your father. But don't cross the bridge. Don't go to the village and mingle with those boys who will grow up to be fishermen like their fathers."

But, but . . . she wanted to object. Jamie McKitrick was a fisher-man's son. He caught tuna—wasn't that more special than ordinary smelly fish?

In early October they flew away to spend the winter in Bermuda. There she had five tutors to teach music, art, English lit, history, and they left all her questions about how babies were born unanswered. "It's not our place to tell you the facts of life," said Miss Cooper, her eyes following Jason as he strolled the beach in front of their small white cottage with five rooms. "Your father is so handsome. I just fin-ished reading his last novel. It was wonderful. I hear it's become a bestseller, and will be made into a movie."

Yes, now that Mama was dead, Daddy was as famous as she'd always wanted him to be. Now Daddy had plenty of money to waste on travel, on new clothes for a daughter who didn't really care that much about clothes.

On the island, during the long bitterly cold winter, Elka and Swen stayed to see Windown House through. They were at the airport when Daddy and she landed near Bangor.

"Hi, Elka, Swen," she called happily, skipping ahead to greet them. But Elka drew back and refused to be won over, refused the hug and kiss she would have readily given.

"It's all right," said Daddy later. "She knows her place is that of a servant. And yours is mistress of the household. Take charge, Lisa, for I don't give a damn about anything but putting words on paper."

Was he being sarcastic? They were words her mother had flung in his face time and again. "And me, don't you care about me?" she asked timidly, so afraid he didn't care enough.

Long and hard he looked at her, then softly said, "Of course I care about you. I made a dreadful mistake with your mother, and neglected her. I promise never to neglect you. If I do, you let me know."

Whenever Daddy drove over the bridge to collect his mail in the post office that was also Jansen's General Store, Lisa made it a point to be at his side. This was her only chance to see Jamie McKitrick. She'd be ten in August. He'd be thirteen in November. She'd loved him at first sight, since she was seven.

But why did he stare with so much admiration and awe and never visit?

Why don't they like us? She wanted to ask Daddy, but refrained. They lived such lonely isolated lives with only a few of his friends coming over to visit in the evenings after she'd gone to bed. Only Dr. Benson knew she had a congenital heart defect. "It's easily enough corrected, Jason. That small extra heart valve can be closed surgically without too much risk."

"I'd die if I lost her too."

"Jason, you owe it to that girl to see she has the option to live out her life normally. You give her no option if you don't permit the surgery."

"There's too much risk now. In a few years the heart specialists will know more, and she'll be stronger. She's frail, Tom, very frail."

Disgruntled, Tom Benson looked away. "As her doctor I urge you not to wait. As your friend I can understand your concern. But Jason, there are other women. You can have other children. Don't put all your eggs in one basket with this one."

"This one is exceptional," Daddy said while she crouched in a hidden place, trapped into eavesdropping from falling asleep behind the sofa.

Puzzled and wondering she wandered down to the shore to stare wishfully toward Berryman Village. Why didn't Jamie come? Was he going to let all their lives pass by before he made his move? Should she do something to force him to come?

Then her heart skipped a beat. Was that his sailboat coming this way? She stood on her toes and took a few running steps toward the dock by the new boathouse. Oh! It was his boat! He was coming!

Jamie, Jamie, Jamie . . . I thought I'd never get to know you. Not until you were claimed by someone prettier, healthier.

Wearing short-shorts, white, her top white too, she stood with her bare feet in the water and watched him skillfully berth his boat. He jumped on the dock and tied knots, all while she stood breathlessly watching his every graceful move. He was so tall, so broad in the shoulders, so lean—so altogether wonderful.

For minutes he did nothing but stare her way, as if words were very difficult for him to find. She was to find out soon enough he was noted for being taciturn, almost stubbornly refusing to talk. "Hi," she called, fiddling nervously with her hair that refused to stay in place. "You're the boy I always see in Jansen's store. You always stare at me so long and hard."

"You stare right back," he answered slowly.

"Why do you stare?"

He shuffled his feet, hung his head, and looked so embarrassed and awkward, she wished now she hadn't asked, yet he surprised her. "You're the prettiest girl I ever saw—and besides, you stare back just as hard, and just as long—what do you see?"

Now she was blushing, and embarrassment made her eyes drop to stare at his bare feet. Such big feet. He was only going on thirteen, and already he had a deep husky voice that sounded mature. "It's taken you a long time to work up the nerve, Jamie McKitrick," she said shyly, flickering her lashes upwards long enough to see him flush again. "If I were a boy and given as much encouragement as I've given you . . . I would have sailed across the bay years and years ago."

His amber eyes widened. He shook his head to flip a lock of hair from his eyes, and then snatched for her hand. Suddenly they were both laughing, naturally at ease with one another. "And I thought this was going to be the most difficult thing I've ever done! Thank you, Lisa Lorraine, for making it so easy. They say you're a snob in the village for not attending our schools. I always knew they were wrong."

From day number one she loved him; as she knew almost certainly he loved her. She never considered it physical attraction. Never thought it was sexual, only wonderful.

"I'll bet if you asked your father if you could go sailing with me he'd say no."

Yes, if she'd asked, he would have said no. But Daddy wasn't going to hear about Jamie until she was ready to tell him.

Two winters passed, one in Florida, one in Arizona, and then she was back on the island and meeting Jamie again secretly. He was always "going on" some age, and as soon as he arrived there, he was "going on" to the next year, so he was always older than chronological years. He was shooting up like the proverbial weed in summertime, nurtured by the sea and sun, while she'd already obtained her height of five foot six. He was going to reach seven feet, she suspected.

"Of course I won't," he objected when she said this. "Gosh, Lisa, I'd look like a freak if I was that tall. I'm only six foot two."

"Going on seven foot two."

He winced. "I wish you wouldn't refer to my height. I'm the tallest boy in my classes, and sometimes I don't enjoy it. Six feet would suit me just fine."

Her arms went around his slender frame. "I like you just as you are, and if you grow up to heaven, just pick me up and take me with you."

Slowly, slowly he inclined his head. She kept staring into his eyes as they came closer, closer. Why green flecks were speckled in the amber, imagine that. Kissing, they were kissing. She felt hot and excited, and pulled away to take his hand in hers. "I'm not yet twelve, Jamie. I was hoping you'd save your first kiss for my sixteenth birthday party."

Laughing, he swept her up in his arms and carried her like she weighed nothing. "Lisa, it's time I met your father. I don't like sneaking around behind his back. When he finds out, and eventually he will, he'll dislike me for doing that."

She feared nothing would make her father like Jamie.

The boy stood before the man who was pruning the roses. He didn't smile or stop what he was doing. "Lisa, you're much too tan without adding more. Have you ever heard the sun is aging to your skin?"

"Daddy, this is Jamie McKitrick."

"I know who he is. I've seen him with you sailing. I wish you'd not take my daughter sailing again, young man, unless you ask my permission first."

"Yes, Mr. Lorraine."

Angered for no reason that Lisa could tell, he threw down his shears and strolled toward the large house that looked like an Alpine chalet. The shears accidentally struck Jamie's bare foot. Aghast, she stared at the blood gushing from the deep gash. "Daddy—you cut Jamie!"

"I'm sorry, but he could have moved his foot."

"It's all right, Lisa," said Jamie, sitting on the grass to press his palm down on the cut. "If you'll run inside the house and bring me a bandage, I'll be getting along home."

She lit into Daddy once she had the chance. "You did that deliberately! Jamie had his head turned. How could he move his foot when he never suspected you'd do anything so mean!"

For a moment it seemed he might explode. "Lisa—what have you been doing with that boy?"

She quivered, grew weak in the knees before the towering power of his unreasonable rage. Why was he staring at her breasts that were just beginning to peek out of her knit tops? Swallowing again, she wanted to run, to hide, and never admit she could feel anything but love for this man who had given so much of himself to her. "Daddy, you almost cut off his little toe."

"What have you been doing with that boy?" he repeated in a harder voice, his eyes narrowing even more suspiciously.

That's when she recovered her spine and stiffened it. "We sail, we walk on the shores, we talk, and I've never had anyone near my age to talk to before—and if all that is criminal then have me locked up in jail."

He started to smile, then forced himself to speak to her sternly. "Lisa, it isn't easy for a man to be both father and mother, and that's what I have been since your mother died. You don't know anything about boys, about what they want from girls."

Anxiously she watched his eyes, wanting him to look at her with love and tenderness again. "I'm not my mother, Daddy, I'm not! I'll never deceive you. I'll always love you. But give me a chance to live, please."

Something in her young lovely face brought tenderness to his eyes, to his mouth, and he spoke more kindly. "I'm sorry about the shears. I was in a rage and cutting down those damn yellow rose bushes your mother planted. I can't bear to look at yellow roses anymore."

I know, she wanted to say, I know why you hate them. I think I hate yellow roses too—because HE sent them to her funeral in the form of his heart and they competed with your heart of yellow.

"We'll plant pink roses there," she said quickly, stepping closer to play fondly with his hair. "Daddy, please don't hate Jamie because his father is a fisherman. Jamie wants to be a veterinarian, even if his father does make him go to sea. Do you know he had his first trip out when he was only twelve?"

Jason drew away. Her fingers seemed to singe him. He lowered his head and gazed blindly at the blotter before him. "Lisa, sit down. It's time we had that talk I've been putting off for months. I look at you, and see how you're beginning to shape into a woman, and I can't put it off any longer. I'm embarrassed and don't know where to begin. I wish now I'd have let one of your tutors tell you, but somehow I was afraid they would put prudish ideas in your head. When you fall in love and marry, I want you to feel free to express what you feel physically. I want you to share your body willingly with the man you love, as you share his—but I don't know if I can say it all without shaming us both." He paused, fiddled with his pens and pencils, then looked up and charmingly smiled. "I'm making a fool of myself, aren't I? I want to tell you not to be ashamed of sensual feelings, while I myself feel embarrassed to talk about them. You see, I was brought up in another generation, when sex was a forbidden topic. Of course it was there; it's always been there, but in the background. Today it's up front, out of the closets and into the books, movies and magazines. Have you ever looked inside of one of those skin flicks?"

Dumbfounded by this unexpected turn of the conversation, she could only sit and shake her head, speechless. Those magazines were in the supermarkets, in the drugstores, and she knew about them. How could decent young women pose naked? In her secret heart she presumed they weren't decent, but cheap.

Jason got up and took a thick book from a high shelf, then opened it on the desk before her. "This is a book on sex in the human being. I want you to take it to your room and read every page. I want you to study the illustrations, and the photographs, and if you have any questions, I'll answer as truthfully as I can." He paused, looked reflective, and reconsidered. "No, read it now, while I'm here and easy to question. For I have the gut feeling you will never ask any-thing."

"Daddy," she said weakly, "do I have to?"

"Lisa," he said with a small smile, "remember when you asked your mother where babies came from? Remember what she told you?"

"Yes. She said they came from hospitals."

"She gave you a half-truth. If you want the full truth on any mat-ter, you have to search for the answers yourself. The book you have before you is one of the best on the subject. It will tell you why a girl starts having periods, why your breasts develop, why your hips swell and your waist diminishes. You'll understand what changes estrogen makes in your body, why you grow hair where you don't have any now. Why a boy changes into a man—and you'll see pictures of naked men—"

"I'd rather look at it alone, Daddy."

"Only if you swear you'll come back to me and discuss it fully. I don't want you left not understanding the ramifications of letting a boy have his way with you."

Oh, gosh! Was this what her mother had meant when she warned not to let any man put his hands on her? Never, never had she felt confident about a man even shaking her hand, lest that was some-thing forbidden to make her pregnant. For Mama had said it was men who made women swell up big and go to the hospital to fetch home the baby.

An hour later she was down the stairs and running into Daddy's arms, crying. "Daddy, Daddy . . . does it have to be that way?"

"What way?"

"Like animals! I thought love meant kissing and holding hands. I didn't know it meant doing all those ugly things. Daddy, I'm never going to love anyone but you! I'm never going to get married! I don't want any children if I have to get them like that!"

He held her, soothed her, kissed her and then took her out to eat in a fine restaurant where the music was soft, and the food divine, and men and women were looking at each other with love lights in their eyes. And to think they'd go back home, strip down to naked, and do those horrible things . . . and some of them didn't even make babies. It was just "fun."

When they were home about nine, he led her into the music room and put a Strauss record on to play. "May I have this waltz, beautiful lady?"

Waltzing along in a dream, that's the way she'd have her life. Waltzing all through life, loving only as she loved Daddy, and never anything gross. No babies ever. No husband ever—not even Jamie. Strange how that made her heart ache.

"This is also love," said Jason after he kissed her good night, and she lay on her bed looking up at him dreamily. "Love comes in many forms, and many disguises, Lisa. Be aware that you are going to be an exceptionally beautiful woman. I see what's happening even now when you go into town with me. The boys are staring, even men much older can't keep their eyes off of you. Soon they'll be wanting to put their hands on your body, and take you to bed. And that doesn't literally mean it has to happen in bed. It can happen any-where, any time of the day. Be aware of this when you are with that fisherman's son. Save yourself for someone fine and noble, someone who has as much beauty to give, as you do."

She dreamed that night of Jamie, and saw him old and over-weight. "Go way, Jamie," she said, and the sound of her voice made her bolt awake. Jamie would never be as huge as that man in her dreams. Yet, yet, she was going to think long and hard before she let him "touch" her.

two

IN THE STRONG CURRENT of the sea that entered the channel, Lisa, at eighteen, lay awake on her bunk. Moonlight filtered through the short casement curtains and fell mistily on her face. It silvered her hair that was honey blond by day. Miserable thoughts made her shift restlessly as she sought a more comfortable position on a narrow bed that wasn't as soft as what she was accustomed to.

Jason was in the small head a few feet back of her head. The noises he made in there he tried to disguise by running the water. The moment he stepped from the head wearing his pajamas, she closed her eyes and feigned sleep. As if he wouldn't be denied, he hovered over her. She could feel the strength of his long gaze as he tried to determine whether or not to wake her and have their usual bedtime talk. Lightly he touched her on her shoulder. "Lisa, are you sleeping?"

"No," she managed to say as sleepily as possible, keeping her eyes closed, "but almost."

"Did you enjoy yourself today?"

"Of course. I always have a wonderful time with you."

"I have a wonderful time with you too."

She had to open her eyes and look at him, strangely, painfully touched by the sincerity in his voice. Their gazes locked and clung while her heart beat faster. He was going to be hurt—again. She'd be the cause—again. And they'd grown so close since her mother died in the accident. All the things she did for him to replace the loss of her mother, now she found, too late, constructed a wall around them, keeping all others out.

"Daddy," she began in the most tentative fearful way, "there's something I've been wanting to tell you."

"Of course," he said, smiling at her kindly as he perched on his bunk three feet across from her own. "You can tell me anything."

Nervously she swallowed. What she had to tell him wasn't going to be easy. "You're very busy with your writing during most of the day, and that gives me lots of free time when I'm not studying . . ."

"You're bored. Why didn't you tell me before? I want you to be happy. I can put this book aside and we can travel." He leaned forward to peer at her more closely in the dimness. "Where do you want to go? Somewhere special? I know you like Hawaii."

"I don't want to go anywhere. That's what I'm trying to tell you, Dad. I haven't been bored. You see . . . you see," and here she had to pause to gather the strength, "there's someone I've met. A man."

He didn't say anything. But even so she could tell he was preparing himself to be wounded. She saw him tense for the blow. "Are you telling me that damned Italian musician who found you so fascinating last winter has gotten in touch with you?"

"No, Daddy. The man I'm talking about is someone I met first, a long time ago."

He stared at her with eyes of disillusionment, with pain, with some anger too. "Don't tell me it's that damned fisherman! I've seen him with you walking on the shores; I've seen him sail to pick you up.

But I presumed you'd have better sense than to take him seriously. You told me, you promised me you wouldn't let any man touch you."

Cringing inside, she tried not to hear the pain in his voice, or see the distress in his eyes. Daddy, Daddy, I'm not ten years old anymore. I'm ready for everything you showed me in that book.

"Are you lovers?" he shot out in a hard voice.

"No!"

"Can I believe you?"

Now she was hurt. She hadn't lied to him about anything. "As long as I live, I will always tell you the truth. I love you, Daddy, but I also love Jamie. I pray to God you are not going to force me to make a choice, you or him. We live in a big house, a wonderful house, large enough for all of us." She ended on a hopeful note. Foolish hope.

"You are never to see him again, hear that, Lisa! Never again!" Hard words, ugly words, enough to make distress and pain fill her eyes until they appeared midnight blue. How had she known in advance that he would behave this way? What look had he given her to suggest that he considered her his property, to do with as he would?

He fell backward on his bunk and stared up at the ceiling, his fast breathing beginning to slow, as if he presumed he'd broken her spirit to resist anything he denied.

"Daddy, before you cut Jamie out of my life, won't you give him a chance to prove himself?"

"He cannot prove himself, that's the whole point. Any man who would sneak around for years, seeing my daughter on the sly, is not a man I can admire."

"But that was my fault, not his!" she cried desperately. "He wanted to come forward and approach you honestly, but I was afraid you'd act just like you're acting now! Daddy, fishing is not dishonest, or anything to be ashamed of."

"I don't want to hear another word on the subject. You are to cut this man out of your life; never see him again, and never speak to me of him again. Now go to sleep!"

Fear. It came again into her life, telling her as it did in all her dreams that she'd never have anything she really wanted. She wanted to cry out and make him see how unreasonable he was acting, how selfishly he put his own opinions above hers, but she could say nothing more. Another day would come. Another opportunity to win him over.

The small gold watch on her wrist seemed to tick like London's Big Ben. Painful minutes passed by, and still sleep purposefully evaded her, as it did him.

Then, as the moonlit waters flooded into their cabin through the loose weave of their draperies, she saw his hand reach toward her. Hovering near her hand, silently pleading, asking forgiveness. She wanted to rebuff him. Wanted to refuse his conciliatory gesture that didn't mean anything, for still he would forbid her Jamie, and want her to live out her life alone on the island with him.

"Lisa, I won't say anything more on the subject tonight. This is the new boat I bought for us to enjoy together. For the remainder of this short holiday, can we declare a truce?"

His hand still waited for hers, not quivering, steady and strong, as if it would stay there forever until she gave in. Then, slowly, even without her conscious consent, her hand slipped from under the covers and moved into his. His fingers closed like iron around hers, clasping tight, so tight it hurt. For a moment she panicked, as if sensing the long battle ahead; then she thought, what is to be will be, and quietly, without further protest she fell into sleep. Her hand still hurting.

Sunlight was in Jason's face when he wakened. The first thing he saw was Lisa's hand, pale and limp, fallen to the floor beside her bunk. It appeared a pale and delicate wounded bird floating on a pool of blood. Gently he reached to lift it from the red carpet. He tucked it neatly beside her. Like a dancer frozen in graceful position, she lay there breathing deep and evenly. With hypnotic rhythm her breasts swelled to fill the bodice of her flimsy nightgown, then flattened, holding him entranced, the hard, darkish peaks of her nipples were definitely obvious. Rage filled him to think she could be having a sensual dream of that damned sardine-catcher!

He headed for the galley seven feet away. Another fisherman to steal from him. Tears stung his eyes. Therese, Therese, I loved you so much, how could you do that to me? While I worked like crazy to write that bestseller you wanted, you deceived me behind my back! Like mother, like daughter.

A vision flashed before him. He was taking his usual early morning stroll, only this time he walked from east to west. There, near the old boathouse, his wife with a man, embraced, passionately kissing— and she wore nothing at all! He'd screamed out his shock, his anger. "Go!" cried Therese, giving the fisherman a shove so he couldn't half see him in the misty fog. He saw only that he was well over six feet tall.

"Who the hell was that?" he demanded when he had hold of her shoulders, and was shaking her so her head rolled. "I thought you loved me, Therese. I believed in you! I have never looked at another woman since we married—and now you—know—"

"Now I what?" she spat directly in his face, flaunting her nudity, and breaking free of his hold that didn't really want to bruise her fair skin. "Go on, say it! Or can't you give voice to the fact that one woman can spit in your face! I have never really loved you, Jason Nathan Lorraine! Never! You stole me from Rudy! You made Rudy kill himself! But for you I'd be living amongst people, not stuck on a miserable island in the middle of nowhere!"

Stunned, he could only stare and let the wild winds tear into his hair, just as her glorious mane was wind tossed.

"You promised me so much when I was married to Rudy! You promised me travel, excitement, glamor, and all I've known is boredom! I hate Maine! I hate that village of stupid idiots! You don't have time to love me, Jason. You only have time to write about love in your stupid novels that don't sell anyway!"

He could have slapped her then. He should have slapped her—maybe then she would have respected him. "Please, Therese," he'd murmured, "don't destroy what I feel for you."

"All right," she said, running to the old boathouse and tugging on her clothes as he watched, "I lied. I did love you in the beginning, when life held some promise of being better. But it's not better, it's worse. I can't stand this isolation—and that's why I took a lover who is the exact opposite of what you are! He hasn't been to college. He doesn't speak eloquently. He isn't gracious, gentle, or even considerate. He takes what he wants, and I like what he wants."

Hate. He was beginning to hate her. Scornfully she whipped away from him, running ahead, back to the house.

In the library they confronted one another. Her beautiful face framed by that mop of honey-colored hair made him ache inside, even as he both loved and despised her.

"You're never going to write a bestseller, Jason, because you just don't have it in you to write gutsy enough! The world doesn't want your literary style—and you don't have enough nerve to cash in on your father's fame. You are stupid enough to use a pen name!—and you won't even touch the money he puts aside for us—for US! Jason, for US!"

"I won't live on my father," he said stiffly.

She came closer, putting her face close to his as she hissed:

"Then I'm leaving you, Sss-irrr Galahad, the noble, the chaste, the faithful. There is no Holy Grail, Jason, there never was. There is no perfect woman, Jason, and never will be. For to have a perfect woman, there has to be a perfect man—and where in the hell do I find one of those?"

"You can leave when you choose, but you will never see your daughter again. From this day forward, she is mine."

She laughed in his face. "You are welcome to her, my love. She is a flawed diamond, remember; one that will steal your life, rob you of hours and hours while she's sick and you tend to her needs. As for me, I'm ridding myself of this island—and Lisa too! Goodbye, my love. It was fun while it lasted, but too soon monotony set in."

That's when he seized hold of her. "I will see you in hell before I see you leave this island! If I have to lock you behind bars, you will not leave me, or your daughter!"

And one week after that scene, one week of pure hell, with the two of them not speaking except when Lisa was around, she'd died in that plunge over the precipice.

And now he'd say the same words to her daughter. He'd see her in hell before he let her marry a fisherman. Blindly he stared before him, aching all the way down to his toes before he turned to strike his forehead on an open cabinet door.

"Oh, hell!" he cursed.

Behind him Lisa tried to smother laughter. "Really, Daddy, you're something to watch. You've spilled the orange juice, let the coffee pot boil over, and now you almost poke out your eye." She reached for a thick robe before she rose from the bunk, pulled it on, stood to tie the sash, and then came swaying into the galley, her glorious head of silky hair a golden nimbus around her pale face. Quickly she mopped up the orange juice, cleaned the coffee from the small range, but only after she'd closed all the cabinet doors. "I think you were deliberately clumsy just so I would awaken and fix your breakfast."

The bruise beside his eye hurt. He accepted the cube of ice she handed him wrapped in a washcloth, and put it to his injured eye. Grateful that she wasn't angry with him, he watched as she laid bacon carefully in a cold pan. "Now you keep an eye on it, turn it over often, and in a sec or two I'll be back to fix you the best breakfast you've eaten outside of Windown House."

Hope sprang eternal. She had forgiven him. Life as normal could go on. He breathed a sigh of relief and sat down to wait for her to come out of the head. In two seconds she came running, scolding him for not watching the bacon, even as she saved it from burning, then put it on a paper towel to keep warm in the oven as she whipped eggs and started his favorite omelet.

"My, you have learned how to cook!" he said fervently when he polished off the last of the two omelets and four slices of bacon, plus two English muffins. "I think I'll fire Elka and hire you."

"Then Swen would go with his wife, and you'd have to do all the handyman work around the yard, and cut the firewood, and paint the gutters, and run the lawnmower, and clean the windows, for I wouldn't have time to cook and do all of that too."

He grunted, ashamed to know how much she knew about him, and his dislike for menial chores. Now that he had written that bestseller Therese had desired so much, the book that would have given him the means to let her live a glamorous life, he decided then and there it was time Lisa and he stayed a few years in Europe. With Charles. She'd like that. And the fisherman would be forgotten.

"Dad," she said, her voice very small, making him think she was going to mention that fisherman again, "there's a man in the village who watches me all the time. The first time I noticed him he was just standing near our bridge, staring over at our island. Now I never go to the village without seeing him staring at me. He has a dark beard and mustache."

He laughed. "You should be accustomed to all men staring at you by now. That man you mention is an artist named Kyle Peters. I bought one of his scenes of our island. He thinks you are the most beautiful woman alive. In fact he asked me last week if you could pose for some church murals he's planning to put in St. John's Cathedral."

Her violet-blue eyes grew wide in surprise. "Why, I didn't know that cathedral had been restored. Didn't it burn a few years ago?"

"To the ground, but it's been reconstructed, and made more impressive. I told him no, since I think we should spend this winter in Rome again, with your grandfather."

"Oh, Daddy! How wonderful! In Rome with Charlie-Pop, and maybe this time you will take me to Vienna, like you did when I was fifteen. I loved that winter."

He laughed, pleased because she was. Happy because she loved their island as much as he did, and loved Charles with a devotion that was touching.

Together they cleaned the galley, she washing, him drying the dishes. An hour later they roamed the dense dark pine forest of Mt. Desert Isle, both armed with cameras. Two of the same age it seemed, trying to out-rival each other by shooting the best shoots, achieving the best lighting.

Suddenly it grew very dark. Glancing upward he saw a bit of sky that had turned gray. Fat cumulus clouds were now stretched out long and lean, driven by high strong winds. When he looked around for Lisa she had disappeared. He called: "Lisa, there's a storm heading this way! We've got to get out, and fast!"

Her bright head popped up from behind a thorny bush. "Dad, look what I've found." In her hands she held a small white dog, a mongrel of some sort. "Isn't he adorable? Let's take him home. Some-one must have gone off and forgotten him, and you know he can't fend for himself in these woods."

Not answering, he seized her up in his arms, the dog seem-ingly too, and ran for the boat docked a mile away. Panting and gasping, as she complained about being carried, he managed to reach the dock just as the rain broke. He wouldn't let her help on the deck, just shoved her down the two steps and ordered her to put on a life-jacket. "And hold onto that damned dog if anything happens."

"Nothing is going to happen with you at the wheel," she said with a complacency that startled and pleased him.

Dry and warm in the thick robe she'd put on, Lisa held the small dog, as she lay curled up and staring out of a small window. She wasn't afraid. Jason would get them all home safely. As much as he scorned fishermen, he was as much at home on the water as they were, as Jamie was. Born and bred to this rocky Maine coast like Jamie.

Jamie, somehow, some way, I'll make him accept you.

three

THE GENTLER, FRIENDLIER WATERS of Birdlane Island welcomed them home as Jason turned his yacht into the cove and sighed with relief. Wet and dripping, he threw open the cabin door and called down to Lisa, "We're home. Now all we have to do is make it up to the house. Unless you'd rather wait here until the worst of this storm is over."

She was curled up on a bunk, shivering as she held the small dog in her arms. The radio was on, predicting the storm would last through the night and possibly half of tomorrow. Despondently she switched it off. How miserable to spend the night in the boat, inside the new boathouse with its unpainted wooden walls, with the water churning restlessly throughout.

"You look cold and pale," he said with concern. "Lisa, are you feeling all right?"

"Sure. But we're out of food, no dinner, no breakfast if we stay."

It seemed thirty degrees colder than this morning, just like winter had returned and wiped out even the memories of spring. He fiddled with the heat control on the wall and tried to make it warmer. Damn! A trial run on a new boat and the heater stopped working. Great! No food either—who'd eaten it all? He struck the heat control, wishing he were good mechanically and could fix the damn thing. She'd turned the fan on high but it was blowing only cold air. Scowling and irritated, he turned to Lisa and asked if she was game for the house. "I'll build a warm fire, Elka will have a hot dinner ready, and you can take a long soak in a hot tub to put some color back in your cheeks."

Nodding, she rose to pull on a purple sweater that reached down to her hips while he held her rain slicker. With his slicker on, the dog in one of his huge pockets, they set off toward the house.

The fierce wind was enough to force them to double their caution. It wasn't easy walking on the rocks even on a beautiful day. This gale blew the wind directly in their faces. He shoved Lisa behind him and told her to cling to his waist. As a boy he'd found this kind of wild weather exciting, now he hated it for what it could do to her. That's all he could think of as he felt her steps leaden, and heard her short gasps for breath even as the small dog whimpered.

That's when he whirled around to pick her up and throw her over his shoulder, though she protested. "I can walk, Dad. It's hard enough for you without carrying me."

It was June, and from the freezing way it felt, snow was possible. He tried to run with his burden, slipping and sliding several times on the wet grass, on the mud, stumbling on the rocks that seemed to move directly in his way. Windown House loomed up ahead, bright with lights.

No sooner had he carried her into the foyer, set her down, taken the dog from his pocket, than Lisa was swaying from side to side, her unfocused blue eyes full of pain as she tried desperately to communicate with him without words. She made some small whimper. A familiar signal of distress. He skimmed off her wet yellow slicker, then his own, supporting her all the while. Again he picked her up and then ran for the stairs. In her room he dropped her on the bed, then ran back into the hall to fetch from a closet the oxygen mask and its tank. In another second he had her mouth and nose covered and he was instructing her to hold that in place while he raced for the hypodermic syringe.

Despite the panic in her eyes, the heaving of her chest, he shoved up the wide arm of her sweater and robe, swabbed her upper arm with alcohol, then plunged in the needle to release the sedative slowly, slowly. He felt as desperate as she did inside, only his panic didn't show. She stared at him with eyes going sleepy, as if he were the only real and solid and dependable factor in a world gone crazy with pain that was inflicted upon her time and again, for no reason she could understand. Why me? Why me?

His fingers stayed on her pulse until she was deeply asleep and breathing regularly, only then could he relax. No sooner had he fallen into a chair, sighed with relief, than he saw the muddy footprints he'd left on her white carpet. He groaned. Not that she'd say anything. It was him who wanted perfection for her. Next he was moving closer to the bed and seeing for the first time her sopping wet white robe. He couldn't allow that to stay on or she'd wake up with pneumonia. He frowned, thinking of Elka downstairs in the kitchen, and started to go for her. There wasn't much closeness between his daughter and his housekeeper, despite all the years they'd lived in the same house. Something peculiar about Elka.

Instead of seeking out Elka's help, he decided he could modestly take care of her himself. Grabbing up several large towels from Lisa's bath, he spread them over her, then drew off her robe by reaching underneath and tugging. He dried her hair, then rubbed at her body with her covering towel. One careless move and he discovered to his surprise that she hadn't put on any underwear beneath the robe. Why the devil hadn't she dressed properly? Nevertheless he tried not to look, tried not to feel as he briskly rubbed her down and then pulled a warm granny gown over her head. Only when the hem touched her feet did he reach under the gown to pull off the damp towels.

He was trembling, strangely weak. He sat, befuddled with embarrassment, wondering what had come over him momentarily. Once more he rose, this time to enter the kitchen and present the problem of the muddy footprints to Elka. Even as he spoke, he picked up a thin slice of raw carrot and began to munch.

Elka was tall and lean, almost de-sexed in her gray uniform. Her pale eyes turned sharp as she turned to him, not at all surprised by his wet disheveled appearance. "Sir," she said in her flat toneless way, "I didn't expect you and Miss Lisa back until tomorrow."

"We were caught in the storm, and she's had a slight attack and is sleeping from the sedative I gave her. But I've ruined her carpet with muddy footprints, and that on the stairs too."

"I'll take care of it, sir," Elka said calmly. "All you've got to do is wait for the mud to dry, then it scrapes off easily."

He'd never seen Elka ruffled, and fully believed the house could blow down and she would stay unperturbed. "I hope that's true, and let's hold back dinner until Lisa's awake. The drug I gave her should wear off in a few hours."

"If you can stand it, sir," she said with wry laconic knowledge of his avid appetite. He gave her his own wry look, picked an olive from her plate of appetizers and left to take a hot shower. After he shaved and dressed he checked again on Lisa who hadn't moved. The mud was still on the carpet. When he used his thumbnail to scrape some away he saw to his relief, perhaps the carpet could be salvaged.

Somehow he couldn't leave her alone. So, she was seeing a fisherman too, just like her mother. Perhaps planning to elope in some romantic way and leave him here. Never guessing how she'd ruin her life. Nine years since Therese had killed herself in that accident, for he liked to think that way, despite himself. Therese, Therese, how could you prefer a fisherman above me?

Beside one of the wide windows near the back balcony he sat

down to stare out toward the sea. It was almost night. The wind had the sapling trees groveling to the ground. He couldn't see the surf that was hundreds of feet down and away, but he could hear the pounding roar on the rocks as a distant rolling drum.

The howling wind, the noise of the surf, the rain, all combined to make a kind of fierce vengeful music. He heard it as similar to the ominous organ music played in a minor key that portended trouble.

Enervated now, he sank backward and rested his head.

Even too tired to think of food, and he was hungry. Wearily he drifted into unhappy sleep. Still, even so, he heard the door open behind him and softly close. Elka's quiet movements as she brushed the dried mud into a dustpan became part of his dream. The cleaning fluid to remove the smudges infiltrated his dream too, and turned the blood blue as the chemical she used. Another noise to bring cold damp air that blew in his face. The dream worsened. Death, so cold, so cold. Rotting bodies. Then as swiftly as the chemical odor had come, as the cold air had come, as thoughts of death had come, everything vanished and a door closed. Elka had vanished. Now he fell into real sleep, deep sleep. Rising and falling, swimming for his life, and up on the shore waited the dream he had too often. Someone ahead was running. Someone he yearned to catch. On and on running. On and on yearning, until suddenly, terrifyingly, he sensed someone desperate was behind him, yearning to catch too.

He had her kind of music on. Lonely and desolate feeling he sat in the library waiting by the fire for her to call, and then he'd carry her down and he could satisfy his appetite. He tried not to think about the young body he'd glimpsed. Tried not to fall asleep and dream again.

Into the library she came drifting, sleepy-eyed, the small new dog at her heels, already hers, already a bed companion to keep her company. Her warm robe was saffron colored, her slippers the same color and fuzzy soft. He wanted to reprimand her for taking the dog to bed, to say nothing of walking so soon after another attack when she knew he would have raced to carry her down. But pity stole his scolding; love made his eyes soft with sympathy when she cuddled up on the sofa and complained that the room was cold, and he'd made the fire just for her.

"I just can't seem to get warm," she complained, then apologetically smiled when their eyes met. "Here I am with my warmest nightgown on, covered with my warmest robe, and still I'm freezing. You should throw me away, Daddy."

"What fool throws away their greatest treasure?" he said lightly. "You should have taken a hot bath." Anxiety puckered his brows as he took notice of her shadowed eyes.

"I did take a hot bath." Shyly she glanced at him, her cheeks rosy with shame. "When I woke up I had on a gown and I don't recall undressing. The last thing I saw was you, all fuzzy and worried looking after you gave me the shot. I'm sorry I'm so much trouble." Her head bowed low so her hair fell forward to cover her face. "Daddy, did you or Elka put this nightgown on me?"

First he lit a cigarette and took a few pulls before he answered calmly: "Could I allow you to sleep in a wet robe? I know I could have called Elka, but that would have taken time; you know how she is, poky. I also know you don't like her very much. She's a cold, but efficient woman. So I took it upon myself to modestly cover you with towels as I managed to slip off your robe, and pull on your gown, and I swear to God I didn't see one thing I shouldn't have."

Her head lifted as she delved his eyes to find the truth in them. A look so penetrating he felt himself grow hot, and he hadn't blushed in years. Her lips parted to object—then she was sneezing violently, one after another.

It was so hot in the room he felt he was roasting. Now she'd have a cold. Perhaps pneumonia. Oh, God, he'd made a terrible mistake coming back. That fisherman was over there waiting his chance. Still he managed a cheerful face as he got up to head for the kitchen. "You just sit where you are and we'll have a picnic dinner in here before the fire."

Filled with incredulity, her eyes widened. "Daddy, you mean you haven't eaten? And it's after nine o'clock."

It hit him then, like a stunning blow from nowhere, why had he waited? He didn't need her company during every meal he ate. He stared at her, ambivalent and troubled. Did he hate her for looking so much like her mother, and love her for being just what he'd wanted for his wife?

Hurriedly he left, to disappear in the kitchen where he dished up the meal Elka kept warming in the oven. When he placed it before her on a TV table, she gave him one of her slow and beguiling, sleepy-eyed smiles that was low voltage as compared to what she could do when she felt well. His heart felt funny, weak and vulnerable, like he too had an extra heart valve that was dysfunctional in the presence of someone female, young, blond and so much like the woman he'd married and adored beyond reason.

Beyond reason, he kept thinking. Be reasonable, hold onto yourself.

Though he was aching inside; though something fine in him had been destroyed the day he found out his wife was unfaithful, he polished off his food with such alacrity Lisa was still pushing her food around on her plate, with only a few bites taken.

"Eat, Lisa," he commanded with a hard edge to his voice, when he wanted to reach out and comfort her and say she'd be fine, just fine. "Stiffen your spine and put that food in your mouth even if it isn't up to your standards of cooking."

She threw him a harassed, bedeviled look before she weakly smiled. "Jason Nathan Lorraine, I think you could eat on your death bed, and possibly in your coffin."

Bitterly he smiled. Was that her idea of a joke? She'd eat when he wanted her to eat. Damned if he'd let her win that way. She wasn't a child to thwart him by refusing food when she didn't get her way. This time he'd keep what he had. This time it would be the fisherman who lost.

four

"YOU NEED A NAP every afternoon," said Jason the day the mailman came unexpectedly to the island and he had to sign for a registered letter. "Go upstairs and rest while I read my mail."

Orders, he was always giving her orders. Resentfully she climbed the stairs. Resentfully she sat on the side of her bed, her eyes fixed on her small watch. She picked up her bedside phone to call Jamie and ask if he couldn't sneak over earlier, and in that way they'd have more time.

But Daddy was on the phone talking to his father. She started to interrupt and greet the grandfather she loved, but the somber way both men were speaking held her tongue mute as her senses quickened. Oh, dear God! No! Charlie-Pop, take all that back! Say it's a lie, please!

The moment she could, she tried to call Jamie. "He's not here," said his father with an odd tone to his voice. (She'd never called Jamie at home before.) "May I tell him who called?"

"Never mind," she said before hanging up.

For long moments she sat on the edge of her bed trying to control her near hysteria. Why was it always this way? Was Fate trying to tell her something? Did she deserve only to lose, always?

Panic made her heart begin hurting with that vague ache. Soon she was feeling the familiar tingling behind her ears and in her fingertips. She reached hastily for the medicine she kept always handy, and swallowed two of the tablets. Sleepy. Next she was so sleepy she couldn't think, didn't want to think.

Dreams came of Windown House. She stood as the wife of the man who had constructed the original log cabin. "Put it down-wind from the northern bluffs," she said in her dream. All those high bluffs would lovingly shield the house on the island that was curiously enough shaped like a bird in flight. Half-awake, she recalled tales of how Swen often had to use the roof-door to shove off the snow that heaped there during a blizzard, though the sharp pitch of the roof was supposed to slide it off. Easily the house could have ended up a monstrosity due to the many amateur architects that had added one wing after another. Fortunately the fur-trappers cabin had a graceful, even dignified exterior, and more important it was sturdy. Above all it had to be sturdy.

Dreams, deeper dreams. Awful dreams, sweet dreams where she and David were running on the beach, laughing, childishly happy just to be alive and out of sight from those who wanted to hold them back from having fun.

"You wear too many clothes, Lisa!" called David, her mother's younger brother, age twelve, when she was seven and deeply in love with him. "See, I don't wear any at all!"

How beautiful he was with his brown body, his curly blond hair, his sparkling blue eyes that teased and mocked, and made her feel wonderfully healthy. She stopped running long enough to pull off her shorts and top, and hesitated only a moment before she stepped out of her panties. Naked as he she ran after him. He put out his foot suddenly, whirling around to trip her up, and down they both went with him on top. He began kissing her with wild abandon. Funny how strange it felt, how exciting when she should say, no! no!

Daddy loomed up dark and menacing, his face livid. Terror! He spoke, his voice hard, cruel: "What the hell are you doing to my daughter?"

"Nothing, nothing," cried David, afraid—why afraid?

Slap!—slap! Daddy was striking David until he reeled, stumbled and fell. "I'll go!" yelled David, scrambling to his feet and backing off, his nose bleeding. "I'll go and you'll never see me again!"

Gone. David had gone, and she could cry ten million rivers of tears and still David would never be seen again.

"He took one of my boats and tried to cross over to the peninsula," explained Daddy when she was home from the hospital after one of her worst attacks. "The ocean currents must have carried him out to sea. That's the opinion of the Coast Guard who searched for ten days. They never found his body."

But Daddy didn't care; she could tell by the way he said, "It was his own fault, Lisa. His own fault."

That's the way it was, your own fault, the weather's fault. Blame the sea, the currents, God or Fate, or just plain bad luck, it was never, never anything you did yourself, never, never.

David was dead and down at the bottom of the sea, all his twelve-year-old bones picked clean by the fish that Jamie set out to catch. Tuna fish put in little cans, choice bits that had once been David with the golden hair, the blue eyes, the tanned body that ran naked in the sunshine.

So David was dead, why did he call? Lisa . . . Lisa . . . Lisa. David, Daddy?

She bolted awake.

Jamie, he could save her. She glanced at her watch. Saw to her dismay that it was almost six o'clock! Would he wait two hours? Please be waiting Jamie! Quickly she slipped on a pair of fresh white shorts and pulled on a clean top before she swiped a brush through her tangled hair, touched powder to her nose and chin, added a bit of lipstick, and then she was out of the western window, on the balcony tiptoeing to the balustrade she straddled, and then she was descending the rose trellis to the ground.

Minutes later she approached their special hidden place for meeting. Ah, there was his boat with the red sails furled, rocking gently on the bay water as the waves lapped the cove shores.

"Jamie!" she called because she couldn't spot him anywhere. "Did you come and leave your boat? Come out from wherever!"

He didn't respond, forcing her to call again.

"No need to yell," he said, coming into view as he sat up and showed above the huge rocks that had shielded him. "You'll wake the dead—and your father if he's sleeping." He rubbed at his eyes with his fists like a small boy, making her expression tender with love. Sleeping while he waited, imagine that. She'd thought he'd grow impatient, angry, or be so eager to hold her, even now he'd jump up and come running. But he only sat there, waiting for her to go to him. "Hi, sleepyhead," she said as she strolled his way. "Hi yourself— latecomer," he said softly.

"I'm sorry about that," she said hoarsely, thinking again of Charlie-Pop.

"So am I sorry. Now I won't have long to stay. It's almost dinner time."

"You can always eat with us."

"Can't. Promised Kate I'd be home. She says I eat too often over here. Your father already thinks I'm a freeloader."

"Freeload all you want. He can afford it," she said as she knelt before him and gave herself into his outstretched arms. Eagerly they kissed. He wasn't David, and she wasn't seven. It was all right now to feel what she was feeling, to love as she loved now. David had come too early into her life, and seduced her wrongly. Jamie never demanded anything she wasn't ready to give. She yielded against him, responding kiss for kiss, with more passion than any she'd shown yet—and why was that—because of what she'd heard when eavesdropping? For the first time she submitted to his caresses that grew ever bolder. By her very silence she gave consent to his rambling explorations of her body. Hands that eagerly felt her breasts and stroked down over her buttocks, then, startlingly, grabbed between her thighs. Sharply she jerked away. Her dazed eyes met his as she blushed. "Don't, Jamie."

"Isn't it time we did more than just hold hands and kiss?"

Was it? Was eighteen old enough? Who would be punished if she allowed him to do more? Not Charlie-Pop, God had decided his fate already. What was it she read the other day? . . . Take what you can while you may for life slips so swiftly away.

Slowly, her eyes holding his, she leaned into his arms again, allowing her lips to part beneath his. Her arms fastened around his neck before her hands rose to his head and her fingers twined into his strong auburn hair. There was a special taste to his lips; a smell to his body, clean, like soap; like he always showered before he came and never, never did he smell of fish. She closed her eyes and allowed him to do what he would. I'm not afraid, she kept telling herself. This isn't wrong. It's all right as long as I love him and he loves me. Love made sex without marriage okay, particularly if they were married eventually.

And during all this thinking Jamie had moved his hands with surprising knowledge to rid her of her knit shirt. Her bra was skillfully unhooked, making her shiver; making her think too he had unfastened many another bra, and she didn't want to think he had. His hands seemed to burn her bare skin as he fondled and kissed, teasing her nipples with his tongue until they were firm and hard. She began to breathe harder, faster, almost as if she were going into an attack, and that couldn't be, could it? Then she jumped. He'd touched the zipper of her shorts. "No! Stop, Jamie! You're going too fast! I'm not ready to give in all the way."

"When will you be ready?" he asked even as he tried to take off her shorts.

Beginning to resist more firmly, she shoved him away.

"Wait! I have to be sure. I have to feel right about this. And I don't want it to be so commonplace, here on the shore." (Like Mama in the boathouse) . . . "When it happens between us, Jamie, it's going to be beautiful."

"I know that," he said stiffly, his passion not as easily turned off as hers. "Anywhere with you would be beautiful, if you loved me enough." She saw his flushed face, heard his heavy breathing, saw the bulge that he tried to hide by turning away.

"Let's talk instead. I have so much to tell you."

"No lovin', no talkin'."

"You don't mean that."

"Oh, yes I do. I'm sailing away tomorrow morning before dawn, won't be home for two weeks or more." His voice was husky, intense, his eyes refusing to look as she put on the clothes he'd just taken off. "I was hoping this time you'd commit yourself, but it seems you never will—or not with me."

Gulls, gannets and guillemots flew overhead. A tern dipped down to walk on the beach only yards away. She kept her eyes on the birds in the sky, the ones who wheeled, glided, soared. Wonder what it was like to be as free as a bird. Free to go where she would, knowing she could, even if she didn't. For they didn't go, the birds of the island. They stayed and they had the wings to go anywhere. Was she like that tree on the bluff twisted and tortured out of shape by all the storms, rooted to one place, and made what she was only because of circumstances? No option, no option . . . Trapped by a heart that had too many valves. Trapped by Daddy's love and his ability to keep her alive. No place to run but to him—or Jamie.

"Jamie, you do understand?"

"Ay-yuh."

Smiling, she turned, only to see his disappointment, his lack of understanding. She ached for him, for herself, for all lovers who had to wait. "Talk to me in your Down East accent."

"Nope. Goin' home. I don't need to sit here and let you make a fool of me again."

"All right, go home. Leave me here feeling ashamed and guilty, and there will never be any lovin', anytime, anyplace."

"That so?" he asked, appearing indifferent. He got up to go, leaving her sitting on the sand staring after him as he untied the knots, tested the wind, and made all the preparations that usually took only seconds. Now he was stalling. "Jamie," she called, knowing he'd never break a silence. "If you can't understand me, I can understand you. For you words don't come easy, while I can rattle on and on incessantly, saying nothing. You always say something of importance. So this time I'm going to talk in your way, honestly. I've never had a lover, and I'm not sure I'm ready for one. But when the time comes, it will be you." She had his attention now, all of it. "I love you, and I'm sorry I can't give you what you want. At least not yet." Gracefully, she rose and beckoned him closer. Reluctantly, he came to stiffly stand before her, allowing her arms to slip around his neck while he fisted his hands and held his emotions under control. His jaw squared more as her finger traced lightly over his lips, and then she was kissing the hollow of his throat.

"Don't toy with me, Lisa! I don't like it!"

"I'm not toying. I'm trying to say I'm sorry."

"I've had enough of this for one day—take your hands off. If you don't really love me, and don't want me, then tell me to get the hell out of your life, and I will. But if you want me to come back, you keep in mind we're no longer kids playing at being in love. This time it's for real—and I want it all."

How could she explain how she felt? He wouldn't understand about David . . . "Jamie, let me try and tell you about my mother when she was very young, just my age when she married a man named Rudy Marshall. Years later she met my father and they fell in love, madly in love. She divorced Rudy and married Daddy, and on their honeymoon Rudy put a shotgun in his mouth and blew off the back of his head. Mama never forgave herself for leaving him. She never forgave Daddy for making her fall in love with him. She told me not to make the same mistake, not to marry too young, but to wait for the kind of man who would keep me happy all my life long."

"I understand," he said coldly. "You want to hang on to me while you look over the field for someone better."

She stepped closer and pressed her soft curves against his hard body, forcing his arms to embrace her, as she cuddled her head on his chest. "Hold tight to me, Jamie. Never let me go! I want you as much as you want me, but I'm scared, and the timing is wrong. Sometimes I feel God is waging a vendetta against me, stealing from me everyone I love. I've told you about David who was lost at sea; you know my grandmother died when Mama, Daddy and I were in Bermuda, and Daddy never forgave himself for being away and not able to attend the funeral. Then Mama was killed in that accident, I've lost three puppies I love, the parakeet you gave me, and now just today, I picked up the telephone to call you, and I heard Daddy talking to my grandfather in Rome. He's coming home, Jamie. My grandfather is dying of lung cancer, and he's coming home to stay until he goes into the ground."

"I'm sorry, so sorry. I know how much you love your grandfather." His strong young arms held her tighter.

"That's why I can't give you what you want, Jamie—at least one of the reasons. I feel everything is slipping away from me, people, time; perhaps the new dog I just found and named Pipkin, he'll be lost too. Then there's my own life, my stupid heart that needs an operation. I wake up at night wondering what's going to happen to me, to you, to Daddy. I'm so terribly afraid somebody else will go out of my life, and I don't know if I can live through another loss."

"You can live through anything, Lisa, for I'll be beside you, loving and supporting you all the rest of your life. Your long, long life."

They clung tighter, holding fast to one another, as she fixed her eyes on the water. Only the bay water, but around the bend of the island was the sea, the cruel pitiless sea.

"Now don't you be thinking I won't come back, for I will. Robbie was the first McKitrick to be lost at sea, and that was because he didn't want to go in the first place. The sea is like an animal, Lisa, it senses fear."

She shuddered and held him closer, so afraid for him. Poor Robbie McKitrick, only twenty-five when he was lost; now in Davy Jones's locker, waiting for Judgment Day . . .

As she embraced him, and he lowered his face into her hair, all the sky turned amber, touching the water with golden crests, etching each wave with silver—and then it was crimson, everything redder than blood.

It was just like her nightmare when she was running on the beach, searching, searching . . .

His boat when he sailed away grew smaller and smaller.

She put her hands to her head, trying to stop the precognition that one day he wouldn't come back—ever.

five

EARLY, BEFORE THE MORNING mists had lifted from the land or sea, when it was more like night than day, the fleet of tuna fishing clippers, trawlers and schooners moved from their home harbors on the peninsula on Frenchman's Bay, then curved gently into the Atlantic, going north. The bluer warm waters of the gulf stream their goal.

The men of these vessels were not averse to catching lesser fish, right down to those sardine size, if such made themselves available, and if their equipment was suitable. But for tuna they were targeted. For tuna was their preferred quarry. For tuna they were prepared and equipped, but empty holds had to be filled with something.

Once fishermen like them had depended largely on their own personal knowledge and skill to locate their elusive quarry, following the ocean currents. Now they had modern electronic listening devices similar to sonar instruments. Some ships used radio beams to bounce off the ocean floor and this information of depth was recorded on graphs. They used charts of the ocean bottom with previously recorded depths of watery valleys and unseen peaks of drowned mountains. By comparing these charts with the recent reading of the fish-finding fathometers the skippers would know a lesser reading of fathoms above a spot that should read greater was either an unrecorded peak or kelp forest—or what they were searching for—fish.

And for the first time, Jamie McKitrick was skipper in charge of his father's new trawler that had cost hundreds of thousands of dollars. At twenty-one, the youngest captain in the fleet.

On his bed, Jason Lorraine heard the mechanical sounds of the fishing fleet's early departure. The mournful wails of the lighthouse foghorn, wistful and somehow sad as they were, nevertheless pleased him. He stilled, lay supine, and turned only his head toward the eastern windows, sponging up the taste and feel of the fresh new day. Seeing the billowing fog, sniffing the salt-brine air, hearing the ghostly cries of the outbound boats did not fail now, as it had never failed in the past, to send an appreciative rippling thrill down his spine. He didn't stir more than blinking eyelids until the last forlorn cry had spread into the muffling morning mists and all boats vanished in the distance. It was for such as this that he loved his island with a passion that could be named obsessive.

He sat up then, all his senses keen. Knowing that today he would be exhilaratingly productive. He inhaled deeply, then stretched before he threw off the covers. Pulling on a robe and thrusting his feet into slippers, he felt eager for the clean white sheets of paper that would take him into adventures he'd never experience in any other way. Then he headed for the back balcony facing the Atlantic.

As new as the day was, his daughter had preceded him there. She didn't turn her head or speak to acknowledge his presence. "Lisa," he had to say twice before she finally turned to him and gave him a tremulous smile of welcome. Why were her eyes brilliant with unshed tears?

"What's wrong, sweetheart?" he asked as he touched his forefinger to the salty drop that clung to her lashes. He lifted that one away, then touched her other eye in the same soft way.

"Jamie's father broke his leg, and now Jamie is taking his place for the first time. Of course he's been going to sea since he was twelve, but to captain a boat in that huge ocean, it scares me."

His mouth gaped open in surprise. She'd said all of that exactly as if her tears and woeful expression were adequately explained. Good God, did she care that much already?

He tried to keep the tone of his voice understanding, kind. "I'm sure he can take care of himself. Now tell me about yourself, how are you feeling health wise?"

After all, the sea was the right place for a fisherman to be, why worry?

"Oh, Daddy, sometimes you annoy me with your silly concern for that stupid extra heart valve. It's functioning properly if that's all that concerns you—but why can't you feel some concern about Jamie? He's young, inexperienced at being in charge of such a huge expensive boat."

"He'll come back," he said tonelessly, thinking of that other fisherman who'd come back too—to steal his wife and be the cause of her death. And nothing had been as good since. Nothing. No woman in his bed for nine long, long years, and to think she'd left it for her coffin. Why had he slept alone? To punish himself for failing her? Had he forced her into the arms of that fisherman? And then the most ironic twist of all, the novel that would bring him millions was published soon after she was buried. But, but, he could have given Therese all the glamour she wanted anyway—if he had chosen. Why hadn't he chosen?

Suddenly he realized from the way Lisa was staring at him that his expression was giving away too much. He tried to smile.

"Daddy! You don't like one thing about Jamie, do you?"

"I wasn't thinking about him. And I've never said that, have I?"

"You don't have to say it with words. With your attitude, your demeanor, you speak eloquently, and have you ever heard one word about him that was not to his credit?"

Indifferently he shrugged while the strong winds whipped her flimsy nightclothes and pasted them to her shapely body. He didn't want to stare, but his eyes couldn't stay away. Her bright silky hair snapped horizontally, like ribbons to forever twine his fate to hers. (Why hadn't she put on a robe, something concealing?)

"Daddy, I am not the child you try to keep me," she began, trying to subdue her hair and hold down her gown at the same time. "I've been your little girl long enough. I'm ready now for what comes next. I want to feel free to marry Jamie."

Something tender and sweet that was just sprouting inside him, the shoots started the day Therese died, shriveled and tried to die. He calmed his rising temper, his terrible wrath to think she could follow in her mother's footsteps. "Lisa, you are not suited to be a fisherman's wife—now you let me have my say, since I allowed you yours!" He spoke more hastily than he'd planned for he could see she was ready to object. "James is your first love, your only love, or so I presume. You feel romantic and generous, hoping to put into his life all the beauty and sensitivity you have to give. I can understand your reasoning, and your attraction. He's a clean-cut good-looking young man—but marriage outside of your class just won't work. You're accustomed to all the luxuries an affluent life has given, and he isn't. Sooner or later he will resent your ability to give to him, and his inability to give to you."

His words made her tremble, look uncertain, before she obviously forced herself to speak with some determination: "Daddy, I believe you are trying to wage a war of attrition. I love Jamie for himself, not for what he can give me. I don't want you to say anything more against him, for it won't make any difference anyway. I'm eighteen years old and legally responsible. And though I appreciate everything you've done for me, you've got to let me live my own life."

"Have you told him about your heart operation and the risks it involves?" He felt cruel to ask, aching when he saw her blanch. She turned from him and hastily retreated up the two steps and into her bedroom suite.

Left disconsolate, he stared after her, watching as she closed the casement windows and then drew the draperies to shut him out completely. Just like it had been with Therese when she told him she was leaving him for that fisherman she called Jack. "I love you more than I love him, Jay, but I cannot live on this island and give up all you expect me to. I don't feel real living here. I look around and see this island as a prison while you see it as paradise."

His hand shook when he pulled cigarettes from his robe pocket. Wondering, as he always wondered, if smoking was really carcinogenic as the warning said was possible. And Charles had smoked heavily once. Lung cancer, spreading down into his stomach. He sighed heavily. Just what he needed, a dying man coming home to complicate his life more.

At the far end of the dining table, not at his right where she usually sat, Lisa did not once allow her eyes to lift and meet with his as they ate breakfast. Elka served them with her usual laconic attitude, then quietly stepped into the kitchen where she could be heard muttering to herself.

Jason marveled that a girl of eighteen could be so clever at her exclusion game. Even when she looked right at him she looked through him, making him feel he was as effective as melted ice in a clear glass of water. For some reason he couldn't define, perhaps to break down her defiance, he told her then of his dying father who would be flying home soon. "I know," she said quietly. "I listened in on your long-distance call, and I've cried until my eyes hurt. But when he comes I'm going to smile so he won't feel sad. I'm going to do everything possible to make all the remaining days of his life happy. I'm going to be like Jamie who knows how to cope with any situation. He's sturdy, Daddy, dependable and firm. His foundation is bedded in rock. He'll never list or collapse for there's not a storm any-where that can sweep Jamie into deep uncontrollable waters."

So, she was deciding on his strength she could lean, and on his bedded-in-rock foundation she would find her own. He pitied her, he loved her, but most of all he felt afraid for her future. Should he tell her about Therese with her fisherman lover? No, he thought, what daughter should be told that her dead mother was capable of deceit? Death put an instant halo above the head of the deceased and sprouted wings on their backs. Even he didn't want to believe. Most certainly he didn't want to even suspect there might have been more than one lover.

His teeth bit down into his lower lip as he watched her use her fingernail to etch a design on the tablecloth. With considerable skill she put the finishing touches to her perishable artwork. He narrowed his eyes. So damn skillful with paintbrushes. His eyes narrowed even more as she cocked her head and tenderly smiled as she studied her faint picture.

Without glancing his way, without excusing herself from the table, she stood, left the dining room with the dog found in the woods trailing close at her heels. Already she'd made him her devoted slave.

No sooner was she out of sight than he was up and bending over to stare at her nail indentations. She'd sketched a small sailboat on choppy waters, sailing off into the sunset. Two were on board, one very obviously a woman.

Furious! The anger that suffused him made his eyes see red! Ruthlessly he rubbed the tablecloth until the boat, the waters, the sunset, the man, and even the woman were all obliterated.

No Paradise, Lisa. Not for me. Nor will there be one for you!

six

JAMIE WAS VERY MUCH on Lisa's mind as she sat beside her father in the airport terminal, awaiting the arrival of the plane bearing her grandfather home from Rome. She jumped to her feet, tugging Jason along with her as she ran toward the wide window wall to watch a plane turn, then head into the wind. She smiled up at her father, realizing this was her first really warm gesture of reconciliation between them since their argument on the balcony.

"So, we're going to be friends again," he said in a relieved way. "Thank God for small favors."

She stood on her toes to kiss his cheek. "Daddy, even when I don't like you, I still can't help loving you. So yes, we will stay friends and in the end you will discover to your amazement that Jamie is not your common variety of fisherman."

Scowling, he drew away. "Don't mention your fisherman to me again. I'm not in the mood to fight more."

"Don't call him my fisherman." That's when she looked again at the newly perched plane to see the passengers already descending. "There he is, Daddy!" she cried out happily.

All Lisa's memories of Charles Lorraine were colored by a nimbus of glamour and excitement. She thought he'd never grow old, dull or stodgy. He seemed to her the epitome of everything exceptional, talented and handsome, and much too wonderful to age as ordinary people did. She liked to think he and Jason lived in their own private creative worlds, improving from year to year in every way. Yet, this time his appearance shocked her. He didn't appear nearly as tall or as straight. Since last Christmas twenty years had been laid on his shoulders. Forcing a smile she ran forward to throw her arms about him.

"Grandfather! How wonderful to have you home again." She kissed his hollowed cheek and stared up into his dark eyes that still sparkled with the same old fire. "If your son isn't just like his father."

Jason winced.

"And I must say, Leedee, you are your mother all over again, too beautiful to describe."

She looked from him to Jason as they embraced, trying to control her emotions. I'm going to do this right, she thought. I'm not going to let him know how much I'm suffering to see him look so gaunt. His last days are going to be his happiest days, no shadows only sunshine.

Still, they were hardly on the highway leading home when the sun clouded over. Brisk high winds pushed long layers of clouds and moved them in confusing opposite directions. Telling her something. The roadside trees were whipped and driven wild by the wind, like dancers gone crazy. They were telling her something too. A fist closed about her heart as Daddy turned onto Hemlock Road. She swallowed and turned to chatter merrily to her grandfather, trying to take everyone's mind off what had happened to her mother on this very road nine years ago.

Rain began to patter down and darken the road ahead. Just like it had rained then—and it began just when they reached the break in the trees where her mother had gone over.

Burned, burned, all that beautiful hair burned off her scalp so they couldn't open the coffin, even if she'd worn a wig. Scarred so badly it was difficult to recognize her. Who had told her that? Dreams? The atmosphere was so heavy she felt smothered by depression. She stared off toward the island which came mistily into view.

Birdlane Island, the home of her heart. Her Paradise on earth, if only, only. On the island she was enchanted, protected, safe. There, time passed, flowers bloomed, fall and winter came and went and nothing changed very much. An eon of time could pass by and still the pounding surf wouldn't erode the bedrock shores of her sanctuary. In the library was a huge old family Bible listing all the births and deaths of the Lorraines, and not one had died on the island, although many a babe had sounded its first cry in Windown House. And many a Lorraine had met his or her death on the mainland, but not on Birdlane.

How wonderful to have a home like Windown House that refused to hear the rattle of death. And this was her comfort, her consolation; death would not come for her there, but only on the mainland where other Lorraines had died. On the island she was inviolate from the vicissitudes of life; on the island she was impregnated by its strength, and with the additional strength Jamie gave, perhaps she would survive to old age.

Jason's long green Lincoln turned onto the island bridge and not one of the three inside could speak of what was on their minds. This was the last time Charles Lorraine would come home.

She fixed her eyes on the high gray waters that almost had the bridge awash. The waves of the bay churned in extreme agitation, hurling the surf with thunderous power to crash against the rock shores. Towering sprays of water arched back upon themselves—and this was safety?—this was her sanctuary and her lonely Paradise?

The wind came and shrieked under the archway of trees leading to the house. Screaming wind that erased Swen's voice as he came to help with the luggage in the garage. Elka stood in the doorway of the kitchen to welcome home the Master and his father. Elka was everything Jason deplored in Jamie McKitrick, and admired in his housekeeper—who knew when to keep her mouth shut, taciturn, but efficient. She was his jewel, his cook, his mainstay when Lisa was sick, and most of all she intimidated her husband so much it seemed Swen just didn't exist at all. "Swen's like a houseplant that surprises you when it moves," Lisa had whispered once to Jason.

"Don't bother," said Lisa when she saw Elka heading toward the dining room with their second-best china. "I'll set the table," and she'd use the best porcelain too, take out her mother's wedding crystal, the sterling silver, do it up right.

"If that's what you want, Miss," said Elka who put the china back in the kitchen cabinets.

Elka had the placement of a drill sergeant when setting a table, lining everything up in precise rows. Even flowers in a vase stood at attention when Elka placed them there.

With the same questing need for a woman's companionship, Lisa stared after Elka longingly. Why didn't Elka like her? Why couldn't she see she needed a mother now that her own mother was gone? And why had her mother chosen Elka above all the other nurses who'd been in the hospital when she was born?

Does Elka see Mama in me, is that it?

Wipe away ugly thoughts by keeping busy. Put the flowers in the low bowl, make it pretty, and only then did she drift to the French windows to stare out at the tempestuous ocean. There it was, beyond the spacious lawns, that huge cold indifferent sea, always a threat, her enemy—and Jamie's. The rain-washed windows blurred her vision, though she imagined she could see Jamie on the slippery deck of the *Seabird*. He'll be all right, she kept telling herself. He's old enough to know what he's doing. A Chummer no longer, hauling up the big fish as soon as one bit the line. Surely all those long years of childhood training would pay off now. He'd find the tuna. He'd fill the holes. He'd come sailing home on the very day he'd promised to return.

Hands were placed lightly on her shoulders, making her start. She swung around, as if to defend herself, then felt silly and embarrassed. It was only Daddy. "How's Granddad?" she asked.

"Fine. He's taking a bath, and then he's going to rest for a while, but he will be joining us for dinner. He's told me he intends to lead as normal a life as possible, as long as he can."

He tucked her hand in the crook of his elbow and led her toward the library where he soon knelt to put a match to the kindling in the fireplace.

"You know, of course," he said while he was still on his knees, using the bellows to hasten the flames into sturdy life, "we won't be able to fly south this fall. This winter you are going to get your dearest wish, we're staying. You'll see it snow, like you always wanted to. You'll learn what real Maine winters are like. Charles doesn't want us to leave, though he hasn't said so, I can tell. So, if you swear to be careful, to obey my orders, I won't send you off to stay with your mother's sister."

Why, she didn't even know her mother's sister! Why was he even suggesting that when he knew she knew he'd never let her go anywhere without him?

Once he was settled in his favorite chair by the fireplace, he opened the *New York Times* he'd purchased at the airport. She watched him with troubled eyes, not understanding something that vibrated from him; some silent communication that told her he was aware of her presence, and he wanted her to stay where she was.

"You're forgetting your New Year's resolution," she said when he lit a cigarette.

"That's what resolutions are for."

He went on reading. She picked up a paperback and opened to her bookmark, but her thoughts kept drifting. All the winters the two of them had spent together since her mother died; spent anywhere but here; Arizona, California, Hawaii, Italy, anywhere but here when the cold came to stay.

In the winters, so the villagers said, the coves froze over with ice projecting out into the bay. Then the Coast Guard ice-breakers had to come to tear up the ice and sweep it into the faster-moving currents of the sea. Certainly this winter they would be more isolated than they'd ever been in the summers. Lonely on this side of the bridge. That expensive bridge he'd had constructed just so he could get her quickly to the peninsula and a doctor or hospital.

Tutors, they came and went in her life, all pretty young women. Every one of them falling in love with Jason. Every one of them ignored by Jason. As if he didn't need any woman after his wife died. Mama, did you steal his manhood? Did you take even his sensuality with you into your grave?

At that moment Jason looked up from the newspaper.

Smoke from his cigarette circled aromatically above his head, weaving toward her lamp. His eyes locked with hers. Then, slowly, charmingly, he smiled. She flushed, half afraid he'd somehow divined her thoughts.

For some uneasy reason she couldn't understand or identify, she put down her book and left the room. Left him staring after her in the oddest way.

seven

Sometime during the night the storm blew out to sea.

When Lisa wakened there was only a residue of dense fog lingering around Birdlane, to shroud the trees with wisps of veils, to impart an otherworldliness to what might have seemed to her ordinary if the weather didn't constantly change her perspective.

She felt happy, healthy, glad to be up and about before anyone else. As soon as she was bathed and dressed she peeked in at her grandfather, afraid somehow he might not be here after all.

Already she'd passed her father's bedroom, and through the open door had seen his rumpled bed. She suspected he'd be in the dining room, but only Pipkin ran to greet her, racing from the music room where she'd established his small bed. For a moment she hugged his small warm body close as he tried to lavish her with wet slurpy kisses. "Now you be quiet," she whispered. "You're my pet and have to be on my side, and not let my father know I'm up and about."

She didn't guess at how he would feel about her leaving the

island. She knew he'd forbid her to do this without him beside her in the small car her grandfather had given her last year as a birthday gift. It wasn't often she had the chance to drive and be alone in her "bone of contention" and this made her smile again. This car would have gone right back to the dealer if Jason had his way. He'd stormed, indignant, offended.

"Charles had no right! He should have asked me! He knows you shouldn't be driving yourself! Lisa, you are never to drive this car alone!"

Refusing to be intimidated, she laughed and caught his hand, and swayed. She'd driven with him cringing beside her, criticizing every time she whipped around the cars ahead, taking curves on two wheels, and all to make him realize he was only irritating her so she wanted to drive dangerously.

"Damn if I can stand a woman driving me around!" he complained when she drew to such an abrupt stop he was thrown forward. "You make me so nervous I'm sweating." She got out and raced to open his door and assist him out. He jerked his elbow from her hand. "What the hell are you trying to prove? I'm not an invalid, or a fool!"

"You make me feel like both, so I'm giving you the chance to wear my shoes—how do they fit?"

"You're just a girl, and I only treat you with courtesy."

"All right, so now you know what it's like to feel female and incompetent, when you taught me to drive in the first place, and you know I am just as capable of good driving as you are." She dropped the car keys in her purse and looked up into his face earnestly as they headed for the specialty wine and cheese store.

"There are times when being assisted in and out of cars and having doors held open for me, sometimes makes me feel pampered and well taken care of. It's sweet too, but you carry it to the extreme. You manage to show condescending superiority when a sensitive man like you should know better."

"Are you telling me in your subtle way I am NOT sensitive? That I am tactless too? Reaching eighteen has gone to your head!"

She smiled to win him back. "I'm much too happy to argue over trifles, so to make up, this shopping spree is on me, Daddy. Help yourself to anything your heart desires."

Helplessly she watched as he set to. There was nothing Jason liked better than shopping for gourmet food—let Elka buy the mundane stuff. By the time he was halfway through the cheese section his anger was over. In the wine shop he bought to such a degree Lisa furtively slipped out her checkbook and blanched.

He grinned at the checkout counter, then pulled out his own checkbook, his smile wicked, and well pleased with himself.

Fog. What difference did it make? She didn't want to think of Daddy who believed love would make her fly away and be free for the first time in her life. I'm happy, despite all he does, even if Charlie-Pop is dying, I have to feel happy when I have Jamie. So seldom did she feel genuine happiness.

Someday she'd give in to Jamie. Perhaps after she was nineteen in August. That would be just the right age.

Sometime during the night the gale blew out to sea, leaving a residue of dense fog. Lisa was up early, skipping breakfast, deciding to eat that on the mainland. Reasoning that if her father knew of her plans, he would inevitably try to change them, and she wasn't in the mood for another argument. Not often did she use the small white car with the red seats that had been her grandfather's birthday gift last year. Her father's face had flushed red with indignation when first the car was delivered. Right back to the agency it would have gone, if she had let him. But for once she had been as adamant as he could sometimes be. Imagine, behaving as if she would immediately jump into the auto and flee forever . . .

Windown House was left behind her, misted mellow by the fog when she turned to look. The thick fog enchanted her, for it had the illusive reality of night dreams lingering too long.

The peninsula shared the same billowing unworldliness until she opened the door of a waterfront cafe and stepped into the hard, yellow light from swinging lanterns on the ceiling. A jukebox in the corner played loudly. The waiter grinned displaying yellow teeth with the two incisors missing. Quickly she glanced toward the bridge to her island which could be seen faintly beyond the parked cars outside.

"Yuh ready t'name yer poison?" asked the waiter who appeared to be about eighteen.

The way he said that made her jump. Nervously she listed off scrambled eggs, bacon, coffee with no cream, no sugar.

"Yuh don't want toast?"

She stared at him blankly before she realized the toast didn't go automatically with the meal—and she'd thought bread was always served. "Yes, toast with butter and jelly."

"What kind of jelly, ma'am?"

"Currant," she said.

"Ain't got none of that kind."

"Bring me what you have then."

He sauntered away, tossing a big smile over his shoulder. She should get up and go. Jason was right, this cafe wasn't fit to eat in. Why, there might be cockroaches in the kitchen.

Second by second as she waited, she grew more apprehensive. Not one man in the place took his eyes away from her. Although the inhabitants of the village knew who she was, who Jason and Charles were, she had met only a few casually. None had ever appeared friendly. This used to hurt when she was a child, to always accept their indifference to her existence. Jamie had tried more than once to explain their attitude.

"It's because your family leaves in the fall, and comes back in the summer. They think it makes all of you seem frail, less hardy than the ones who stay, the ones who endure the weather, come what may."

And none of them knew she couldn't endure . . .

Secrets, an island of secrets. Not a paradise like Jason believed, like her mother refused to believe. Lost in her thoughts, she came back to the cafe with a start. The skin on her neck prickled. Thoughtlessly she turned her head to squarely meet the brown eyes of that man with the beard. That same man who always stared.

She shifted her eyes, feeling a visual rending, and tried to ignore what she saw him doing next. In her peripheral vision she watched this shabby young man gain his feet. He spoke in a low voice to the two men with him at his table, then picked up his plate, cup and saucer—and headed her way! Unbelievable!

I won't speak. I'll ignore him.

"Now don't look so scared. I don't bite. I've come to protect you from all the leers. I just told my two companions you came to meet me, and in a way I don't think that's an absolute lie. Fate has sent you into my life, Lisa Lorraine."

Very surprised, somewhat caught off guard, she stared as he placed his plate, flatware, cup and saucer on her table. Nothing like this had ever happened to her before. Always she was under the protective wing of her father. A strange panic began in her heart, and yet, and yet . . . she was oddly fascinated with this young man whose laughing brown eyes spoke directly of the sensual pleasures he had in mind. If his eyes hadn't mocked her and made light of the situation she might have answered differently, or not at all.

"You have the advantage. I don't know who you are."

Again he looked her over, as if now that he was up close he'd make the most of it.

"Why should you know me, Lisa? I'm nobody."

"Everyone is somebody."

"That's true in a way," he said as he sat down to pick up his fork and stab into his stack of griddle cakes. "But I'm nobody special like you, and that's what I mean. You're the beautiful princess who lives in a mysterious castle on an enchanted isle."

Frowning, she said slowly, "An island you've taken to prowling, and that's trespassing. My father could have you arrested."

He said nothing, offering no excuses, just continued to eat, all the while watching her facial expressions, her body movements, as if he'd never see enough. She went on more nervously, "And even nobodies have names—especially nobodies who paint pictures. Or else how would somebodies know which nobody was responsible for the art?"

Pleasure sparkled in his eyes even more. "So-oo, you've noticed me after all. I'm honored to introduce myself as Kyle Peters. I hail from a long-long way from here."

He didn't have to say that, just his soft mellow voice told of his differences from those native to this storm-driven rocky coast. "Hello, Mr. Peters," she said with a certain intuition that she knew she was saying hello to more than just a brief acquaintance.

"Hello, Lisa. I've waited a long time to say that to you. You're so seldom alone. I couldn't believe my good fortune when you walked in here without your father in tow."

Something earnest in his voice, in his eyes, made her eyes drop shyly, thinking even then that Jamie wouldn't like the events of this morning. And she mustn't hurt Jamie, never. Nor was she sure she liked this man's easy familiarity, eating with her as casually as a man who'd lived with her for years on end. Was this what was called a "pickup"?

"You don't look like any girl I've ever seen before."

"Is that a compliment or a criticism?"

"Take your pick," he answered as she put the last of her dry toast into her mouth. She smiled, then answered, "You don't look like anyone I've seen before either." Her eyes met his squarely then, enjoying his look of perplexity.

"How so?" His left eyebrow lifted quizzically.

Deliberately she finished her meal before she answered. "You're all hair with that beard and mustache. I can't see your face. Are you in disguise, Mr. Peters, hiding?"

Disconcertion wasn't his even briefly. "Everyone is in disguise in one way or another, even you."

Now she was disconcerted, but she sought to hide that by cocking her head to one side in an imitation of his manner, and mimicking his voice she said, "How so? My face is without hair, shining forth for all the world to see. My clothes aren't so large they hide even my figure, like you hide yours."

He put his elbows on the table and leaned forward until his hairy face was only inches from hers. She shrank backward, wanting to dodge his penetrating long gaze.

"Even beautiful bare faces like yours can be in disguise, hiding from themselves."

"Oh," she sighed, a small fear fluttering her pulses, "you can't possibly know that much about me. Even if you do sneak around on our island spying, you can't know anything. And please stop prying into what is none of your business!"

Without embarrassment or chagrin he smiled easily. "I know all about you, Lisa Carol Lorraine, going on nineteen in August. I've made it my business to find out all about you."

She shivered. Something cold and scary made her dislike his implications, his prying, his confident demeanor. She stood, placing her napkin on the table before she took change from her purse and put it beside her plate.

"People are very dull when you know everything about them. So, I'll leave you now, Mr. Peters, before my predictability begins to bore you." Not waiting for his reactions, or looking to see his expression, she went swiftly to the cashier's cage to pay her bill.

When she slammed the cafe door it seemed to echo.

On impulse she decided to stop by and see Jamie's father who was confined to shore life now that his leg was in a cast to his hip.

John McKitrick sat comfortably on the back porch of his saltbox home, with his casted leg propped on a hassock. Crutches leaned against the house. It seemed to her ironic that an accidental fall on a wet kitchen floor would put him down for the first time in his life, and he was a man of the sea, accustomed to rolling decks. She knew him only slightly since he was very seldom home.

"Hello there, Lass," he called cheerfully as she ascended the steps. "If you aren't the prettiest thing I've seen since the last time you were here. Jim told me to expect you to drop by, but somehow I didn't think you would."

She smiled before she leaned to hug the large sandy-haired man with his sea-chafed skin. His blue eyes were blurred by the brightness of the sun on the ocean, looking at it year after year. Now she didn't know what to say.

"Jamie told me about your wife, Mr. McKitrick . . ." she began haltingly. "I hope she comes back soon."

"Call me John," he said with a hard tone to his voice, as if his wife's leaving was something he didn't want to discuss.

Rowina McKitrick with the blue-black raven-wing hair, so much like her daughter's. Rowina who hated the sea, hated when her two sons and husband put out to sea and stayed for weeks on end, leaving her lonely, worried, praying every night they'd come home safely. And her eldest son had gone overboard during a storm, his body never recovered. Poor Robbie McKitrick, dead so young.

Jamie had told her: "She just pinned a note to her pillow the night after his memorial services, telling us she couldn't stay on and worry another day. When we woke up she was gone. She said too she wasn't going to hang around and grow older while she waited for another of her men to die."

Now John said: "No need to feel sorry for me, Lisa. I have my son, and I have my daughter, and I have the sea. He gave her a shrewd look. "It's not easy to love a man of the sea, I hope you know that."

"Yes, I know," she said weakly, and started to get up and go, suddenly very uneasy. "Sit and stay awhile," he said, pulling out a checkerboard from under a stack of magazines.

"I suspect you didn't come to just see me, so I'll get on with tales of my son. He radios me every day, and he's doing fine. He told me to tell you not to worry. His navigational ability far exceeds mine. Jim knows the ocean currents like he knows the streets of this village. He'll come home, you can bet on that." His blue eyes sparkled as he smiled and leaned closer. "Any young man would come back to you, Lisa."

"But, but . . ." she sputtered, knowing she should say nothing more, "Jamie adores his mother. She hurts him too by leaving."

"Aye, but that's the name of the game, didn't you know? Before you make a permanent commitment to my son, Lisa, you think a long time about my wife, and how she felt about the sea. She wasn't born to it, like the other village women. Nor are you born to it. Take the best out of life, lass, before you grow old and the best has passed you by."

"But Jamie is the best!" she flared, oddly angry that he should try to discourage her.

He looked at her with soft eyes of pity before he touched her hair. "Such soft, soft hair. Such a beautiful rich color, not gold, not wheat, not auburn, but a combination of all three. Only you and your mother . . ."

"I think my mother's hair was a bit lighter . . ."

"Was it?" he asked with a faraway look.

She would have said yes, but at that moment Kate McKitrick came into view carrying two bags of groceries. A frown puckered Kate's dark brows when she saw Lisa. Her long hair was jet black, her eyes dark too, her manner brisk and no-nonsense. Only two years older than Jamie, she seemed almost ten years older in mannerisms.

"Hi, Lisa," she said without warmth. "Will you be leaving again this October for some warm place where people do nothing but play in the sun and seek to amuse themselves by constant partying?"

Why was everyone trying to hurt her? Lisa rose to go.

"No, Kate, we won't be leaving this fall. My grandfather has come home and wants to spend the winter on the island."

"That must be terribly disappointing and such a bore," said Kate before she flipped through the kitchen screen door and let it slam behind her. She could be seen through a porch window placing food in the refrigerator and on the cupboard shelves.

It was Lisa's first impulse to run away, to leave before Kate had the chance to wound her more, but this time she forced herself to enter the kitchen, and there she told Kate in a low voice, "I won't be disappointed or bored to spend my first winter here. I'm looking forward to the snow and being with Jamie. But I am not anticipating the death of my grandfather. For his doctors say he won't live another year."

Her pretty face flushed, Kate threw her a quick look of apology. "I feel ashamed, Lisa, and sorry I said what I did. Jamie told us your grandfather was sick, but he didn't tell us it was anything serious."

Of course Jamie wouldn't betray their secret. He could be trusted to keep a confidence. "Kate, I know you don't like me very much, or maybe not at all. But I love your brother and I hope to become friends with you." She regretted this frankness when Kate turned away, but nevertheless she went on with determination. "So, if you like me even a little, and you trust your brother's judgment even a little more, then when Jamie's home again, will you and your father come with Jamie to our island and have dinner with us? Don't tell me I should have invited you years and years ago, I know that now. But my father likes his isolation, his privacy, and has become somewhat reclusive. I am hoping you and I can become friends. I want Jamie's family to like me."

Irritatingly, Kate continued to fiddle with the precise arrangement of her cans of peas, tomatoes and corn. She threw Lisa a different kind of appraising look, something new glittering in her hard eyes.

"Your father is very handsome and young looking. It's hard to think he could be your father. So, maybe we will come, if you ask us again and set a specific date and time."

No matter the reason, Lisa sighed in relief. Let Kate come.

Daddy wouldn't like her. He never liked any of her tutors, and all of them had been more feminine than Kate.

On the island, Charles and Jason had moved their chairs from the flagstone terrace out onto the lawn facing the Atlantic. A steamship could be seen on the horizon. Jason stared at that and not at Pipkin who chased after a new rubber ball that Lisa had given him. The moment the dog saw her, he dropped the red ball and went flying in her direction, yipping happily all the way, his tail a frantically waving flag. She swooped him up and in a wild display of affection the two of them lost themselves.

Jason grew impatient. "Where have you been, Lisa?" he asked coldly. She jumped. Why was he glaring at her—what had she done to deserve such a look?

She didn't dare do anything but ignore his attitude and his question. Greeting Charles, she pulled a chair close to his and watched the squirming puppy playing at her feet.

"Yes, Leedee," said Charles, reaching to hold her hand, "it does feel good to be home again in all this fresh invigorating salt air. Already I feel better, and every time I look your way I see you're lovelier, more beautiful than your mother, if that is possible."

Why did Jason wince?

"Where the hell have you been?" he demanded again. He snuffed out his cigarette, glaring at her suspiciously.

Trying to control her emotions of panic, she watched Pipkin play by scattering a flock of chickadees into flight from the birdfeeder. She didn't want to tell him anything, but the silence grew so loud she said faintly, "I drove into the village."

"Why?"

"Does it matter?"

"Of course it matters! Suppose you had an attack while alone in the car, driving over that bridge. Who would be there to keep you from going over into the water? Who would be there to take care of you in case you didn't go into the bay?—that is if you didn't die first from the attack. And you left without eating your breakfast. Now don't lie and tell me you did. I've already questioned Elka and she told me you didn't eat. Lisa, I won't have you being so careless with your health."

Now she was quivering, on edge, as talk of her health always made her nervous. Why couldn't he let her forget it? She didn't look his way as she explained slowly how she'd driven carefully, and she had eaten at a cafe (though she didn't tell him which one), ". . . and it's time I started doing things on my own, without you beside me every second."

"You went to see him, didn't you?" Jason snapped angrily. "What other reason would you have for disobeying my specific order for you never to drive alone?"

That fragile strength she tried to retain began to dissolve before the onslaught of his rage that grew to more frightening heights with each of his words. She squeezed her eyelids tight, thinking of Jamie and what he would think of her if she let her father overrule her even on small things.

"You know you had an attack just the other day, and here you go off alone, risking your life, without regard to the consequences."

She blanched and bowed her head, trying to regain control of a situation that was raging toward a tempest. "Father, I've had only one small attack in three years, and you speak as if I have one every day. You're embarrassing me in front of my grandfather, and I want you to stop it."

"I will stop it. When YOU stop and consider just what obligations you owe me! When you remember that I've devoted the major portion of my life to taking care of you and keeping you alive, you will realize you have to do your share by weighing the risks you take for some petty reason."

Suddenly she could stand no more. She jumped to her feet and flared in his face: "All right! Every time I need something in a drug-store, or need to visit the beauty parlor, I'll ask for your permission, and demand that you go with me and sit in the car and wait—and I hope you are very happy while you sit there bored stiff!"

"Did you have your hair done?" he asked, rising to his feet to intimidate her with his towering height. "It appears to me very much as it looks every day, so if you had your hair washed and set, I'd demand my money back."

She started to go, but he held her with his voice. "You were lying, weren't you? You didn't go to a beauty parlor. You don't like the way they do your hair. You had something else in mind when you drove off without me. Now don't think you can escape so easily by promising to do differently. Saying you will obey my orders just isn't enough. You have to swear you will never go off this island unless I am with you."

Frozen in flight, she turned slowly toward him, disbelieving her ears. Her eyes met briefly with her grandfather's and saw his sympathy and understanding of her plight. I won't say anything more, she thought as she headed for the French doors of the library. I have to think about Charlie-Pop.

"LISA!" called Jason loudly. "I want your promise!"

It wasn't a request, but a demand. She spun around to face him, her face as flushed and angry as his. She saw him as she'd never seen him before, all the softness, all the compassion gone from his eyes, from his lips that were set in a hard grim line. She'd seen that expression before in her dreams, her terrifying dreams. She visualized him day after day, forcing her to make promise after promise, on and on into eternity like a figure in a mirror looking into another mirror that looked into yet another mirror . . .

She swallowed over the hard lump that rose in her throat. "I don't make promises unless I intend to keep them," she said stiffly.

Dark wrath filled his dark eyes. Sanguine color made his skin flame redder. "Are you saying now that you refuse to promise? Are you openly defying me—refusing to obey even this simple request that will keep you alive and healthy?"

What was wrong with him? Who was he?—a stranger she'd never seen before! She tried to control her trembling voice and lost the struggle.

"Daddy, I do appreciate all you've done for me. I'm ashamed I have to talk like this to you, and in front of your father, but I'm not going to allow you to dominate over every aspect in my life, for it is my life and not yours! I'll take as good care of myself as possible, and that's all I can promise."

Jason glanced at his father as if he'd completely forgotten his presence. His clenched fists relaxed. Had he meant to strike her? No, certainly he'd never do that. "Dad, I'm sorry about this, sorry you have to hear . . ."

Without replying, Charles reached to pet Pipkin's head, as if he sensed the puppy's uneasiness and was trying to comfort him. Again Jason turned his attention to the girl who lingered in the framework of the French doors, appearing on the verge of fainting, but regardless, he was going to have his say.

"Lisa, don't you say one more word to me. I want you to go upstairs and stay in your room until you can reconsider your attitude, and recognize the rashness of what you did this morning."

Rashness? What had she done? Her first meal on her own, and then a visit to a man with a broken leg—and all of this was rash? But of course, none of that had anything to do with his fury. It was Jamie. He wanted to use this small infraction of his rules and enlarge it into mammoth size so he could forbid her access to the mainland without him. Forbid her, even more importantly, access to Jamie.

She bit down on her tongue to keep from screaming this out and further increasing his anger. Pivoting about, she raced into the house. For the first time something akin to hate rose up to make her feel sick. How could she hate the very man she'd always loved most? That was, until Jamie came sailing over to her island in the sea.

Breathing hard, she leaned back against her bedroom door. That was it too. This was also his island, and everything on it belonged to him. The same as her mother had belonged to him. And Mama had escaped only by dying.

eight

HARSH WORDS WERE ON the tip of Jason's tongue, ready to lash out and strike down Lisa's rebellion that left him feeling unbelievably hurt and angry. He trembled with a rage so huge he wanted to strike out and hurt someone as he'd been hurt the day he knew Therese was having an affair with a fisherman. A common, coarse fisherman!

Then, still trembling, he sank into his chair. What am I doing? he asked himself. She's not her mother. But why did it have to be a fisherman? Any other man wouldn't have angered him, but to waste herself like that was so incredibly . . . so incredibly what? History repeating itself? His head dropped into his hands; his fingers stabbed into his hair as he felt shame and guilt wash over him.

Then the question, the question he dreaded. "Jay, just what are you trying to do to your daughter?"

His head lifted. His eyes stared blankly at Charles. "What did you say?"

The question was repeated, louder, more sharply.

"I'm trying to keep her alive, that's all."

He heard Charles sigh as if from miles away. Why was it a sigh that always irritated him? "Jay, you've always been one to see everything from your own perspective. You're not trying to give life to Lisa. You're trying to keep life away from her."

He spoke angrily: "You speak without knowing the full facts. Everything I do, I do to keep her healthy and alive!"

"All right. If I don't know the full facts, then tell them to me. You and Lisa are all I have left. I'd like to help, if I can."

Jason slumped lower in his chair and stared off toward the sea, not seeing it, but always feeling its presence, ominous. Why didn't he hate it? "You have your problems, Dad, I have mine."

"Son, I'm an old man," said Charles as he edged his chair closer. "I've lived a rich and full life, most of it rather pleasant. I have my regrets, who doesn't? The main one is I know I didn't make your mother as happy as I might have if I had given up music and stayed here with you and her. So, most of the unhappiness in my life was of my own doing. Don't follow in my footsteps. Allow me to help. Let me live to see the day both you and Lisa are on the road to happiness."

"We were happy until—" and here Jason broke off.

"Until what?"

He wished Charles wouldn't persist. "Until she fell in love!— that's what!"

A flashing impression loaned his father's face a temporary youthful appearance when he smiled. "Jay, have you forgotten what it's like to be young and in love? Do you want to rob your daughter of life's greatest moments?"

"I don't want to deny her anything," he said bitterly. "I wouldn't object at all if she'd chosen the right man."

"Jay, I marvel that Lisa found any man at all with you standing watchdog at her heels."

"You don't know him, Dad. He stands six foot five and earns his living catching tuna! And that's not the worst of it. He's only twenty-one, and already he's inflexible. She thinks she can change him, and take him away from the sea, but he won't change. She'll be the one who has to fit into the mold he shapes. In the end he'll break her, ruin her, and worst of all, waste her. Look at what she is, delicate, talented, beautiful enough to be a movie queen, and she wants to live in a fishing village and spend the best years of her life alone, with a brood of children to raise alone. Most of his life will be spent at sea while she waits for him to come home—and you know what that will do to her heart." He bit down on his lower lip, hoping to restrain himself with the blood he brought to the surface. "Why, when I think of his huge hands handling her, I want to . . ." He paused, then considered better.

But he'd said too much already. Strange how his father looked at him, so long and intensely he fidgeted and felt transparent, just as he had when he was a boy and facing up to this man. He shoved Pipkin from sniffing at his shoe just for something to do. "Take a look at that mutt. We found that dog on Mt. Desert Isle, and she took a liking to him mainly because he has amber-colored hair—like his."

"His?" asked Charles. "Can't you even use his name? And look again at your daughter's hair color—it's only a few shades lighter than amber."

"You don't understand!" flared Jason angrily. "He's a fisherman!"

"Come now, you make yourself sound so snobbish, and our pedigree isn't two yards long. We've just been lucky enough to have been born with certain talents."

"Talent isn't enough, you know that. You've worked, and I've worked damned hard to achieve success."

"Yes, you're right. We've worked hard, made our sacrifices, paid our dues, so now we reap the rewards; but there are other worthwhile crafts other than the arts."

"It's not that," said Jason, looking uneasy, even as he hedged in his own mind, not understanding anything about the way he felt except the sense of being betrayed twice. Mother and daughter both betraying him, and in the same way.

"Jay, don't stare off into space. If it's not that, then what is it? Lisa is of marriageable age. She's mature enough mentally, emotionally."

"What do you know about her, Charles? You see her now and then; I live with her day in and day out. And how can I list the faults I find in what she plans to do? There are so many odds against her marriage to a fisherman working out. He'll be out there, God knows where," he gestured toward the Atlantic, "and she'll be stuck in some little village shanty, surrounded by people without her education, without her sense of the aesthetic; night and day she'll worry about whether or not he'll come home, and then will come the babies, one after another the way they do it over there—God knows, sometimes I think I'd rather see her dead than trapped in an intolerable situation like that!"

Charles appeared appalled and shocked, tiny lines seemed to etch deeper around his already hollowed eyes. He searched Jason's face, making his son squirm in an uncomfortable way, and seeing this only intensified Charles's concern. Eventually he had to speak. His voice was soft. "Jay, certainly you can't mean what you just said. You're letting passion run away with your common sense."

Jason couldn't look at his father but briefly. Haunted eyes that flashed then lowered to stare at his shoes. His voice was a hoarse whisper when he spoke: "No, I didn't mean it. I love her, God knows I love her. I want the best for her—but it seems she wants the worst."

The bright sun on the grass, the play of birds in the tree shade, the surf splashing against the rocks of the shore hundreds of yards away somehow trapped Jason in a weighted oppression that couldn't be lifted by the beauty of the scenery all around him. He had reached a plateau in his life, having all he ever desired . . . all but a wife. He tried to dispel his melancholia and put on a pleasant expression, if only to deceive his father. But his need for a dim isolated place where his inner bleakness could smolder, mingle and merge into like

surroundings jumped him suddenly to his feet. He mumbled inco-
herently, thinking he'd said an apology for his abrupt departure, and
literally ran into the house.

In his study that faced north, he threw himself down and stared
at the wall before him. In the half-light, with the draperies drawn, he
felt lost, totally alone in a world that had turned hostile. Therese,
Therese, he moaned inwardly, the world is no good without you.
Where did I go wrong? I tried, honestly I tried.

His hand of its own volition stole to the bottom drawer where
he'd carefully placed the professional photograph of the woman who
had represented to him everything noble and feminine. He stared at
her beautiful paper face that only vaguely resembled the perfection
of the original. She was young in this photo, only a little older than
Lisa. Her blue eyes stared at him with a wistful expression, so haunt-
ingly wistful and yearning he pressed the hard glass to his cheek and
choked, "Lisa, I'm sorry, so sorry."

He'd said the wrong name. His mistake hung in the air to encir-
cle him with a choking feeling of helplessness. Why was Fate waging
a vendetta of infidelity against him, why? Tears streaked his cheeks.
The first tears he'd shed since that awful day when he'd viewed the
scarred and ruined body of his wife, and had turned away in shock.
Had a fisherman lover been worth it? Had it, Therese?

Not until he'd spent his aged and intensified grief did he dry his
tears, and the name he'd whispered wrongly he put away from him,
like he put outgrown shoes into the far dark end of his closet, someday to bring them out again and make a decision whether or not to
wear them too tight, or throw them out. Funny, he could never throw
away his old shoes, old pictures, old friends, anything once beloved.
But some memories he could stash and never take out again.

Freshly showered and shaved, he went to her door and softly
tapped, listening for the classical music she should have been playing. He'd missed lunch, and he never missed meals. Impatiently he
waited. "Lisa," he called in a tender tone, "I've come to apologize. I

never want to see that look of someone betrayed on your face again. I'll try to do better. I'll try to understand, if you can help me understand what you can find appealing in a fisherman."

No one came to the door. When he looked inside her room, all pale blue paneling, with a white carpet and sheers, he was startled to find her gone. And he'd ordered her to stay until he came. Fresh anger washed over him—where the hell had she gone now? Was it going to happen all over again? Would he hear the telephone ring, hear again the impersonal voice that told him his beloved had been involved in an accident? Lisa, Lisa, Lisa! Don't be dead! Stay alive! Let me do something right just once!

Already Elka was busy preparing dinner as Swen mowed the lawn out back.

"Of course I don't know where she's gone. But Miss Lisa did prepare a lunch for herself to eat on the shore."

Elka couldn't tell him, however, which shore, east or west.

"I don't ask questions, sir."

It was near sunset, and knowing her as he did, he ignored the ocean side and headed for the bay. As he strolled he packed a pipe she'd given him last Christmas. If he had to search every one of the coves that meandered in and out, he'd lose days. But he had his memories of where they used to linger and talk soon after her mother died, and it was toward that cove he headed.

Here and there were little inland pools of fresh water where dark lines of alewives swam along like nervous nebulous ribbons pulled by unseen hands. He tromped over swampy places where speckled alder grew, places where thorn apples sprouted in deep holes.

"And when the island is all covered with blueberry blossoms, I love it best of all," said seven-year-old Lisa when she clung to his hand, and was eager then for his advice. "If there's one place I'd rather be, it's here, Daddy, just you and me."

"What about your mother?" he'd asked.

"But she doesn't like it here, and that spoils it. She doesn't see what we do, or feel what we feel. She thinks it's lonely here, isolated and scary. I think this could be the mold from which heaven was made."

"You are quoting your grandmother," he'd answered and smiled. "You're like your grandmother. When I was a boy she walked with me like this, and we talked as you and I are talking."

Fool, fool to care so much. Fool to remember all the sweetness of a girl who'd grown into a woman who'd make the same mistakes as her mother, and what could he do to stop her?

In the spring, that heart operation. But the operation was another pair of too tight shoes that had to remain unworn in the dark far end of his closet.

Before the ending of day all the island birds went frantic, shrieking, shrilling their ravenous wants into the air. He heard their orchestra tuning up and felt the beat of their wings as they lifted, displaced by his prowling through the long grass, sumac and shadbush. Where was she hiding? How long since he'd been here? The cove somehow looked different, smaller, more intimate.

If he called she'd sit quiet and unmoving, and let him pass her by. There were huge boulders that would shield her from his sight. What would he say when he did see her? Dress her down for disobeying twice in one day?

"Lisa!" he called, knowing she'd ignore him. But, if she did, another didn't. The new puppy came bounding his way, leaping and trying to seize his hand. With just one pat on the head to reassure him, Pipkin raced toward a retreating wave—and in so doing, told him where she was.

Seated on the sand, her back against a rock, she sketched on in silence, not even lifting her head to acknowledge his presence. He marveled at her sure strokes, her young hands that didn't tremble or fear his punishment. Was she really that confident? Then she made a mistake. From what he could tell, only a minor one. But she tore off the sheet of heavy watercolor paper, balled it into a wad and tried to hurl it into the water. Pipkin snatched it up and ran to a distant place to play a game of rip and tear. And the watercolor had been almost finished; a beautiful scene of the bay on a peaceful summer day.

Because he sat down beside her, she methodically began to gather up all her equipment and stow it in her blue canvas tote. He watched, again feeling helpless, wondering how to approach her, and keep her here, when obviously she didn't intend to stay.

The day before Therese's death, she'd been with him in this very spot. "I'm going, Jay. Not because I don't love you, more because I do. If I stay you'll make me hate you, and I don't want to hate you."

"You're not making good sense."

"You don't know the first thing about compromising, Jason Nathan Lorraine! You know only what you want, never what I want. You want to take from me, while you give nothing of yourself. You absorb the best that's in me, making me feel depleted; making me feel a thing that's only used, never really loved for what I am."

"What are you?" he'd asked, completely bewildered.

"Only a woman who wants to feel really needed."

He'd thought that ridiculous then, as he thought it ridiculous now. What more could he have done to express how he needed her always with him?

Now Lisa's carryall was packed with the small folding easel, with everything. She tensed her muscles to rise, making them fill the tight faded fabric of her jeans, her breasts swelling the too small red-striped knit shirt.

"I'm thinking back to a day when you were seven," he said as if he hadn't noticed her preparations for departure. "I remember the sand castle we built together. You used to pray at night to wake up a princess, and I said you already were a princess."

Nothing from her, but her muscles relaxed. The strap of the canvas bag wasn't hefted to her shoulder.

"I make mistakes; every day of my life I make mistakes. I made many with your mother, and she left me . . ."

Her head turned then. Her eyes large and darkly violet blue with an unasked question. What did she know?

"There's something you don't know, Lisa. Your mother was leaving me to run away with a village fisherman."

"No, Daddy!" she cried, anguish darkening her eyes even more. "Mama loved you. She would never have left you and stayed. But you should have given her a little more freedom to come and go. She needed her own car, just as I need the one I have."

"You're right, I know that, too late. I wanted her always near so if I suddenly needed her, she'd be there. It was selfish, I know that now. I don't want to make the same mistakes with you."

Her head bowed as if heavily weighted, until the long loose waves of her hair covered all of her profile. "You could find someone else. You're only forty-four. You don't need me nearly as much as you think you do. You have to let me go or else you will force me into actions both of us will regret."

"So you too will leave me for a fisherman," he said bitterly. "There was a time when you were younger I thought you'd never leave this island, or me. You appeared happy, helping me with my research, learning to cook to please my appetite, learning all the ways to make my life comfortable. Did you do all of that just as practice to please some other man?"

Oh, the look on her face when she lifted her head and flung her hair from her face so it fell in a wild mop to frame her suddenly very pale face, so scared looking.

"I would never hurt you, if I could keep from it. I would stay forever, just to repay you for all you've done to keep me alive, and make me happy—but there's Jamie, and he needs me too."

"What about your grandfather?" he asked, a coil of wire in his chest tightening. "Will you stay as long as he lives?"

Had he said the right thing? Was she taking some small light from those words? Suddenly her arms were flung about his neck, and her head was on his chest.

"I hate having ugly thoughts about you, Daddy," she cried. "I would stay with you forever, if you would let Jamie come and live with us after we marry."

God, he thought sourly, always it came back to that. Every new road he traveled headed ultimately, inevitably, invariably, toward the same detested goal.

"Will you?" she insisted.

"When the need arises, we'll discuss it then."

She drew away from him sharply, her voice small, the look in her eyes suspicious. "If you won't let Jamie live here with us, then I'll be forced to live with him on the peninsula."

Something hard as ice wanted to blast out and tell her about her mother, how she'd died from thinking she could have her cake and eat it too. Despite his thoughts, the hope in her eyes, the child she still was, reached out and touched him and made him speak tenderly: "Darling, don't you know there's a whole wide world of men outside of this island? A girl such as you are can pick and choose. You don't need to settle for the first one who comes your way."

Silently she rose to her feet and bent to pick up the canvas sack which had slipped from her shoulder.

"I see. You have already decided that I can never have Jamie. And I have already decided I have no life worth living without him. So I will go, and you will stay, and Grandfather will understand. When I come for visits, I'll make sure you don't see me."

"Lisa! What about this island? Have you lost your belief in this island's ability to keep you alive?"

She shrugged to heft the bag more securely on her shoulder, then tossed her hair again. Something about the way she backed off told him when she left, she'd never again be as she was now—all his—in all the ways that counted.

"Sorry, Daddy. I don't believe in magic islands anymore. You made this island a sanctuary when I was young enough to believe in everything you said. You convinced me I would die if I stayed too long away from Birdlane, but now I think you were self-serving. That was your ploy to keep me here forever; your ploy to postpone the heart operation forever, your ploy to keep me from loving any man but my father—but it won't work. Thank God for the day Jamie had the courage to sail over to set me free."

Free? Like her mother had been set free?

He jumped to his feet to follow, and yanked the canvas tote from her shoulder and carried it himself. "All right, you're not a child anymore. You've made your point very well. Congratulations! I've lost, and you've won. You may marry Jamie anytime you choose—and he can come here and live after you marry."

"You won't change your mind?" she asked, her eyes shadowed with doubts, with distrust.

"If he's willing to come, I won't object."

She smiled and skipped ahead, laughing over her shoulder, appearing as if ten tons had been taken away from her, while he felt the tons crush down on him.

A fool, a fool, a fool he'd been to promise so much. Nevertheless he sensed the new peace that came into Windown House. Lisa glowed, her radiance so bright he couldn't bear to look her way, knowing instinctively he was going to be the one to smother that radiance. The world would end before he saw her married to a fisherman.

And yet, and yet, it was sweet to see her smiling so often, to watch her quick graceful steps, to hear her practicing with Charles in the music room. Their two violins alternating as one or the other took the lead, played the melody, and the other performed the variations. She was benefitting from being with Charles, intent on learning from him as if one day she'd be on stage—when he knew damn well her heart couldn't stand the pace of being a professional musician.

Then one morning, not long before Lisa's nineteenth birthday on August eighteenth, he was sitting at his desk and watching a small battered red car swing onto the curving drive to the house. A strange car he didn't recognize as belonging to a friend. Ironically he smiled, for he had only one good friend in the village, Lisa's doctor. A friend from his own childhood.

The door chimes sounded, though from his study he couldn't see who got out of the car. Elka's raspy voice came to him.

"Sir, there's a gentleman here who says his name is Kyle Peters. You want to see him or not?"

Quickly he left his desk and strode toward the foyer, stretching out his hand to the good-looking young man who had shaved off his thick clump of beard and mustache, had his hair stylishly trimmed, and was, for the first time since he'd seen him, wearing respectable clothes.

"What a difference a shave and a haircut make," said Jason as he shook hands. "I would never have known you if Elka hadn't called out your name."

In the library they settled down, with Kyle Peters quickly coming to the point of his visit, even as he looked around, as if searching to see something, or someone.

"Remember when I approached you about using your daughter to model for my church murals? I heard so many tales in the village about what a recluse you are, I decided to draw a few sketches and win you over to my side. A girl like your daughter should not live and die without being painted for all posterity to admire."

The sketches were remarkably good, forcing Jason to reconsider, for it would be wonderful to have her forever as she was now, so young, fresh, and vulnerable.

"The finished murals will be like these sketches?"

"More or less. Only minor alterations."

Jason eyed the young man wisely. "All the painting would have to be done on this island, naturally."

At this point Kyle frowned and leaned forward to speak intensely. "I have what you would call a shack on the Bayfront. It's loaded with painting equipment that will have to be transported to the cathedral.

To do the murals on this island would be impossible. I'm talking about frescoes directly painted onto fresh lime plaster." He spread his hands expressively. "The painting has to be done on site."

"It's here, or nowhere," said Jason, faintly smiling.

As if hedging, Kyle tried again. "I guess I could do the murals on canvas, and figure out a way to attach the canvases later to the walls—but you won't have a room with a northern exposure that's large enough, and it's messy work."

The cathedral was a good 30 miles away from the village. Even stretching his imagination Jason couldn't picture Lisa driving that distance back and forth every day—and he couldn't go with her and waste that much time. Plus many other objections he could think of.

"There's a simple solution. You can make your sketches here, then transfer them to the walls, and do your painting as you originally intended, on the fresh plaster."

"May I call you Jay?" asked Kyle, looking ruefully depreciative. "I have an honest confession. I am very new at portrait and mural painting, and therefore, cheap. The church directors were unwilling to splurge on a recognized artist, so they chose me. Still, I want to give them the best job I am capable of producing. Maybe topnotch artists don't feel a need to have the live model before them at every stage, but being a novice, I feel I'll need Lisa from the first preliminary charcoal sketch, right down to the last highlight."

Looking reflective, Jason mentioned the old boathouse that might be ideal, all the while guessing Kyle exaggerated his need for a live model when good sketches would serve the purpose. Still he liked his frankness, his direct approach, and the way he looked now in his expensive three-piece suit.

"Its only heat is a coal stove that's not altogether adequate when the weather's near zero. But perhaps you'll be finished before it's too far into winter. We had a gardener once who made out very well there—but he was a hardy soul who was unaccustomed to creature comforts."

An odd smile curved the artist's lips when he'd settled back in his chair, as if everything had been settled.

"I'm a hardy soul too, which you'd know if you saw my shack." He glanced toward the music room from which romantic music could be heard, two violins accompanying a recording that Charles had made himself. "Don't you think the major participant in this venture should be brought into this discussion?"

In a second he'd summoned her on his phone. In silence they sat and waited, somehow suspended in time, as if all this had been planned long, long ago. The music in the distant room came to an abrupt halt. Kyle sat up straighter, to adjust his tie, to brush his hair back before he looked toward the foyer expectantly.

Quick light footsteps in the hall. Lisa there in the framework of the double doors, smiling at him, appearing startled to see he wasn't alone. Only then did it hit him, seldom did they invite anyone to visit. And even this visitor hadn't been invited.

Along with Kyle Peters he rose to his feet, wondering why even as he did—a show of respect for the beautiful image she presented? What a fool he was to admire her type, after Therese . . .

She advanced toward Kyle, holding his eyes, faintly smiling as she put forth her hand. "Can you possibly be that savage-looking hippie type I saw in Pete's Grill?"

"The very same," said Kyle, "only this time I'm not hiding overtly. My bare face is showing, and I hope, shining."

"It does look clean."

"Then this time you approve?"

Laughter sparkled her blue eyes as Jason narrowed his. What the hell was this? Had they met before?

"I can't truly say, Mr. Peters. As you once remarked yourself, even bare and clean faces can be in disguise too."

Kyle sighed in overacted modest defeat. "Then all my efforts to please have been in vain."

Jason watched, he listened, he connived, thinking just as he'd plot a book how to reach the conclusion he wanted, and when he had the chance, he intervened: "Lisa, why don't you show Mr. Peters the old boathouse—since you've agreed to model for his murals."

The look she gave him was so wise, so unnaturally wise.

"I don't think it's really necessary, Father," she said with a cool sophistication that surprised him. "Mr. Peters had made himself comfortable on our island before, but if you prefer, YOU show him the way. I'm going back to my grandfather who's waiting to conclude today's music lesson." She smiled at Kyle and stood. "Goodbye, Mr. Peters. And I do approve of your new disguise. It's much friendlier. Less threatening than that bearded face and those shapeless clothes that made me think you were overweight."

On that note, she left both men staring after her, both speechless.

The Do-It-Yourself Romance: "Love's Savage Desire"

FOR YEARS THERE HAVE been rumors that Virginia Andrews published romance stories under a pseudonym. None has ever been found. One of the most widely speculated-on stories was a mystery titled "I Slept with My Uncle on My Wedding Night," supposedly written years before *Flowers in the Attic*.

The following rendition of it was part of a submission on May 2, 1982, to *The Do-It-Yourself Romance*, created by the publishers who had done *The Do-It-Yourself Bestseller*. In spite of her massive success at that point, Virginia had been flattered by the request and wanted to publish her story. She titled this version "Love's Savage Desire."

No one has yet located a copy of the original short story, "I Slept with My Uncle on My Wedding Night," which was supposedly published in a romance magazine. No one in the family had ever heard of it, and few were even aware of the excerpt of the "Love's Savage Desire" version presented here.

She was to submit only a beginning and an ending for consideration, and what follows was her submission.

TITLE: Love's Savage Desire

<u>OPENING (two paragraphs or more):</u>

There wasn't a light to be seen, no farmlands were tilled and ready for spring planting. Peering through the window of the carriage which careened drunkenly over the rocky and rutted dirt road heading obviously for that highest mountain with the dark castle riding its top, Tarella Lewellyn sought some other sign of human inhabitation. It was then she heard the lonely and somehow frightening wail of an animal, not quite wolf or dog.

Troubled thoughts ran through her head. Who was this man who claimed to be her father's uncle?—when she knew her father had been an only child. Had it been a mistake to lie and tell the authorities she did remember an uncle? Why had he sent for her? And would that high and forbidding castle be a better home than the misery of the orphanage she'd just escaped?

An hour later she was standing before a massive wooden door that was barred across with iron. The night was bitterly cold. The wind whipped her raven tresses free of her bonnet. Her thin clothes felt inadequate as she waited for someone to respond to the driver's urgent pounding. Resting beside her feet was her single bag, containing all the pitiful possessions she'd managed to acquire in her seventeen years. Her heart pounded madly with the expectations of seeing someone like her father when the door opened. But when it did, the man that stood there sent a terrifying shiver down her spine. Her lips parted to sound a scream that she quickly smothered.

CLOSING (one paragraph):

On the highest rampart of the castle Tara stared toward the west from which he'd come—if he still lived. She'd been seventeen when first she met him, and had almost screamed when she beheld him. In his castle she'd found terror beyond belief, and love beyond her expectations, which had been small. And if given the option to live again through the terror, she would ten times over again, if only she knew he lived. Hour after hour she waited there, the wind whipping her dark locks until the failing day left only a hint of promised dawn in the coming night. I'll forgive him everything, she thought, forgive him anything, if only he comes back to me.

But when the moon was riding high, she was on her knees still praying, bowed down with grief . . . for he'd be back before dark, if he still lived. Then, as she sagged, all hopes gone, she heard again that lonely, heart-wrenching wail of an animal, not dog or wolf. Coming over the hills toward home . . . he was coming back. "I'm coming, Tara," she thought she heard him cry, but she was up and running to meet him halfway, ready and eager to be crushed this time in his arms, and this time her lips would be just as savagely demanding as his.

Virginia Andrews
May 2, 1982

Two Poems by Virginia Andrews

THE FOLLOWING POEMS HAVE been transcribed from the original document housed in the V.C. Andrews special collection at the Howard Gotlieb Archival Research Center at Boston University.

"Golden Things" (poem)
By Virginia Andrews

Oh. he promised me rings . . . and golden things,
   And a house looking over the sea . . .
But I never said once, to that boy at my side,
That all I wanted was him . . . next to me . . .
He gave me his dreams, his exalted schemes,
Of the hopes that he planned to make true,
But I never said once, to that boy trying so—
That my love, demanded no due . . .
He gave what he could . . . and I took what I should . . .
And our days, were long and green . . .
But I never said once, to the boy wanting me—
That it was love, gave life its sheen . . .
How the years wash away . . .
Like the waves in the Bay . . .
Love for him, is a game to play
For his dreams became things—
And his schemes were the means,
Of making every wish come my way . . .

But I lost him somewhere . . . as he climbed up the stair . . .
    Where's the boy my man used to be?
With his rings on my hands—and his gold shining 'round . . .
    I'm alone in my house by the sea,
For I should have said once—to this man that I loved . . .
That all I wanted . . . was him . . . loving me.

"Regretting" (song lyric)
By Virginia Andrews
July 13, 1971

Summer comes . . . and summer goes—like my dreams of old,
Autumn gold turns into winter snow—like my dreams gone cold—
I should have taken the grape, not waited for wine—
I should have tasted at least
While I sat at the feast—
And when the wine came my way,
I shouldn't have let it pass by
Because the cup didn't shine . . .
Now,
Summer comes . . . and summer goes—there is a tear in my eye,
Autumn gold turns into winter snow—for my youth has gone by.
Where are my spring days,
My daffodil time?
Where are the bird songs,
My bells that should chime?
Where is the green grass,
And the love that was mine?
So,
Summer comes . . . and summer goes—and I walk alone,
Autumn gold turns into winter snow—and I would give all I own—
For just one yesterday—
And the chance to play—
The game . . . another way.

acknowledgments

MOST OF THIS BIOGRAPHY was made possible by the help of the Andrews family, whose love of Virginia is why her remaining papers, letters, pictures, and documents were cherished and made available to give us a truly personal picture of her life and work.

A special acknowledgment as well must go to Douglas E. Winter, who convinced Virginia Andrews to do her most in-depth personal interview in existence and whose comments about Virginia, her mother, and her work are quite appreciated by her family and fans.

Thanks, too, to Adam Wilson, who has been my editor for many V.C. Andrews novels.

bibliography

Andrews, V.C. "A Writer's Way to Profit from Memories." Originally published as "Turning a Profit from Memories." *The Writer* magazine, November 1982.

Aurthur, Kate. "The Ghost of V.C. Andrews: The Life, Death, and Afterlife of the Mysterious 'Flowers in the Attic' Author." *BuzzFeed*, January 15, 2014.

Bohlman, Lynn. "Wilson Grad Writes Bestseller." Wilson High School Newsletter, n.d.

Germanotta, Tony. "Cancer Kills V.C. Andrews, Best Selling Local Novelist." *Virginian-Pilot* and *Ledger-Star*, December 20, 1986.

Hall, Harriet. "Who Was Mary Shelley and What Inspired Frankenstein?" *Independent*, September 17, 2018.

Huggins, Renee. Review of *My Sweet Audrina*. ReneesBookCase.com, April 24, 2019.

Janas, Nikki. "Portsmouth Author Colors Hope Yellow." Review of *Flowers in the Attic*. *Panorama*, November 4, 1979.

Jarvis, Kay. "Banished to an Attic of Hatred." Review of *Flowers in the Attic*. *San Diego Tribune*, November 18, 1979.

Johnson, Deanie. "Road from Concession Mags to Bestseller Is Sweet." Review of *Flowers in the Attic*. *Norcom Gazette*, February 1980.

Langdon, Dolly. "Have You Read a Bestselling Gothic Lately? Chances Are It Was by a Recluse Named V.C. Andrews." *People*, October 6, 1980.

Pocket Books. Press release for *Dark Angel*. November 1986.

Robertson, Nan. "Behind the Best Sellers; '*If There Be Thorns*.'" *New York Times*, June 14, 1981.

Rosen, Jackie. "'Flowers' Blooming for Area Author." *Times Herald*, November 2, 1979.

Rubin, Stephen. "Blooms of Darkness." *Washington Post*, September 20, 1981.

Ruehlmann, William. "Spinner of Strange Tales, Flies High with Her Newest, *Dark Angel*." *Virginian-Pilot*, November 28, 1986.

USA Today, 1986. (Family scrapbook, n.d.)

Winter, Douglas E. *Faces of Fear*. New York: Berkley Trade, 1985.

Winters, Shirley. "Bestselling Author Due at Library Program." *Currents*, September 8, 1980.

Index

Adams, Jeb Stuart, 143

Andrews, Arthur (Virginia's uncle), 4

Andrews, Brad (Virginia's nephew), xxv, xxvii, 63–64, 68, 86–87, 91, 101, 111, 116, 119–20, 124–25

Andrews, Eugene ("Gene"; Virginia's brother), 3, 11, 26, 33, 52, 145

Andrews, Glenn (Virginia's nephew), 64, 68, 101

Andrews, Joan (Virginia's sister-in-law), xviii, 118, 145

Andrews, Lillian (née Parker; Virginia's mother), xx–xxi, 6, 14, 61
conservatism/prudishness of, 3, 24, 50
as a Depression-era homemaker, 24–26

dominance over Virginia, 50, 53–54, 60, 66–67, 70–72, 80–81
personality of, 2–4
reaction to Flowers in the Attic, 24, 85–86, 98
response to Virginia's disability, xx, 44–45, 53, 61, 65, 85
Virginia's artwork promoted by, 35, 58–59

Andrews, Mary ("Baby Sis"; Virginia's sister-in-law), 3, 24, 43–44, 59, 68, 78, 85, 145

Andrews, V.C. (Virginia), xxi–xxii
adolescence of, 7, 11, 23–26, 38–39
appearance of, xix–xx, 60–61
as an artist, xxiii, 8–10, 35–36, 57–59, 61–63, 65–66, 68

Andrews, V.C. (Virginia) (*cont.*)
  birth of, 2, 4
  books' importance to, 16–17, 33–
    34, 37–38, 64–65, 100
  childhood of, xxiii, 15, 19, 26–28
  clairvoyance/psychic visions of,
    5–7
  confidence of, 20, 91–92, 110–11
  death of, 41, 67–68, 146
  death of, letter to mother
    regarding, 138–39
  depression of, xxv, 67–69
  development as a writer, 36–39,
    62–63, 83, 85–87
  on dreams and goals, 2, 17, 102
  ESP of, xxiii, 61
  fame of, xx–xxi, xxvi–xxvii, 1, 42, 66–
    67, 92–93, 99–100, 114–15, 123
  family, experiences/success
    shared with, 103, 106–7
  fan letters to, 113, 140–41
  financial concerns of, 13–14,
    19–20, 109–10
  financial success of, 30, 62–63,
    110, 118–19, 126
  frustration of, 12, 54, 59, 67,
    74–75, 110
  "Golden Things," 247–48
  Hollywood trip by, 66–67, 128–36
  imagination of, 17, 22, 31, 35, 39,
    61, 79, 86–88, 101–2, 106
  independence sought by, 71, 91
  influences on, 9, 15, 17, 20, 32,
    34, 50, 62
  "I Slept with My Uncle on My
    Wedding Night," 109, 243–45

on isolation and writing, 86
London–Paris trip by, 120–21, 123–26
Love's Savage Desire, 243–45
on marriage, 12, 82–83
monument to, 1–2
mother's control of, 50, 53–54,
  60, 66–67, 70–72, 80–81
on novels with happy endings,
  88–89
obituary for, 146
personality of, 7, 15, 59–60
in Portsmouth, 19–20, 62–63, 72
premonition of her father's death,
  6, 61
privacy of, xii–xiii, xxvi
pseudonym of, xv–xvi
public exposure of, 115–16
"Regretting," 248
reincarnation, belief in, xxiii, 5,
  48, 50
relationship with Eugene, 26–27
relationship with father, 7, 61
relationship with mother, 31,
  53–54, 66, 85, 126
relationships with men, 46, 80–83,
  101
religious views and church
  attendance of, 47–50
reticence of, 42–43, 99
in Rochester, 4
schooling of, 8–9, 21, 25, 32–33
sensitivity about her age, xiii, 99
sexuality of, 23–24, 38
shift from art to writing, 62–63
on "V.C. Andrews," use of, 87, 93,
  111–12

"A Writer's Way to Profit from
Memories," 51, 54–55, 77–78,
83, 100–101, 127
writing habits of, xvii–xviii
Andrews, Virginia, disability/
illnesses of, xiii, xix–xxiii
arthritis/ankylosing spondylitis,
23–24, 41, 43, 54, 74, 85
arthrodesis, 52
body cast, 46, 52, 55, 74
bone spurs, 43–46, 85, 119
breast cancer, xxi, xxvii, 41, 145
corrective surgeries, 43, 45–46, 50, 55
crutches and wheelchairs, 52, 55
depression due to, 58
disability benefits, 14
doctors' dismissal of symptoms, 45
hospital bed, 66, 68
Lillian's response to, xx, 44–45,
53, 61, 65, 85
pleurisy, 144
pneumonia, 144–45
restrictions due to, 7, 44–45, 50,
53–55, 57–59, 100, 114–15
rumors about, 42
stairway accident, 22–23, 39,
41–44, 54
Virginia as a victim of medical
mistakes, 74
Virginia's acceptance of, 60
Virginia's reticence and
exaggerations about, 42–43, 99
Andrews, Virginia, interviews with
Ledger-Star, 7, 17, 63
People, xiii–xv, 55, 99, 124
Publishers Weekly, 141

Times of London, 123–24
Virginian-Pilot, 7, 16–17, 34, 38,
63, 75, 79
Washington Post, 12, 43, 97–99, 102
Winter (see Faces of Fear)
Andrews, V.C. (Virginia), novels by
Dark Angel, 36, 39, 50, 92, 105,
137, 140, 149
Garden of Shadows, 29–30, 140
Gods of Green Mountain, 92, 143
If There Be Thorns, 95, 116–17, 119
My Sweet Audrina, xxv, 22, 32, 36,
41, 92, 101, 105, 119, 126–28
Petals on the Wind, xxii, 6, 39, 95,
113, 115–17, 119
Seeds of Yesterday, 92, 95, 127, 136
See also Flowers in the Attic;
Heaven; The Obsessed
Andrews, William, Jr. ("Bill"; Virginia's
brother), 3–4, 52, 110–11
Andrews, William Henry, Sr.
(Virginia's father), xxi, xxiii,
2–4, 6–7, 14, 19, 21, 25, 61

Begun, Jeff, 128, 130
Bloom, Jeffrey, 141
"Blooms of Darkness" (Rubin), 12,
43, 97–99, 102

Charles, Milton, 104–5, 117
child abuse, 32, 96–97
Clowning in Rome (Nouwen), 91
Craven, Wes, 141

Dark Angel (V.C. Andrews), 36, 39,
50, 92, 105, 137, 140, 149

Diamant, Anita, xi–xii, 78, 84, 88, 91, 120–21, 123–24, 126

Dickens, Charles, 17

Faces of Fear interview with Virginia (Winter), xiii, xxvi
  on age, xiii
  on art classes at junior college, 9–10
  on child abuse, 97
  on fairy tales, 33–34
  on fear in her novels, 75
  on focusing on one talent, 62
  persuading Virginia to be interviewed, xiv–xv
  on privacy, xxvi
  on reincarnation and clairvoyance, 5–6, 48
  on writing to entertain, 89

Fletcher, Louise, 142–43

Flowers in the Attic (film; 1987), xxii, 66–67, 93, 128–30, 134–35, 140–43

Flowers in the Attic (film; 2014), 99

Flowers in the Attic (V.C. Andrews)
  audience for, 103
  banning of, xvi–xvii, 95–98
  Cathy in, 5–6, 10–11, 24, 32, 51, 76–77, 79, 95
  child abuse in, 95–96
  Chris in, xxi, 52, 62, 75–76, 79, 85, 101
  Christopher Sr.'s debt/death, 13, 19, 29
  color use in, 90
  copies in print/sold, 94, 96, 105, 117, 143
  Corrine in, 13, 17, 19, 29, 47–50, 97–98
  cover art for, 104–5
  critical reception of, 105–6
  dark family relationships in, 36
  dedication of, xxi
  descriptions in, 101
  Diamant as agent for, 85–86, 88, 110
  doctor's story as a source for, 46–47, 52
  Dollanganger name, source for, 51
  fear in, 75–76
  genre of, 18, 78–79, 111–12
  incest in, 24, 47–48, 95–98
  income from, 82, 109–10, 112–13
  Lillian's reaction to, 24, 85–86, 98
  Malcolm in, 30, 47–48, 95
  Olivia in, 29–31, 34, 47–48, 50–51, 85, 95, 105, 143
  parallels with Virginia's life, 11–13, 17, 19, 27, 47–52, 76–78, 81, 84–85
  parent-child relationship explored in, 75, 78, 88–89
  pitch letter for, 78, 84
  plot, 84
  popularity/success of, xvi–xvii, xxii, 85, 91–96, 99, 105–6
  premise of children locked in a mansion for years, 73, 78
  publication of, 91, 93–94, 97
  publicity events/press release for, 8, 94, 105, 115, 117–18
  punishment in, 96
  religion in, 48–50, 95–96
  setting in, 37, 142
  theme of cruelty and love, 103–4

Virginia's feelings about, 77–78
Virginia's purpose in writing, 88–89
Virginia's response to success of,
    93–95
women's status in, 29
writing of, 47, 77, 89–90, 102
Frankenstein (Shelley), 18, 117
Fries, Chuck, 128–29, 132, 134

Garden of Shadows (V.C. Andrews),
    29–30, 140
Gods of Green Mountain (V.C.
    Andrews), 92, 143
"Golden Things" (Virginia
    Andrews), 247–48
Goldstein, William, 141
Great Depression, 12–14, 20–21,
    24–27, 142
Guille, Iris (Virginia's aunt), 28, 59

Heaven (V.C. Andrews), 92
    characters in, 136–37
    cover art for, 105
    descriptions in, 101
    family relationships in, 32, 36, 89
    religion in, 50
    success of, 137
    weather used to set mood in, 34–35
Hills, Gillian, 104–5, 117
Huntley, E. D., 37

If There Be Thorns (V.C. Andrews),
    95, 116–17, 119
"I Slept with My Uncle on My
    Wedding Night" (Virginia
    Andrews), 109, 243–45

Janas, Nikki, 106
Jarvis, Kay, 106
Jenkins, John Philip, 97
Johnson, Deanie, 106

Ledger-Star, 7, 17, 63
Levin, Sy, 128–31, 134
Lifetime, xxiv
literary agents, 83–84
    See also Diamant, Anita
Lolita syndrome, 38–39
Love's Savage Desire (Virginia
    Andrews), 243–45

Mock, Pat (Virginia's cousin), 14, 24
    on *Flowers in the Attic*, 46
    on Lillian's father, 3–4, 28
    on Lillian's response to Virginia's
        disability, 85
    living with Lillian and Virginia,
        53–54, 68–71
    memories of/relationship with
        Virginia, xiv, 60, 69–72
    on Virginia's disability, 44–45
Myers, Suzanne Andrews (Virginia's
    niece)
    on Lillian's reactions to Virginia's
        premonitions, 6
    memories of Lillian, 65–67
    memories of Virginia, 63–67,
        76–77, 145–46
    sex talk with Virginia, 79–80
    on Virginia's appearance, xx
    on Virginia's art and writing, 62–63
    on Virginia's London–Paris trip,
        125–26

Myers, Suzanne Andrews (Virginia's
    niece) (*cont.*)
  on Virginia's love of fables, 34
My Sweet Audrina (V.C. Andrews),
    xxv, 22, 32, 36, 41, 92, 101,
    105, 119, 126–28

Nabokov, Vladimir, 38–39
Neiderman, Andrew, xii
Nouwen, Henri J. M., 91

The Obsessed (V.C. Andrews;
    unfinished manuscript), 149–
    245
  prologue, 153–57
  chapter one, 159–72
  chapter two, 173–82
  chapter three, 183–89
  chapter four, 191–99
  chapter five, 201–6
  chapter six, 207–12
  chapter seven, 213–26
  chapter eight, 227–41

Pagán, Camille Noe, 45
Parker, Lucy (Virginia's
    grandmother), 25–26, 28–29, 59
Petals on the Wind (V.C. Andrews),
    xxii, 6, 39, 95, 113, 115–17, 119
Pocket Books, 91, 93–94, 96
Portsmouth (Virginia), 5, 20–21
punishment, 73–74, 96

"Regretting" (Virginia Andrews),
    247–48
Robertson, Nan, 116–17

Rochester (New York), 4–5, 20
Rubin, Stephen, 12, 43, 97–99, 102

Seeds of Yesterday (V.C. Andrews),
    92, 95, 127, 136
Shelley, Mary Wollstonecraft, 18,
    117
Simon & Schuster, 96–97, 117
  See also Pocket Books
Sisters (Neiderman), xii
Swanson, Kristy, 143

Tennant, Victoria, 143

Universal Pictures, 66–67, 129–30,
    133–34

Virginian-Pilot, 7, 16–17, 34, 38,
    63, 75, 79, 146

Washington Post, 12, 43, 97–99, 102
Winter, Douglas E., 18
  See also *Faces of Fear* interview
    with Virginia
women
  education of, 28–29
  marriage by, 29
  in medical settings, vs. men, 45
  voting rights of, 2
  in the workplace, 13
Wright, Frank Lloyd, 8, 101
writers, 83–84, 86, 101–2
"A Writer's Way to Profit from
    Memories" (V.C. Andrews), 51,
    54–55, 77–78, 83, 100–101, 127
writing vs. acting, 36–37

about the author

Andrew Neiderman is the author of numerous novels of suspense and terror, including *Deficiency*, *The Baby Squad*, *Under Abduction*, *Dead Time*, *Curse*, *In Double Jeopardy*, *The Dark*, *Surrogate Child*, and *The Devil's Advocate*, which was made into a major motion picture starring Al Pacino, Keanu Reeves, and Charlize Theron. He lives in Palm Springs, California, with his wife, Diane. Visit his website at Neiderman.com.

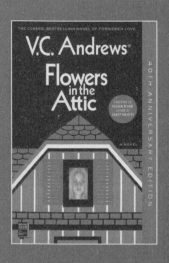

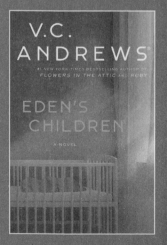
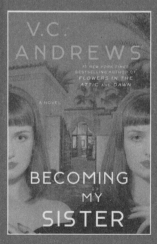
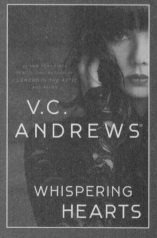